ENGLAND
AND ENGLISHNESS

ENGLAND AND ENGLISHNESS

Ideas of Nationhood in English Poetry

1688–1900

John Lucas

University of Iowa Press
Iowa City

University of Iowa Press, Iowa City 52242

Copyright © 1990 by John Lucas
All rights reserved
First edition, 1990

International Standard Book Number 0–87745–275–X
Library of Congress Catalog Card Number 89–51574

Printed in Great Britain

For John Goode and David Howard

'*Where shall we sometimes meet, and by the fire*
Help wast a sullen day; what may be won
From the hard season gaining . . .'

CONTENTS

ACKNOWLEDGEMENTS

Many people helped me in my work on this book. Some answered queries. Others made useful suggestions or drew my attention to material I had overlooked or of which I had been ignorant. Still others read portions of the manuscript and offered advice and criticism. They include Maureen Bell, Robin Butlin, Angus Calder, Victor Crowther, Denis Cosgrove, the late Ian Fletcher, Carol Gardiner, John Goode, David Howard, Roger Hubank, John McClelland, Mona McKay, Bill Overton, George Parfitt, Arnold Rattenbury, John Squires and Jenny Taylor.

Thanks are due to the Carcanet Press, who first published a version of the section on Goldsmith.

I owe a great debt of gratitude to Jenny Uglow. Whatever the faults of *England and Englishness*, they would have been considerably worse without her vigilance and unfailingly helpful editorial advice.

Thus from a Mixture of all Kinds began,
That Hetrogeneous *Thing*, an *Englishman*.

Daniel Defoe, *The True-Born Englishman*

These vague allusions to a country's wrongs,
    Where one says 'Ay' and others answer 'No'
In contradiction from a thousand tongues,
    Till like to prison-cells her freedoms grow
Becobwebbed with these oft-repeated songs
    Of peace and plenty in the midst of woe.

John Clare, *England, 1830*

'But, asking pardon, laws is made for the good of the nation, not for your good or mine.'

Daniel could not stand this. He laid down his pipe, opened his eyes, stared straight at Philip before speaking, in order to enforce his words, and then said slowly –

'Nation heere! nation theere! I'm a man and yo're another, but nation's nowheere.'

Elizabeth Gaskell, *Sylvia's Lovers*

As to the name itself, he did not borrow it but compiled it, seeking for something that sounded solidly English ... The rootless, non-dialect speakers of the public-school élite are apt to over-value nationality, just as exiles do. It did not surprise me once I'd considered it that Scots-descended, Anglo-Indian, Etonian Eric Blair would like to be accepted as English.

Jack Common's recollections in *Orwell Remembered*, edited by Audrey Coppard and Bernard Crick

INTRODUCTION

This book spans roughly two centuries, from 1700 to 1900. It explores some of the ways in which poets came to write about England and Englishness, and it offers explanations for their different and often conflicting visions and versions. The fact that I begin at the end of the seventeenth century does not mean that I think poets before then had had no interest in imagining England. Quite the contrary. Any number of earlier writers had produced accounts of England's origins, its growth and 'divine' purpose and destiny; and they had speculated about the Englishness of the English. There is nevertheless a difference between them and the writers with whom I am concerned. Very simply, 1688 marks the beginning of England as a distinctively modern nation. This is not necessarily to suggest that the poets of that time saw the matter in these terms. It is, however, to say that they felt a special responsibility to identify nationhood in a manner that was new. It is also to say that what they identified as 'England' did not necessarily meet with their approval.

This leads to a further point. The self-consciousness entailed in the poets' imaginings inevitably produced a good deal of theorising about the nature of poetry and the identity of the poet, or POET. By what right *did* the poet speak for England? Who or what gave him the authority to do so? In the pages that follow there will be much to say about these and other, related, matters. Here, I will remark only that the focus of the book on poetry and poets is quite deliberate. Novelists increasingly developed their own ways of imagining England, but until the middle of the nineteenth century the novel was not typically considered as an art form. As a result, novelists did not have the authority or responsibilities of poets. This of course gave them very different responsibilities and opportunities, but to have tried to explore what those were would have led to a different and much longer work. To a lesser extent, the same is true for dramatists. For better or worse, then, my concern is with poets and with what they made of a distinctively modern or modernising nation.

Anthony Giddens has suggested that a key factor in distinguishing pre-modern from modern states it that the former have frontiers while the latter have borders. Frontiers are vague, contestable areas, borders are precise, readily identifiable. The threat to a modern state is usually identified as coming from beyond the border, whereas a pre-modern state is threatened by rival groups within its frontiers, endlessly struggling for power. The transition to the modern state occurs when such power becomes legitimised or is assumed, or said, to have the authority of the nation behind it. At this point borders can be drawn, and enemies identified as those beyond, while inside them the nation is proclaimed as being at one.

But to produce this nationally sanctioned authority, this at-oneness, not only requires the kind of surveillance to which Giddens draws attention, it also requires a homogenising of culture in its broadest aspects. Ernest Gellner rightly argues that the development of this homogenisation is therefore an essential feature of the modern state, so much so that without it the state could not exist. Gellner sees the development of nations and nationalism as inextricably bound up with, because required by, the processes of industrialisation, whose success is dependent upon the people within the borders of a nation agreeing with or being brought to accept the implementation of such processes. There has to be at least the pretence of a common purpose, and this purpose is linked to and expressed by means of nationalism. 'Essential' national characteristics are then discovered and celebrated. They are what 'we' have in common.[1]

In 1688, where this study begins, those who thought themselves entitled to speak for the nation represented a remarkably small constituency, one that excluded far more than it included. As the endlessly reproduced term 'Augusta' implies, the idea of England among those who saw themselves as Augustan was focused on the model of the city-state. They were upholders of the tradition to which 'Augusta' referred. They were the enfranchised, the free citizens. They alone could be trusted disinterestedly to pursue and safeguard the nation's concerns.

Nor did they have to wish their nation to be a republic. According to John Dennis, writing just after the turn of the century:

> As the *Athenians* had Liberty with a Common-wealth, the *English* enjoy the very same Liberty under the Government of the best of Queens, and in so doing are the happiest People in the World . . . Liberty is Liberty under a limited Monarchy, as much as under a Common-wealth.[2]

The People to whom Dennis refers are by no means the population as a whole. As we shall see, it is in the gradual extension of the term 'the people', its coming to apply to more of the population, that struggles over the definition of liberty begin to emerge. Later poets would therefore mean very different things by their appeal to liberty for 'the people'. The new meanings led to the unsurprising insistence that many English people did not in fact have much in the way of liberty.

The frequent elision of *England* into *Britain*, as with the use of the term *Albion*, obscures tensions which the Act of Union of 1707, between England and Scotland, did not resolve. I have not had a great deal to say about these tensions, but I have tried to be mindful of their existence; and I am acutely aware of the fact that when English poets speak of Britain as a nation of the free they usually mean England.

Claims to disinterestedness can mask aggressive self-interest. Nevertheless, Pope's desire to uphold an ideal of benevolence as appropriate to the free citizen, an ideal about which I shall have something to say in the first chapter, has its justification. It is a plea for social responsibility. If it takes its stand on the acceptance of a hierarchically structured society, it also puts the case for citizenry as enjoining civic virtues. It therefore implicitly rejects the desirability of epic virtues. Epic virtues are potentially dangerous. They are divisive, or at the service of divisive energies. They centre on bravery and daring, they are the virtues of battle, and they are intimately associated with the difficult task of making a nation. As such, they are bound to be an unwelcome reminder of England's recent problems. This is why Pope's use of mock-epic is so crucial. By adopting a form which both pays tribute to the power of epic and at the same time treats it as a merely literary mode, to be imitated and parodied, Pope implies that it has no greater contemporary relevance than as a sport, which is what his versions of Homer amount to: sport poems of genius. Pope's dismissal of epic is his contribution to the suppression of radical republicanism. The verse epistle comes to stand as the typical poetic utterance of the time, its Horatianism at the service of those civilising values of friendship and a common cultural inheritance without which discourse becomes impossible.

I suggest that among the ambitions which prompted the literary tactics of 'Augustan' poets, the desire to make Milton more or less invisible was pre-eminent. Failing that, he had to be tamed. Hence those (often illustrated) editions of *Paradise Lost* which reproduced the poem in a manner that could accommodate it to humanist ideals.[3] Yet this was always difficult to do. For many eighteenth-century writers Milton remained an uncomfortable, because uncompromising, presence. And his frank partisanship raised awkward questions about the nature of the poet's authority, his disinterestedness.

Pope was especially alert to such questions. They discomfort him and may be said truly to discompose some of his best poems. I shall spend some time discussing the ordering (and disordering) of the last two ethic epistles, on the Use of Riches, because they so revealingly show his uneasiness about the moral, political and social propriety, of benevolence. The moral worth of benevolence has to be argued for in a context of need. Why should it be required? What makes the argument tricky is that Pope is deeply aware of and yet implicated in the concealments of self-interest which lie beneath the appeal of civilised disinterestedness (where what is civilised is aligned with those cultural values specifically drawn from the idea of the city-state). That is why the case of Stephen Duck is important; for what Duck has to say can hardly be accommodated to the image of social relations which Pope's poems endorse, an image which is deeply indebted to the Pastoral, as I try to show.

The ultimate sanction for Pastoral lies with Virgil. Not the Virgil of the *Aeneid*, but the Virgil of the *Eclogues* and, more importantly, the *Georgics*. In the sense in which I use the term, Pastoral implies a vision of social relationships, harmoniously structured, hierarchically ordered, and succoured by full creativity (which is why the *Georgics* are so usable). A literary tradition is granted a general cultural and political validity. Labour is content with its subservience because work guarantees plenitude. Initially, this vision includes benevolence, because without the care benevolence implies – its pastoral responsibilities – things might fall apart. But later the promise of plenitude is offered in so self-confident a manner as to make any appeal to benevolence unnecessary. This is the confidence of James Thomson and the mid-eighteenth-century 'Georgic' poets. Their praise of 'rich industry' makes for an absolute coincidence of self- and national interest. 'Industry' here is both those who labour and those who direct labour. All are rich. Work for one is wealth for all. Wealth for one is work for all.

But the uninflected ardour of this new, *laissez-faire* dream of England comes at the same time as, and almost certainly prompts, the work of other poets, more doubting, troubled and deeply anxious than Thomson could ever be. This is most especially true of Thomas Gray and William Collins, poets who have not been properly appreciated, perhaps because they have been seen as set apart from contemporary issues to do with Englishness and the role of the poet which, I suggest, bear powerfully and perplexingly in on them. It is significant that with them come the first, faint stirrings of recovered possibilities for epic poetry (though to be sure they are ill at ease with these). It is also significant that they are self-divided, hesitant about where, with whom and with what they belong; and this is true whether the focus is on 'merely' literary traditions or matters of wider cultural reference. It is still further significant that they are much exercised about the term 'liberty', which Thomson had taken as a vindication of economic self-interest. And it is of the greatest significance that they both, but Gray in particular, feel the need to 'waken' the voices of those who have been silent or outlawed from poetry. These voices come from the margins of Britannia. They are Welsh, Scottish, Gaelic. They are northern, Gothic, barbaric. They speak, or are said to speak, prophetically, as inspired representatives of the people. And now that phrase, 'the people', has a very different meaning from the one to which John Dennis appealed. It no longer signifies free citizens within the dreamed-of city-state. The people are now those who are *not* citizens, who come from beyond the city-state, or for whom that ideal has no meaning except as a way of denying their own claims to identity, national or otherwise.

Consideration of these issues leads me to say something, although less than I would like, about 'mad' Christopher Smart. Smart literally broke down his identity as a self-conscious 'Augustan' poet and emerged as an 'inspired enthusiast', for whom the Bible replaced 'classical' literature as the source of inspiration and truth. The Bible is the book of the people, and Smart wished to be the people's poet, the poet of the dispossessed.

Oliver Goldsmith did not wish that, but he undoubtedly wrote on behalf of the people, in the newer, wider sense of that term. Goldsmith has been misread by commentators. Irish critics more or less dismiss him as a Tom Moore before his time, a time-server who was content to supply sweet songs for his English paymasters. English critics tend to confirm this. They happily endorse Thackeray's praise of him as the 'most beloved of English writers'. Beneath such praise one detects a sigh of relief. Goldsmith is not going to disturb English complacencies in the manner of Swift. Nor does he. But he is a good deal more cunning, and cunningly subversive, than has been habitually recognised. This is not to deny that he can go through the routine drill of 'disinterested' commentator, speaking to and from a set of culturally orthodox values. But he also, crucially, deflates the idea of a responsible commonwealth as being dependent on the monarchy. And he understands, better than Gray and Collins did, the cant of 'liberty'. In Goldsmith's best work liberty is a contested term rather than an agreed one.

It is for these reasons that Blake recognised Goldsmith as the possessor of virtues which set him apart from the literary and artistic set with whom he associated and among whom it is still customary to place him. But Blake was unlike Goldsmith in that he was truly of the people. In him, the unmistakable voice of popular radicalism is once again heard: the virtues he celebrates are those epic virtues he found in Milton and which for so long had been banished from English poetry, as somehow not English. Blake was well aware of the debt he owed to Gray and Collins. He took over their concerns with the Gothic, the northern, the Ossianic. He *is* their voice of the bard, but not geographically marginalised – he came from London – even though he was an artisan, the son of artisan parents, and thus *socially* marginalised.

Political and social developments of the late years of the eighteenth century made the emergence of Blake's voice possible. Nevertheless, it is worth recalling how long it took before his greatness was properly acknowledged. Post-war English critics were still condescending to him. D. G. James called him rash, Allan Rodway explained him away as an 'intuitive introvert', and in a book that claimed to be about the Romantic poets Graham Hough solved the difficulty of not knowing what to do with him by doing nothing at all.[4] F.R. Leavis apart, Blake's early champions were either outsiders like Rossetti and Yeats (the coincidence of Yeats's work on Blake in the 1890s and his developing concern with the cause of Irish nationalism has not, so far as I am aware, been noted), or Americans. The significance of this hardly needs to be emphasised.

Blake's heroic ambitions ended in partial defeat. The England he imagined refused to make itself real. To the end, however, he remained true to his epic dream. The same cannot be said of Wordsworth. Like Blake he began by wanting to give utterance to those who had been denied their own voices. Such people were no longer to be treated as objects of contemplation, usually from afar, as in the distancing techniques of Thomson's abstractions. Instead, they became subjects: speaking, experiencing. But then Wordsworth began to retreat, figuratively and literally. He altered the words of his subjects or withheld them. He became the authority on them and permitted no challenge to that authority. And so, whereas in the *Lyrical Ballads* he had thrown into radical doubt any reductive idea of a unitary image of 'the people' and, by implication, of England and Englishness, only a few years later he began to move towards endorsing those very abstractions which his great work had held up to criticism, even to ridicule. And as he retreated towards this kind of authority, so he retreated from city to country. Pastoral was once again offered as an image of ideal social arrangements. The concealments and evasions necessary for Wordsworth to produce this version of England are matters I shall spend some time on, and they lead to necessary re-readings of some famous, and familiar, poems.

There is no need for such a re-reading of Shelley. It is, however, necessary to register a problem of which he was insufficiently aware. His 'men of England' are the people in their widest frame of reference. Shelley's knowledge of them was inevitably limited: by exile and by class. But there is also the problem of regionalism. It is a vastly complicated problem, and I am under no illusions that I have addressed it satisfactorily. But I think it important at least to draw attention to some of its major constituents. One is that for entirely understandable reasons historians of the left have consistently underplayed its importance as a determining factor in the development of working-class consciousness. Another is that because of this there has been a great deal of confusion about the value to be attached to such concepts as 'rootedness' and 'dwelling'. Are these good or bad things? My suggestion is that rootedness is always something wished on others, as a way of fixing them unproblematically, whether socially or economically, or both. Those who are rooted are not free. In particular, they are not free to wander. They are actually forbidden from wandering. The 'rooted' pose no threat.

From a radical point of view an acceptable alternative to rootedness may then seem to be dwelling. Dwelling has to do with occupation as well as abode, and both of these may be freely chosen. Wordsworth was free to choose his dwelling and rejoiced in the fact.

But this conceivable ideal collapses as soon as we consider the case of John Clare. Clare was not free to choose. Like many other English people he felt his chief loyalties to be to the local or regional, especially since these could seem to nurture a sense of freedom from national affairs. But this was bound to prove delusive. National affairs – affairs decided at a national level, as matters of enclosure for example were – took freedom away, removed the possibilities of wandering, and thus constrained or made impossible an unambiguous commitment to the local, the regional. And at the very time this was happening, an intensification of the desirability of 'rootedness' became apparent in much of the literature of cultural and political orthodoxy, including that of Wordsworth. It is this which helps to explain the production and encouragement of 'peasant poetry'. Hence the manufacturing of the 'Peasant Poet', John Clare.

Clare suffered from the language of Wordsworthian Romanticism, inherited from Gray and others and suitably reworked. This proclaimed the poet's 'essential' nature and hence his identity. Clare, however, was being made into a special kind of poet, the 'peasant poet'. This identity, which he did not seek but which was conferred on him, both belied the idea of an 'essential' poetic identity and enforced his recognition that he was not what he was, nor even what he did, because his work was suppressed or reworked in ways that denied him any sure sense of selfhood. His poems were required to be 'peasant poems'. Clare's experience was, and is, in no sense exceptional. Being English could typically come to mean a set of complementary but more often contradictory awarenesses, including those of class, regionalism, and perhaps gender (although I admit that my concerns are almost exclusively with the construction of an English*man* and that the term English*woman* will need to be investigated by feminist historians – assuming that they think it worth their while to do so).

Regionalism is a form of false consciousness, but it operates as a very powerful one. In the middle years of the nineteenth century patriotism was equally powerful, given that it was identified with the loved body of Victoria. Just how and why this identification occurred is beyond the scope of my present enquiry.[5] It can, however, be said that at the time when Shelley imagined an England of the future as sceptreless, he was voicing a widely shared expectation. A great many people assumed that Princess Victoria would become plain 'Miss Guelph'. Republicanism was by no means confined to a few, extreme democrats. But during the 1840s monarchism recovered. As it did so Milton's fortunes once again, and most significantly, began to undergo a change. It now became usual to praise him as a religious poet who set his face against vaulting ambition. He could also be praised as a master of style.

Not everyone was content to accept this, any more than they accepted the re-reading of the reigns of Charles I and his son which the newly-confident monarchist tendencies required. The middle years of the seventeenth century were therefore much investigated and fought over. Browning's sardonic 'Cavalier Tunes' are a product of this as, from a markedly different perspective, is Arnold's 'Cromwell'. Dickens's account of the period, in his *Child's History of England*, has, however, gone virtually unremarked. Of Charles I's execution, Dickens says, 'With all my sorrow for him, I cannot agree with him that he died "the martyr of the people"; for the people had been martyrs to him, and to his ideas of a King's rights, long before.' Charles II is accounted for in a chapter which must be one of the most blistering and potentially seditious attacks on the English monarchy ever written. Quotation cannot possibly do justice to its wonderful wit and audacity, but the fact that Dickens began writing and publishing the *Child's History* in 1851 is clearly of importance.

1851 was the year of the Great Exhibition. It was also the year in which Tennyson became Poet Laureate. Poets had authority, novelists didn't. (Imagine Charles, Lord Dickens.) The novel was not an art form. To force a distinction, then, we might call Dickens the spokesperson of the people; by the same token Tennyson would be the champion of royalty. The Poet Laureate was called upon to produce images of England which would endorse the nation as essentially 'Queen and Country': the people united under their monarch. That Tennyson was sometimes ill at ease with this there can be little doubt. He was made even more uneasy by the mantle of poetic authority which Hallam had wrapped round him and which in a number of key poems he tried to throw off. But he was not fully equal to the effort, and in this he differed from his great contemporary, Browning.

Browning's radicalism needs to be given its due weight if we are to understand the extent of his campaign to free poetry from the kinds of authority which he recognised as both impositional and delusive. That same radicalism will also help us to understand the animosity shown towards him by critics like Walter Bagehot. The Brownings' decision to leave England and to settle in Florence is integral to their determination to deny the kind of Englishness which might be expected of poets. Equally important, the way in which Browning ordered the sequences of his poems is self-consciously anti-authoritarian, although this seems never to have been understood. It has also gone unnoticed that he continued the radical work of the great Romantic poets by allowing a range of different voices into his work; and by juxtaposing them, one against the other, he denied his readers the opportunity to take any one of them on trust. The society of voices he presents is endlessly problematic. And when he himself appears in one of his poems, as for example in 'A Light Woman', it is as part of the problem rather than as the problem's resolution.

I would claim Browning as a kind of city poet. By this I mean that in their implied synchronicity his voices register both multiplicity and simultaneity, the tangled hubbub of *Gesellschaft*. Moreover, his typical absence from his own poems suggests the poet as a recording, invisible *flâneur*, who may be thought to characterise a distinctively modern type of writer, the writer in the city.[6]

It was not, however, until the twentieth century that the possibilities which Browning opened up were taken further. His contemporaries and immediate successors were unable to draw on his strengths, which they saw indeed as weaknesses. The major reason for this is that they and their supporters felt unhappy about any suggestion that poets, the practitioners of high art and thus the upholders of culture, should be seen to surrender their poetic authority. This is especially true of Matthew Arnold. Arnold had a very definite sense of what England ought to be, and it did not include the right to utterance by a wide variety of voices. Such a right was the equivalent of 'Doing As One Likes' (the title of a famous chapter in *Culture and Anarchy*). Arnold would have understood Browning's heteroglossia as a form of anarchy, the clamour of the barbarians at the gates.[7]

Others disagreed with Arnold's particular vision of the good society, but by and large they shared his detestation of mass democracy, of city society. *Demos* spoke with the voice of the beast. The most openly reactionary poets clung to a pastoral vision of England. The rest, reactionaries and radicals alike, committed themselves to that vision of primitivism which emerged in the later years of the century as a regenerative alternative to the decadence of the society of the city. (The late-nineteenth-century city-state was to be feared rather than welcomed.) With the exception of Kipling, that odd, special case, poets typically made the voices of English people inaudible. They also made the England of city life invisible.

By the end of the nineteenth century most English people lived in cities. To be English was not to be English.

CHAPTER 1

Englishmen and Citizens of the World

I

One of the minor, if predictable, consequences of the 'bloodless revolution' of 1688 was that it cost Dryden his post as Poet Laureate. A Catholic convert (he was admitted to the church in 1686), Dryden was deeply committed to a vision of the state which took for granted an idealised role for monarchical absolutism. This vision is most powerfully worked through in *The Hind and the Panther*. Here, Dryden opposes the unifying powers of Roman Catholicism to the schismatic and sectarian tendencies of other religions: 'Not sparklets shattered into sects like you:/One is the church, and must be, to be true.' The combination of disdain and emphatic utterance make the Hind's words central to the poem's meaning. This is the voice of true authority and it inaugurates a manner which, heard here for perhaps the first time in English literature, comes to dominate much later writing. Such a tone implies its user's unassailable authority, his rightful possession of the credentials without which one has no right to speak for England. Dryden here uses a 'correct' rather than a 'plain' style.

To say this is to suggest that *The Hind and the Panther* is as much about politics as it is about religion. I cannot agree with William Myers, one of the poem's best commentators, who goes so far as to say that it 'is not primarily about ideas at all', but I share his feeling that it is undoubtedly taken up with 'specific and pressing political problems . . . its major preoccupation is with divisions of power within the kingdom as a whole'.[1] The quarrel between the king and the squirearchy makes for an especially deep division. Myers' subtle account is of great importance to a full understanding of the poem. However, I want to put the emphasis elsewhere. The failure of religious toleration which the poem investigates requires some people to be less than fully English, for that is what the Exclusion laws mean. Besides, Dryden is aware that the spirit of sectarianism, strengthened by exclusion, spreads to Anglicans themselves. The Commons splits apart from what it perceives to be the Roman Catholic dominated court of James II.

The departure of Catholic James and the arrival of Protestant William and Mary might have seemed to provide the ideal opportunity to suture this split. The last fears or hopes of monarchical absolutism left England with James. In its place came a constitutional monarchy. But another split then opens up: between Protestant England and Catholic Europe. The new monarchy brought with it wars against France which were to last until well into the nineteenth century and which, if they made good financial sense to some commoners, meant for others the wreck of a grander dream of orderliness and peace. Dryden had pleaded for 'common quiet [as] mankind's concern'. His desire for sweet submission is replaced by the newer watchword of 'liberty', a watchword which Dryden had seen as the spirit of the sectarianism he so feared. Of course, liberty of conscience and action were to become and remain endlessly problematic (as well as frequently illusory). Nevertheless, in the early years of the eighteenth century, liberty and Englishness become synonymous concepts and virtually interchangeable terms, and it is in response to this that the construction of a national literature was and would continue to be so important.

Raymond Williams notes that the term *Nationalliteratur* first appears in Germany in the 1780s, and he remarks that 'histories of national literatures . . . were being written in German, French and English from the same period in which there was a major change in ideas both of "the nation" and of "cultural nationality"'.[2] This is plainly true, but it is necessary to make the additional if obvious point that the writing of history comes later than the writing of literature. There must be something out of which to construct a history. In the period after 1688, writers tended to see themselves as specifically 'writing for England', by which I mean that they thought of their work as contributing to and even defining cultural nationality.

The consequences of this new ambition, or new responsibility, are plain enough. The best-known history of English literature in the eighteenth century is Johnson's *Lives of the Poets*, and this work is as famous for what it omits as for what it includes. It collaborates with and endorses the notion of cultural nationality that Dryden had virtually inaugurated, and it therefore has to leave out of account, or downgrade, writers who implicitly or explicitly contest that notion. Milton is more or less anathematised, Bunyan – the author of some very remarkable poems – ignored.

It is not hard to see why. Both great writers are frankly divisive in their claim to speak for certain values and ideas of nationality which are necessarily oppositional. Above all, they champion that private conscience whose fruit, in Dryden's terms, was 'occasioned by great zeal and little thought'. Dryden neatly denies validity to the history of intellectual debate in which Milton was engaged throughout his life: the spirit of the Commonwealth is identified as ignorant, rancorous, 'zealous', and endlessly threatening to wreck the dream of a united nation. As indeed it must, if that dream is taken to be dependent on throne and established Church. It is here that English radicalism takes its stand.

For obvious reasons, then, Dryden and Johnson were ill at ease with Milton. But Shakespeare was a different matter. He *could* be accommodated within their comparable visions of England and its national literature. An Anglican Johnson may have been, but his absolutism – 'Sir, the King cannot have too much power' – brings him very close to Dryden's position. Johnson has nothing to say of Shakespeare in the *Lives*, but for all that he was a preoccupation. In the poem he wrote for the re-opening of the Drury Lane Theatre in 1747 under Garrick's management, Johnson suggests that Shakespeare coincided with 'learning's triumphs o'er its barbarous foes'. Elsewhere he rather lets go of that argument and says that Shakespeare did not need learning, he could rely on 'nature'. But nature is a suspect ally. Johnson therefore agrees with Dryden that Shakespeare's art and especially his language can lapse into semi-barbarity. He came before the full achievement of that Englishness which Johnson significantly places after the Restoration. Such Englishness is both a matter of politics and of language, the two necessarily intertwined. Shakespeare pre-dates the terrible fall into the Commonwealth and is not to be implicated in it. But his barbarisms must be sheared off if he is to be made acceptable to a post-1660 England.

Dryden had seen it as his duty to rewrite and reshape – 'civilise' – Shakespeare. Only then could Shakespeare take his place in the national literature. The same held true of Chaucer, which was why Dryden undertook to 'translate' Chaucer's work. He says of *The Canterbury Tales* that 'We have our Fore-fathers and Great Grand-dames all before us as they were in Chaucer's Days; their general Characters are still remaining in Mankind, and even in England, though they are call'd by other names . . . For Mankind is ever the same . . .'[3] In this context it is clear that the construction of a national literature is self-consciously concerned with whatever can be lifted free of the accidental, the local, the time-bound, or of divisive politics. All literature which is worthy to be part of the culture must be timeless, universal and indeed classical. (In the double sense: connected to the literatures of Greece and Rome by the rules of art and at the same time, and as those rules make possible, built to last.) *Antony and Cleopatra* thus becomes *All for Love*, a play which obeys the unities. Johnson could be more relaxed about Shakespeare's ignoring the unities: as he noted, the play takes place on stage, and the audience can as easily imagine itself in Rome as in Alexandria. But if he here exonerates Shakespeare's practice by a 'common-sense' appeal to nature, he elsewhere berates him for failing to abide by the need for moral instruction. Shakespeare is then seen as irresponsible in his presumed role as law-giver to the nation. But this is because he comes at a moment before the responsibilities of the writer were properly understood. Dryden recognised that Antony's dereliction of civic duties was – or at least ought to have been – the real centre of Shakespeare's play. Compared with that, the unities are of small importance.

For all the differences between them, Dryden and Johnson have much in common. Above all, Johnson shares Dryden's concern for critical standards to measure the value of a work. This is why he calls Dryden the father of English criticism, because he 'is the writer who first taught us to determine upon principles the merit of composition'. Such principles come 'partly from the Ancients, and partly from the Italians and French'. Dryden thus 'imported his science, and gave his country what it wanted before; or rather, he imported only the materials, and manufactured them by his own skill'. In addition, Dryden gave England a 'poetical diction, [a] system of words at once refined from the grossness of domestick use, and free of the harshness of terms appropriate to particular arts'. As with human nature, so, then, with language: it is at its truest when freed from history. Dryden's praise of Chaucer's characters is matched by Johnson's praise of Shakespeare. 'His drama is the mirror of life . . . His story requires Romans or kings, but he thinks only on men . . . a poet overlooks the casual distinction of country and condition . . .' By such means Shakespeare can be made to fit into the idea of a national literature.

It is in this context that we need to consider the significance of Dryden's translations of the Roman poets, in particular his translations of Virgil. Why did he undertake them? In his *Life* of Dryden Johnson grandly asserted that 'The nation considered its honour as interested in the event.' By 'nation', Johnson means that element within it which can be identified as full citizens. This is to think of the nation as modelled on the Graeco-Roman city-state, with free men as those who alone have an interest in the state's welfare, which will include all matters of cultural importance. It is for them that Dryden undertakes his translations. Such citizens will in all probability realise that the age of epic is past. For epics coincide with or are about the birth of a nation, and in common with other citizens Dryden does not wish to stir up trouble by re-opening the question of how the English nation in which he and they live has come to be formed. True, he says in the Dedication to his *Juvenal* (1693) that it had been his early ambition to write an epic 'intended chiefly for the Honour of my Native Country', but he adds that 'want' has prevented the writing of such a poem. Hardly. Dryden, after all, was never poorer than Milton. But Milton's epic ambitions were not for the honour of the nation as Dryden and Johnson after him understood that term. Milton had the forming of a very different nation in mind.

Dryden's *Aeneid* is, however, an epic made available to the nation of free citizens. It indicates the possibilities of continuity with that cultural identity which became known in contemporary debates through the term 'the ancients'. England and Catholic Europe are now made part of a continuum that reaches back behind and beyond the fissures of more 'local' politics. It is the assumption that such a continuum existed – in space as well as time – which allows T. S. Eliot, whose critical ambitions and ideological commitments are in many ways those of a wished-for Johnson – to propose Marvell as a more 'European' poet than Milton. According to Eliot, Marvell, 'more a man of the century than a Puritan, speaks more clearly and unequivocally with the voice of his literary age than does Milton'. This voice is apparently European and, specifically, French. Moreover, given that the theme of 'To his Coy Mistress' is 'one of the great traditional commonplaces of European literature', Marvell can also be recruited for Augustanism. Dryden and Pope use 'Augustan', a revitalising of the Roman term for London, so as to promote an image of Rome as model for the ideal city-state. Augustan Rome existed at a moment of history where the civic and liberal arts could flourish under the benign influence of an all-powerful and thus peace-ensuring emperor. It is largely beside the point to argue that Dryden's London was no more like that than Augustus' Rome had been. Dryden – and Pope after him – could usefully appeal to the myth as a way of indicating the dangers of duncery, which threatened 'civilisation'.

At its best the myth of London/Augusta is one of generous intent. It imagines a modern city-state risen phoenix-like from the ashes of the fire of London, built in a manner to outlast immortal Rome, but *like* immortal Rome (its architecture a palimpsest beneath whose contemporaneity we can read the work of Palladio and the civic buildings of Augustus' Rome). Its literature would likewise be palimpsestic: hence, for example, Pope's *Imitations of Horace*, especially the First Epistle of the Second Book, with its dedication to Augustus. Literature was also to be public, social, responsible, its characteristic forms including the ethic epistle and, very importantly, heroic drama, a form which endorses civic virtues, the individual as realised and vindicated through activities which declare him to be the model citizen. Verse satire ('to lash the follies of the age') and 'imitation' ('the dead living into counsel call[ed]'), are also characteristic forms.

Music, domestic architecture and the visual arts had also to play their parts. As John Dennis noted, 'There is nothing in Nature that is great and beautiful, without Rule and Order; and the more Rule and Order, and Harmony, we find in the Objects that strike our senses, the more Worthy and Noble we esteem them.' The coerciveness of this is as apparent as is the inserted term 'Harmony', which allows Dennis fully to politicise his aesthetics, and in doing so to sweeten them. Rule and Order make for Harmony, and this is to be expected whether 'we' are rulers and orderers or the ruled and ordered. A. R. Humphreys offers an intriguing gloss on Carlyle's praise for Wren's Chelsea Hospital, a building which Carlyle had apparently passed by for years, until he realised that it had always given him a certain pleasure: it was quiet and dignified and the work of a gentleman. 'In other words,' Humphreys says, 'it considers its company, is clear without pedantry, and has a self-command which comes not from lack of spirit but from an instinct for social order.'[4]

It was central to the achievement of the Commonwealth period that such 'instinct' had been turned upside down: 'When Adam delved and Eve span/Who was then the gentleman?' And it should therefore come as no surprise that the Commonwealth's great epic, *Paradise Lost*, is later produced in a manner that will make it reveal precisely that 'instinct' for social order – and hence submissiveness – that Milton challenged. You might not be able to ignore his poem, but at least you could do your best to tame it. In 1688 Jacob Tonson completed his purchase of the rights to *Paradise Lost* and that same year produced an illustrated edition of the poem. His choice of Joseph Medina as illustrator has puzzled some commentators, given that Medina, who was of Spanish family, born in Brussels and at work in London from 1686, was basically 'a painter of history, landscapes and portraits'.[5] But if we put together Tonson's Toryism[6] and Medina's probable Catholicism, it becomes clear that, commercial considerations apart (and Tonson claimed that he made more by *Paradise Lost* than by any other poem), the radical intention of Milton's work is being deliberately subverted, or undercut.

This is especially obvious in the final, most crucial illustration, of the unparadised Adam and Eve. It explicitly harks back to Michelangelo, who like Masaccio insists on the terrible grief of the lost pair. Milton very probably saw one or both of these images when he was in Italy. His determination to have Adam and Eve leave Paradise 'hand in hand' is, then, a calculated break with such a tradition. It insists on the paradox of a happy fall, and gives Adam and Eve a measure of human independence and resolve which is implicitly anti-authoritarian and also by implication, libertarian. Their 'wandering steps', while acknowledging their fall into a world of sin, implies a measure of freedom which the image of the driven, grief-overborne pair denies.

The full development of this paradox, these implications, has to wait for Blake's revolutionary revisiting of Milton's radicalism and of the new confidence which is read into 'wandering', a subject which will be taken up in Chapter 4. But enough has been said to show why the epic was bound to be a troubling form. Dryden might translate Virgil and Pope Homer, but if their labours succeeded in demonstrating the fact of a continuum they were also meant to mark out the distance between then and now. The epic is a poem of and for the people, it is about the struggles to found a nation or the struggles that come at a nation's inception. In England such struggles had to be confined to the past. To write a modern epic would be to awaken all those contentious issues which the events of 1660 and 1688 were supposed to have put to rest.

There is another consideration. Epic virtues might not necessarily be civic virtues. Courage, daring, unappeasable anger: these were potentially dangerous qualities, enlistable in contentious causes. As we shall see later, benevolence rather than bravery becomes identified as the truly civic virtue. (Bravery can be seen as positively anti-civic because self-interested; epic virtue then becomes un- or pre-civilised.) In short, although epic was commonly agreed to be the highest of poetic forms, it might not be socially the most acceptable. It is true that John Dennis praised Milton for having resolved 'for his Country's Honour and his own, to present the World with an Original Poem', but we have seen that Dennis also emphasised the need for harmony and order and he has therefore to reconcile Milton's epic with these terms. He does this by concentrating on what he regards as its formal achievement. By comparing it to the work of Homer and Virgil he is able, so he says, to derive 'the Laws . . . of a True Epick Poem'. He carefully avoids any suggestion that *Paradise Lost* might not subscribe to what he sets out as the true end of poetry, which is 'to instruct and reform the World, that is, to bring Mankind from Irregularity, Extravagance and Confusion, to Rule and Order'.[7]

Johnson knew better than to try to tame *Paradise Lost* by such tricks.

I I

Yet 1688 marks the beginning of the end for that particular dream of order which Humphreys reads into the Chelsea Hospital. Both Dennis and Johnson, in their respective appeals to 'the Country' and 'the Nation', are seeking to identify a wider constituency than Dryden would have considered appropriate to his vision of the state. By comparison with these later writers, Dryden, indeed, begins to look out of date. It is not merely that his absolutism is against the times; more significant, and vulnerable, is his concern to uphold the city-state and its citizens as model for the developing England. Dryden finishes his career as a displaced, an 'unofficial' poet. His *Aeneid* was completed in the 1690s, by which time he no longer spoke 'for England'. His replacement as Poet Laureate was his old enemy, that embodiment of 'dullness' and duncery, Thomas Shadwell. And while Shadwell, who was by no means the dullard of Dryden's invention, might not have been a political libertarian, he was quite prepared to adopt a Whiggish stance in his paeans to the new king. In his loyal poem for 1692, 'On His Majesty's Conquests in Ireland', Shadwell makes William into a kind of Cromwell *redivivus*:

> To distant realms his conquering arms he bears,
> And hostile lands are made the seat of wars.
> On him and us these blessings are bestow'd,
> Peace flourishes at home, and war abroad.
> Disdainful princes are compell'd to bow;
> And haughty France begins to feel us now.

The defeat of the French fleet near Cape la Hogue on 19 May 1692 meant that James could no longer maintain communications with France. After crushing the Irish, William was therefore free to move on to those wars against the French which would last on and off for over a century. 'Peace flourishes at home and war abroad.' This is both precise and chilling. Shadwell's enthusiasm for war is loaded with that xenophobia which, while it may seek some justification in fear of reactionary France, is nevertheless a way of justifying aggressive expansionism.

It is also narrowly patriotic. It implies that an especial set of virtues runs in the blood of Englishmen, and that these are characteristically expressed through militaristic valour. Defoe's *The True-Born Englishman* of 1701 sets out vigorously to demolish the racist myth of Englishness. The English are, he says, the 'mix'd Relics' of 'all the Nations under Heaven', and especially of their 'Barbarous offspring'.

> From this Amphibious Ill-Born mob began
> *That vain ill-natur'd thing*, an English-man . . .
> By which with easie search you may distinguish
> Your *Roman-Saxon-Danish-Norman* English.

A hectically comic account of the history of England leads Defoe to the conclusion that 'we have been *Europe's* Sink, the *Jakes* where She/Voids all her Offal Out-cast Progeny'. Defoe's poem is a satire directed against those who claimed that William could not be considered for the English throne because he wasn't of pure English blood. It has the further aim of justifying expansionism by its tacit appeal to William's hybrid virtues.

Such expansionism begins at home. More important than the crushing of the Irish was the Act of Union of 1707, for this gave new force to the term 'British', suggesting a united people – 'the island race' – posed against Europe. (Though as Defoe among others well understood, the Act of Union effectively turned Scotland into a province of England, a matter which the Scots quickly and bitterly recognised.)[8] Even Pope seems to share Shadwell's exuberance when in *Windsor Forest* he imagines that in Lansdown's song 'Should vanquish'd *France* appear,/[It would] bleed for ever under *Britain's* spear', and foresees how 'Kings shall sue, and suppliant States be seen/Once more to bow before a British Queen'.

The bullishness of some of this may be due to the fact that the lines were written fairly early in the century (the composition of the poem was spread over the years 1704–12). But by the time Pope came to write the latter part of *Windsor Forest*, the Treaty of Utrecht had been signed. He was therefore keen to separate the monarchy from the kind of bloodthirstiness Shadwell had endorsed.

> At length great ANNA said – let Discord cease!
> She said, the World obey'd, and all was *Peace*!

The editors of the Twickenham Pope refer us to a possible source for these lines in John Philips' *Cyder*, where Anna is made to say 'Let there be UNION.'

Even if Pope does not intend this, it is significant that the unmistakable echo of the divine proclamation should be put into the mouth of the monarch. For this is to hint at 'divine rights' which the creation of a constitutional monarchy had firmly banished. It is also mystificatory. Peace was achieved not so much by Anne herself as by her Minister of War, George Lansdown, to whom Pope dedicated *Windsor Forest*. But Pope could justify his tactic on the grounds that it was Anne who in 1710 had had much to do with Lansdown's being brought in to replace Sir Robert Walpole (who was dedicated to the war as a sound commercial venture); and it was Anne who in 1712 created twelve new peers as a way of saving the Tory ministry and thus the peace (Lansdown was one of the twelve). Suppliant states therefore become like courtiers: they pay homage to their 'natural' head. In submission is peace, order and a vision of a united Europe.

The peace so achieved was as bitterly resented as was the Act of Union. And it may well be that Pope's frequent switching of terms in the poem – 'Albion', 'Britain', 'Augusta' – is an attempt to confuse or fuse political realities and so create an acceptable myth. 'Albion' conveniently identifies the most ancient name of Britain with a sense of unbroken history while at the same time allowing for its identification with England (as it often was so identified) and ultimately with Augusta/London.

It was this kind of carefully manufactured, seamless, image of a reconciled nation which Dryden had done so much to create, and which he appealed to in 'Threnodia Augustalis', his elegy for Charles 11. Charles had not merely been an ideal authority figure:

> Not Foreign or Domestick Treachery,
> Could Warp thy Soul to their Unjust Decree.
> So much thy Foes thy manly Mind mistook,
> Who judg'd it by the Mildness of thy look:
> Like a well-temper'd Sword, it bent at will;
> But kept the Native toughness of the Steel.

> (ll. 321–326)

Here, the blend of tolerance and strength imputed to Charles is identified as uniquely valuable and proper to the king-as-ruler. His restoration to the throne has brought with it arts of 'purest and well winnow'd Grain/As Britain never knew before'. This image of the husbanding of art is then pursued through the poem in a familiar enough trope: Charles as farmer. But behind it is the appeal to that European continuum, and in particular to the *Georgics*, which is as unmistakable as it is politically propagandist. The king 'Plough'd and Sow'd and Till'd,/The Thorns he rooted out, the Rubbish clear'd,/And blest th'obedient Field'. It is an almost wearily familiar literary tactic, although we should note that blessing the obedient field comes rather more easily in the poem than it had in fact.

Of much greater interest is the connection Dryden makes between husbandry and sexual potency. Not that this is unique in poems about Charles. But the idea of England as a woman, responding 'fruitfully' to her royal master, carries with it a heavily loaded charge in the songs of *King Arthur* (1691), a work which was, so Dryden said, 'the last piece of service' he could do for Charles. Here, Aeolus sings of Britannia as 'Serene and calm, and void of fear,/The Queen of Islands . . .' England as a female body generously loved by her late king, England as Britannia: these are crucial extensions of the language of the *Georgics*. There is, too, the ghost of a private joke in the compliment to Charles and his loved woman. The image of Britannia, as she reappeared on coins from 1672, was modelled on the king's favourite mistress, the Duchess of Richmond, Frances Stewart.[9] Britannia's shield bears the crosses of St George and St Andrew. The olive branch which at this period begins to be placed in her hands links her with Athena, goddess both of wisdom and war, and of peace and cultural fruitfulness. Britannia is given 'classical' status and at the same time made to connect with and even embody a developing, composite image of Britannia/ Albion as the nation whose centre, London, is modelled on the ideal city-state.

Dryden had made another appeal to the image and potentialities of Britannia in his last poem as Poet Laureate. 'Britannia Rediviva: A Poem on the Birth of the Prince' was published in June 1688 to celebrate the birth of James Edward, Prince of Wales, the 'Old Pretender'. Ironically, it was the birth of a son to a Catholic king which proved, as Christopher Hill has remarked, 'the last straw. An invitation was sent to William of Orange to invade England.'[10] It is entirely probable that Dryden feared this turn of events. His poem seems desperately anxious to read Heavenly assurances into the royal birth. He appeals to St George as 'th'adopted Patron of our Isle', to smile on the infant, and insists that 'The Pledge of Heav'n . . . dropping from above/Secures our Bliss.' But the poem is haunted by the fear of 'Dire Rebellion'; and this is far stronger than the assertion that 'Kind Heav'n, to make us *English-Men* again,/No less can give us than a Patriarch's Reign'. It peers through the lines where Dryden dares to foresee 'A Harvest ripening for another Reign,/Of which this Royal Babe *may* reap the Grain' (my italics). James Edward was to be no royal farmer, and it was not grain he was to reap but a bitter wind. Dryden is expecting Britannia to accomplish the impossible: guard against the overthrow of a by now deeply unpopular king and one who had not, despite Dryden's wishful thinking, 'Three Realms united'. The songs of *King Arthur* are not about contemporary actualities, for those had gone painfully against Dryden's hopes. Instead, they outline a dream of peaceful fruitfulness necessarily – from Dryden's point of view – at odds with the kinds of abrasive intolerance and aggressions characteristic of the reign of William and Mary.

This is why the accession of Anne provides Pope with the ideal opportunity for bringing together ideas about the state, order, fruitfulness, peace; and to identify them with the loved body whose centre Anne is (as 'Anna' is the heart of 'Britannia'). Pope develops Dryden's theme. The Act of Union makes it now entirely proper for Britannia's shield to carry the crosses of George and Andrew, just as the newly-achieved supremacy of the seas allows for the propriety of adopting the legend whereby Neptune was said to have yielded Britannia his sceptre (a fancy first mooted in 1652). Britannia ruled the waves before Thomson and Arne between them composed the song for their masque *King Alfred* of 1740. She rules them in *Windsor Forest*.

The image of Anne which Pope constructs in this poem is complex and subtle.

> Here *Ceres'* Gifts in waving Prospect stand,
> And nodding tempt the joyful Reaper's Hand,
> Rich Industry sits smiling on the Plains,
> And Peace and Plenty tell, a STUART reigns.

The Roman goddess of harvest is naturalised in the English landscape, through identification with the British queen; and the peace and plenty for which she is responsible cancel at a stroke wars abroad and work at home. Industry 'sits smiling', and the reaper's joy comes from gifts which put themselves invitingly on offer. He doesn't have to go in search of them, nor is there any possibility that he might be violating their peace. The passage as a whole is derived from or bonded to *Georgics II*, especially those lines where Virgil praised Caesar for making possible Italy's unrivalled fruitfulness through 'secur[ing] our peace at home' (I quote Dryden's version).

In *Pope's Dunciad and the Queen of the Night*, Douglas Brooks-Davies argues for Pope as a Jacobite. The poet would be the more ready to praise Anne because she, too, was strongly Jacobite in her sympathies. Brooks-Davies suggests that before her death Anne was suspected, and not without some justification, of having put her Stuart blood before her Protestant faith by secretly sending funds over to France in support of the Old Pretender. 'Shortly after her succession she had made another vitally significant gesture by adopting Elizabeth, the Virgin Queen's, poignant yet defiant motto, *semper eadem*, for her own. She addressed her first parliament wearing robes modelled on those in a portrait of Elizabeth.'[11] The fact that Elizabeth was a Tudor queen doesn't hurt Brooks-Davies's argument, for the Tudor/Stuart lineage of the monarchy could be presented as both seamless and harmonious (Rule and Order); and besides, there is a body of evidence to show that certain of Pope's contemporaries thought of Elizabeth as the ideal monarch. Brooks-Davies very usefully refers to a comment of Swift's, made in 1701, that 'About the middle of Queen Elizabeth's Reign, I take the Power between Nobles and Commons, to have been in more equal Ballance than it was ever before or since.'

Pope's Anna/Britannia is, then, an image to be read with as much care as has to be taken in 'reading' Wren's London. It is another palimpsest and in it may be seen not merely an accretion of past images which endorse a particular version of the harmonious state, but a promise for the future. At the end of a section of *Windsor Forest* in which Pope has justified the deaths of William I and his son, William Rufus, as tyrannic oppressors, he says: 'Succeeding Monarchs heard the Subjects Cries,/Nor saw displeas'd the peaceful Cottage rise.' A new peaceable order follows, where husbandry and tillage are suggestive of both fruitfulness and a blended body politic.

> Then gath'ring Flocks on unknown Mountains fed
> O'er sandy Wilds were yellow Harvests spread,
> The Forests wonder'd at th'unusual Grain
> And secret Transport touch'd the conscious Swain.
> Fair *Liberty*, *Britannia's* Goddess, rears
> Her cheerful Head, and leads the golden Years.
>
> (ll. 87–92)

A formerly barren land is now given over to cultivation, and this includes the grafting of new onto old. 'Th'unusual Grain' echoes Virgil's discussion of grafting in the *Georgics II*, but also implies a social grafting: the forest which had been exclusively reserved for a king's hunting is now set free for all to enjoy. At this point Liberty becomes identified as Britannia's goddess, and in triumph leads the newly emparadised nation towards a future of even greater peace and plenty. ('Golden Years' invokes an endless succession both of ripe harvests and of material wealth.) But it is this very spirit of liberty which will lead to the fall of 'the peaceful Cottage', a matter which Pope obviously does not wish to consider even though it is bound to be of the first importance to the conscious Swain. The appropriation of the land is a subject about which Pope has very little to say.

A possible explanation for his glossing over or mystification of the tensions within the image of the goddess Liberty is that the problem of enclosure, whether for emparkment or farming, became acute only later in the century. Then again, since *Windsor Forest* is an attempt to create a mythic ideal, rather than to provide a look at the worst, Pope's ultimate responsibility is to produce a poem which will vindicate the ambition. It is a highly elaborate, intensely self-conscious production, at once about an ideal and an embodiment of it. It therefore needs fit readers. Conscious Swains need not apply. And if we then ask who the fit reader is likely to be, the answer, I suggest, is – the citizen of the world.

III

This term needs to be both explained and justified. I do not have in mind Goldsmith's *faux naïf* outsider who 'innocently' records his impressions of European civilisations and in so doing reveals its follies and vices. (Montesquieu's *Lettres Persanes*, 1721, is commonly agreed to be the starting point for this kind of satiric exercise.) On the contrary, my citizen of the world is a descendant of Dryden's ideal reader, the 'urbane' upholder of order whose cultural preferences and possessions, presented as unhesitatingly 'correct', make him the embodiment of what, for Dryden, constitutes an ideal of the national identity. He is the kind of 'civilised gentleman' – learned in the classics, politically Tory, with an instinct for social order – who as a largely mythic construct is nevertheless produced and/or appealed to by Pope, his circle and their followers, because he can be identified as anti-Shadwell, anti-Walpole, anti-commerce. He will therefore be resistant to that developing connection between commercialism and patriotism – commercialism defining itself *as* patriotism – which is one aspect of Liberty, Britannia's goddess, and which can also be an expression of 'Englishness'.

The citizen of the world is likely to be wary of the claims made by such as Andrew Freeport. Addison, Freeport's creator, describes him as a man of 'natural Eloquence, good sense, and Probity of Mind', 'of indefatigable Industry, strong Reason, and great Experience', who 'will tell you that it is a stupid and barbarous way to extend dominion by arms; for true power is got by arts and industry'. Addison was writing these words in 1710–11, and by then many Whigs and merchants were prepared for peace against France. (Though many *weren't*: hence the twelve new peers of 1712.) But although Freeport may here speak against extending dominion by arms, the fact is that successive Whig ministries did their best to use arms in order to gain dominion. His claim that power is to be got by arts and industry therefore sounds as though he proposes a continuation of war by other means. This is perhaps why he claims to find 'a general trader of good sense . . . pleasanter company than a general scholar' (*Spectator* nos 2 and 549). For general scholar read citizen of the world.

Or read, perhaps, a man such as Anthony Ashley Cooper, third Earl of Shaftesbury. Shaftesbury has not been especially well served by recent accounts of the period. Pat Rogers disposes of him with the information that he was 'a valetudinarian, with desultory Whig politics and a talent for making friends', although he concedes that his *Characteristics* 'still makes lively reading by reason of the author's passionate eloquence'. But the final verdict is that Shaftesbury was no more than an 'amiable amateur' who yet oddly became something of a 'culture-hero', enjoying 'very great renown – and it was an esteem the Romantics could later share'.[12] Rogers does not, however, explain that the Romantics admired Shaftesbury for the same reason as did his contemporaries: his concern with liberty.

This is admittedly to say very little. Liberty is a term which can be used in moment concerned, liberty comes to be associated with and appropriated by a newly-emergent class, one which typically identifies with a constitutional newly-emergent class, one which typically identifies with a constitutional monarchy, with the Hanoverian succession, and with parliamentary power. Steele directs his political journal *The Englishman*, successor to the *Guardian*, precisely to this class. He wrote and published *The Englishman* between the key years 1713–15. In the fifth number of the journal he calls the Pretender 'a Traytor to this Nation' who is justly excluded from 'the Birthright and Freedom of an Englishman'; and he repeatedly invokes the Constitution as the safeguard of an Englishman's liberty. Probably the most detailed exposition of this occurs in the twenty-second and twenty-third papers, written in September 1715 in response to Lord Mar's proclamation in Scotland of the Rebellion. Here, Steele sets out King George's claims to the throne and concludes that 'our Gracious Sovereign is arrived at the Throne of *Great-Britain*, which Title none can think to molest, but Men whose Consciences are so monstrously turned, as to prompt them to swear to a Prince in order to find Means to destroy him, and abjure a Pretender, in order to introduce him'.[13] Rae Blanchard rightly notes in the introduction to his edition of *The Englishman*, that Steele is a man of '"Revolution Principles". The justice of the Revolution of 1688, which had ejected a king ruling by divine hereditary right, and the legality of the Convention Parliament of 1689, which had created by a law a new succession, were the continually recurring subjects in *The Englishman*.[14] Blanchard might have added that Steele sees in this new succession a guarantee of liberty for his class and its interests. Here, the term can be taken to mean both freedom from an absolute monarchy and freedom to develop largely mercantile concerns and an interest in political affairs. In this lies the inevitability of future tensions.

Shaftesbury's use of the word 'liberty' matters because it shows that at this moment it was still possible for those who might at first assume they had little in common politically to share in a vision of cultural attainment which would support an 'Englishness' as inclusive as it was desirable. From the perspective of conventional politics Pope and Shaftesbury can appear to be antitypes. One was Catholic, private, Tory, even Jacobite. The other was a public figure, Protestant, with Whig sympathies. But more joined them than divided them. Their essentially European viewpoint has at its sustaining centre a vision of continuity, nurtured by the liberty of the truly free man. Steele and even Addison could on occasions share this vision with their political opponents. Steele's Englishman speaks of the good 'critick' as one who 'throws himself back into ancient Time, lives a thousand Years of

Criticism in a Month, and without stirring from his Closet, is a *Greek*, a *Roman*, a *Frenchman*, and a *Briton*'.[15] Addison views with genial contempt the kind of country squire who, as a ferocious critic of foreigners, remarks that 'he scarce ever knew a Traveller in his life who had not forsook his principles, and lost his hunting seat'.[16] He delights in showing himself as more truly urbane than the Tory gentry he here rebukes. But beyond the scoring of points is a more substantial concern to uphold the model of world citizen, praise of general traders notwithstanding. Although Freeport often acts as Addison's spokesman, he isn't to be confused with Addison himself. He merely provides Addison with the opportunity to prick the skins of complacent Tories. This is a form of Horatian irony, and one of its outstanding exponents is Shaftesbury.

In his excellent account of Shaftesbury in *To The Palace of Wisdom*, Martin Price points out the use of an allegorical engraving of 'the triumph of liberty' as a frontispiece for Shaftesbury's book-length essay *The Moralists*. He further notes that Shaftesbury 'chose to have [it] appear in all three volumes of the second edition of his comprehensive work, the *Characteristics of Men, Manners, Times* etc'.[17] Shaftesbury is well aware that the concept poses more problems than it solves, and it is not possible to follow him into all his arguments, doubts and speculations about what these may be. However, as Price rightly remarks, Shaftesbury's mind is 'saturated in that philosophy he calls Socratic, civil, social, and theistic'. For this reason he makes much of what he identifies as Horace's characteristic cast of mind – a kind of poised, Socratic irony. He is also deeply sceptical of and resistant to the Calvinistic emphasis on human depravity and the Hobbesian account of human nature. His way of writing, by turns playful, sardonic, enquiring, enacts in its rejection of dogmatics a concept of the truly 'civilised'. And this may in turn be called Socratic or Horatian, or, at a pinch, Voltairean. While Geoffrey Holmes is surely correct in calling him 'that austere critic of his party's principles and standards', Shaftesbury's prose testifies to a mental quality which can be identified with the smile of reason.[18] And in its wide-ranging allusiveness and appeal to essentially classical models, it proclaims itself the voice of what I call the citizen of the world. Shaftesbury was a frequent visitor to Holland, and although he was an ardent supporter of the wars against the French, was keenly attuned to European ideas. His is the opposite of that sectarian voice of aggressive self-interest which can be called Freeportian, even if Freeport himself doesn't speak like it.

The account of Shaftesbury I am here offering will no doubt help to explain why the Romantics chose to admire him. Yet his view of Europe is not theirs, any more than his concept of liberty anticipates developments that come later in the century. Shaftesbury is very much the Enlightenment humanist. For him, the free man is the enfranchised man. His thinking about the nation-state is derived from the classical model of the city-state.

Only those who are enfranchised can be truly disinterested in desiring the best for the state, and they will use their freedom to the best advantage if they have the faculty for judgement which is based on wide and deep knowledge of other states. In the *Characteristics* Shaftesbury speaks of the truly free men as those who

> have seen *the World*, and inform'd themselves of the *Manners* and *Customs* of the several Nations of EUROPE, search'd into their *Antiquitys* and *Records* . . . observ'd the Situation, Strength, and Ornaments of their *Citys*, their principal *Arts* . . . *Architecture, Sculpture, Painting, Musick* . . . *Poetry, Learning, Language,* and *Conversation* . . .

These are the citizens of the world. Their freedom includes a freedom from self-interest. It even includes a freedom from patriotism. Bolingbroke, Shaftesbury's admirer, remarked that 'a wise man looks on himself as a citizen of the world: and, if you ask him where his country lies, points, like ANAXAGORAS, to the heavens'.[19]

Shaftesbury thought self-interest tolerable only in so far as it could be reconciled with the interests of others: co-operation rather than competition typifies his dream of civility. Virtue consists in following what he calls our natural affections, those founded 'in Love, Complacency, Good-Will, and in a Sympathy with the Kind or Species'.[20] We will find an echo of this in the *Essay on Man*, where Pope writes that 'true *Self-Love* and *Social* are the Same'. At its furthest reach this conviction is necessarily anti-patriotic, because it requires man to be 'tribeless and nationless', to quote Shelley. But more typically it mutates into benevolence.

Here, an interesting fact emerges. Among those who held most passionately to the particular version of liberty I am outlining were a number, Pope and Swift among them, who in different ways may be considered to have become increasingly marginalised by events. It can be argued that their investment in the kind of liberty as a result of which they become citizens of the world was made possible by the fact that they had no hope of 'buying into' England. But it can equally be argued that in choosing their identity they proclaim themselves free citizens. And this will then give further authority to their argument that liberty is inconceivable without order, a position which is certainly taken by Shaftesbury, who on one occasion speaks in praise of 'that chief liberty, which is learned by obedience and submission'. Like Pope, Shaftesbury took for granted 'order in variety' as requiring a hierarchical structure, so that although 'all things differ, all agree'. The agreement of some is neither more nor less than agreement to submit to others.

This is not to imply that Shaftesbury had any desire to restore an absolute monarchy. He was a good friend to William III, and we may assume that had the king lived longer Shaftesbury's influence at court would have increased.

Had it done so, it would have been used on behalf of constitutionalism. Yet the liberty learned by obedience and submission fits snugly into that evocation of the pattern of 'ideal' social relations identified with the country house. Here again what joins Shaftesbury and Pope is more significant than what separates them. (Shaftesbury's own family seat was at St Giles's in Dorset, and he also had a house at Reigate, in Surrey.) It is usually taken for granted that the country house ideal is opposed to mercantilism; that it may legitimately be set against liberty as commercial self-interest or personal aggrandisement. As Penshurst was not built for envious show (according to Jonson's mythicising), so, according to Pope in the fourth of his Moral Essays, 'Of the Use of Riches', Burlington shows us that 'Rome was glorious, not Profuse,/And pompous buildings once were things of Use'; moreover, his 'chearful Tenants bless their yearly toil./Yet to their Lord owe more than to the soil'. 'Use' and 'toil' are not to be thought of as in any sense exploited labour. On the contrary, what the tenants 'owe' isn't so much rent as gratitude for their lord's exercise of benevolent orderliness.

Raymond Williams has remarked that such orderliness is 'a matter for conscious moral teaching. The house is properly subsidiary to the uses of money and productive investment, the creation rather than the celebration of Nature.' Williams calls this teaching a 'conscious bourgeois ethic'.[21] So it is. But there is something reductive about Williams's reading, which may work for the Man of Ross but hardly for Burlington. Williams ignores Pope's desire to produce Burlington as a citizen of the world. The glory that was Rome, as presented in the poem, requires an entirely civic awareness. Burlington therefore takes his place not merely as a good landlord, but as one whose Virgilian credentials argue for, or assert, a grander sense of 'use' than Williams will allow. Burlington became the dedicatee of the poem because of 'his Publishing Palladio's designs of the Baths, Arches, Theatres, etc of Ancient Rome', and although F. W. Bateson has criticised the poem for being 'something of a hotch-potch, one third philosophy, one third gardening, and one third architectural compliment',[22] it can be argued that Pope strives for rather more unity than Bateson acknowledges. This is why Burlington is central to the poem. He is a citizen of the world who operates as a living reproof to the failure of civic virtues wherever they are to be found: in ornate buildings imposed on a landscape. Such buildings are erected at vast expense but with no account taken of the 'genius of the place'. Their owners' fickle 'taste' therefore implies an entire failure of 'sense' and responsibility. Harmonious relations between man and nature have then an obvious political resonance. They are the outcome of a series of delicate negotiations between persons and place which image an ideal of the body politic. Order in variety is as valid for landscape architecture as for the state. Harmony is order is hierarchy.

A clear and direct line leads from *Windsor Forest* to the 'Epistle to

Burlington'. The 'conscious Swain' of the one become the 'chearful Tenants' of the other. But there is nevertheless an important difference. In the first place, the word 'Tenants', so much more precise than 'Swain', alerts us to numbers of English people whose right to the land was becoming increasingly precarious at this period. In the second, Burlington is produced as an exceptional figure, for the poem suggests that the majority of those with 'splendour' lack both taste and sense. They are also likely to be exploiters of the land – 'improvers' – who, in failing to consult 'the genius of the place', not only rape the land but effect a decisive rupture of its 'natural' human relations, where these rely on a freely accepted concept of order. And this serves to remind us that Shaftesbury died as early as 1713, so that his playful confidence can be seen, like *Windsor Forest*, to belong to a moment which, at the time Pope came to write the 'Epistle to Burlington', was already consigned to the past. By 1731 Walpole's government had been in office for well over a decade, and its corruptions, the wealth it generated and the power it could command, were bound to be seen by Pope and his friends as a dystopic reversal, or especially grim fulfilment, of the vision of '*Thames's* Glory'.

Yet, in the final analysis, the poems are different less because the times have changed than because Pope's strategy has. *Windsor Forest* had rightly hailed a golden dawn for Britain as a peaceful and peace-making European nation. 'Of the Use of Riches' is directed towards some of those who have gained from the nation's triumphs and are in danger of forgetting their larger responsibilities. As a matter of tactics, Pope has to marginalise Burlington, he has to make him exceptional. This being so, it follows that the most obvious as well as the most sensible way to read the poem is as an attack on 'city' values, and this is indeed how Bateson and others do read it.

But matters are not as simple as that. Although *Windsor Forest* wishes to look forward it in fact looks back. It is a last appeal to that sense of a united nation, of a shared 'Englishness', which could *only* be made at a time when, partly by his genius for synthesising traditions and conventions through appeal to that cultural continuum which Dryden had done so much to create, and partly because of the historical accidents – the peace of Utrecht, the possibilities of imaging Anne as a highly complex figure – Pope could produce a poem which offered a mythic vision of an endlessly conciliating Britannia. And this might, just might, have some connection with present fact and a plausible future. But the vision was bound to fade. From now on the image of Britannia, however composed, becomes increasingly abstract or contentious. And Pope's own vision contracts to the point where he no longer feels able to 'speak for England'. Or rather, he offers an ideal Englishman – the type I choose to call the citizen of the world – in the knowledge that this type is losing out to others.

And there is a still further problem. Pope's construction houses an unresolved and unresolvable paradox. His citizen of the world is also a self-interested Englishman, one, moreover, for whom the claim of 'dwelling' can not be made as Jonson (very dubiously) made it for the lord of Penshurst. This is why The 'Epistle to Burlington' does not merely present us with a binary opposition of city (bad) and country (good). Money made in the city was being spent in the country. Hence the very large number of country houses built during this period. The money which came from the conquest of the seas and from successful wars, in particular against the French, could be used to endorse a certain image of Britain – Britannia – that developed at this time. Dryden had anticipated as much in some especially bitter lines in the Second Part of *The Hind and the Panther*.

> Here let my sorrow give my satyr place,
> To raise new blushes on my *British* race;
> Our sayling Ships like common shoars we use,
> And through our distant Colonies diffuse
> The draughts of Dungeons and the stench of stews,
> Whom, when their home-bred honesty is lost,
> We disembogue on some far *Indian* coast;
> Thieves, Pandars, Palliards, sins of ev'ry sort;
> Those are the manufactures we export. . .
>
> (ll. 556–64)

If there is nothing like this in Pope it is partly because he included among his friends some who gained from those very 'sayling Ships' whose 'use' Dryden anathematises. True, he had imagined in *Windsor Forest* a time when 'Conquest [shall] cease, and Slavery be no more', and when 'the freed *Indians* in their native Groves/Reap their own fruits, and woo their Sable loves'. These lines seem humanely optimistic, until we realise that at the Treaty of Utrecht Great Britain and the South Sea Company were given 'for the term of thirty years the sole right of importing negroes into Spanish America . . . and that Pope put some of his money into the company'.[23] No wonder that he should have to turn his attention to 'use' as it reveals itself, or may be ideally manifested, in those social relationships based on order which are to be located in an England whose ultimate reference point is Rome, and especially the prevailing image of Virgilian Rome. But this now feels very literary, a determinedly and hence evasive mythic assertion. ''Tis Use alone that sanctifies Expence.' That Pope felt some guilt or at least anxiety about his connections with 'Expence' may be inferred from his appeal to so grand a word as 'sanctify' (Johnson defines it as 'To free from the power of sin for the time to come'). And the reason for this is apparent as soon as we ask what was the source of the money that made such expense possible. For obvious reasons it was a question about which Pope felt uneasy. He therefore concentrates on 'use' and implies that his ideal man – the Man of Ross, perhaps – is marginalised, pushed aside by the rush of forces which are frankly partisan, secular, and which can never be sanctified.

Pope's ultimate retreat is, then, into that Horatianism which it had earlier seemed possible to embrace as a model of Englishness attainable by all 'civilised' men, whether Whig or Tory. Not now. The Shaftesburyan moment has passed. In an especially sharp paradox, the garden replaces the city as the centre for urbanity. It becomes the focus for the version of cultural continuity which in *Windsor Forest* had been triumphantly read into a new Whitehall where 'Temples rise, the beauteous Works of Peace', but which now can be only flickeringly sustained by Burlington's efforts. Pope however pays very little attention to Burlington's city work. Instead, the focus has shifted decisively to the country house. It is *here* that the paradoxical image of the rooted Englishman as citizen of the world is to triumph.

If this account of Pope's shifting stances is less than fully sympathetic to him it is because, compared with Dryden, there are elements in his work that reveal themselves as being part of a scarcely honest strategy. Such a strategy may be viewed tolerantly as a form of subtle shading. Viewed less tolerantly, it looks like shiftiness. It is to be doubted whether Dryden, at least in his last years, would have had any truck with sanctifying an 'Expence' that was so often a product of 'sayling Ships'. And yet, to be fair to Pope, it can be said that even if we leave aside the matter of the source of some of his income he had different problems to face. Above all, he had to fashion a means of keeping faith with the concept of a largely classical culture which might free England from the narrow self-interests he saw it moving inexorably towards. Or, if that seems unwarrantably vague, it may be said that he tries to offer a vision of those larger cultural possibilities without which 'Expence' would provide a haven for duncery. Either way, the Britannia of *Windsor Forest*, in which country and city are linked together and both are connected to a classic tradition which, it is suggested, is alive and healthy, has shrunk in the 'Epistle to Burlington' to a few friends and the exceptional country house. The Man of Ross can be produced as virtually unique in his roles of benefactor and patron, his house and grounds designed to be at once a delight and of use, his wealth distributed in ways which indicate true civic responsibility:

> Behold the Market-place with poor o'erspread!
> The MAN of Ross divides his weekly bread:
> Behold yon Alms-house, neat, but void of state,
> Where Age and Want sit smiling at the gate:
> Him portion'd maids, apprentic'd orphans blest,
> The young who labour, and the old who rest.
>
> ('Epistle to Bathurst', ll. 263–8)

This seems to offer an image of present achievement which later in the century, in Goldsmith's *The Deserted Village*, for example, will be strategically located in the past. But given that the Epistle was first published in 1733, and that John Kyrle, the original of the Man of Ross, had died in 1724, the precariousness of his achievement is delicately implied. It is as though his disinterested benevolence is taken to belong to an earlier age, and not to 'the actual England Pope knew', in Reuben Brower's words.[24] This 'actual' England is more typically characterised by the city men whom Pope excoriates in the 'Epistle to Burlington', a matter which undoubtedly explains why, although it was written earlier than the 'Epistle to Bathurst' and was first published in 1731, it appears as 'Epistle IV' in the collected edition of *The Works of Mr Alexander Pope*, Vol II (1735), and thus takes its place *after* the 'Epistle to Bathurst'.

In the 'Epistle to Bathurst' Pope emerges as the apologist, even the champion, of proto-capitalism. The expansionism of *Windsor Forest* here yields to a different argument, that it is somehow God's will that 'the ruling Passion' implanted in certain minds must lead to the kind of economic activity whose results, whether intended or not, produce increased pleasure and employment for increased numbers. This is the kind of amoralism which is openly avowed by Mandeville; and elsewhere in the poem Pope is sufficiently aware of it to satirise those uses of riches which he has implied are authorised by God's providence. In short, the Epistle is a thoroughly confused poem. On the one hand, Pope registers a sense of the social process which 'inevitably' marks in England an emergent capitalism. Yet at the same time he protests against this, partly through the satiric presentation of old Cotta and his son, who are offered as contrasting, reprehensible types (miser and spendthrift), and partly through the benevolence of the Man of Ross. He therefore places the earlier-written 'Epistle to Burlington' after the 'Epistle to Bathurst', because in Burlington he can more securely oppose against economic individualism that ideal of the good man whose blend of virtues makes him the citizen of the world, especially since this is *not* defined by benevolence which, I am by no means the first to note, is an ambiguous virtue: however desirable, it is the product of economic arrangements for which the benevolent are responsible.

Maynard Mack quotes approvingly Earl Wasserman's remark that Walpole is 'in the background of the entire [fourth Epistle], just as [he] hovered over the politico-economic morality of the age'.[25] Walpole himself is probably intended in the allusion to Sir Visto (Sir Shylock in early editions of the poem).

> What brought Sir Visto's ill got wealth to waste?
> Some Daemon whisper'd, 'Visto! have a Taste.'
> Heav'n visits with a Taste the wealthy fool,
> And needs no Rod but Ripley with a Rule.
>
> ('Epistle to Burlington', ll. 15–19)

By 1731 much of Walpole's fortune had been expended on the country seat, Houghton, designed by Ripley. Even if we agree with Bateson that Visto may not be intended for Walpole himself,[26] Pope's detestation of the great commoner and the corruption that by now was attached to him and his party is clear enough. In his study of *Pope's Horatian Poems* Thomas Maresca notes how such detestation darkens the tones of the later work, and he rightly suggests that Pope links George II and Walpole as joint agents in 'the destruction of traditional English liberties'.[27] The new, unashamed avarice is motivated by private greed which is endlessly hostile or indifferent to public interest.

The dream of civic, responsible order has, then, retreated to the margins of English life. This is paradoxical enough. It might also be thought paradoxical that where in *Windsor Forest* Pope had seen London in utopian terms, by the time of *The Dunciad* 'Augusta' has become a threatening, dystopic vision of dark chaos. The Great Anarch embodies an absolute threat to the realisation of cultural, social and political harmony on which the earlier poetry had been predicated. The explanation for this is that the anarchy Pope has in mind includes the emergent strengths of what are finally economic and social forces, given authority by the politics of the new nation in a way that makes a mockery of the hope that disinterestedness could direct the progress of nationhood. The emergent forces are those of self-interest, naked and unashamed, as benevolence, for all its compromises, was not. Against such powerful self-interests benevolence can do very little.

The model of the city-state has, then, lost its potency. In addition, whatever lies beyond the city is vulnerable to the money and power which the city generates. Pope continues to uphold his model, if for no other reason than that it enables him to create the new London as an image of 'decline and fall' from its former great possibilities.[28] But other, contemporary, poets refuse to identify with his pessimism. For them self-interest is in the national interest. This points us to the next chapter.

CHAPTER 2

Contesting Voices

I

In his book *On Modern Authority*, Thomas Docherty argues that Swift and Pope fear critical activity when it is directed towards them because it threatens their sense of 'self-stability'. For the 'dunces' to be given a voice is to challenge the authority of those writers who call them dunces.[1] There is some truth in this, but in his eagerness to unsettle all claims to authority Docherty misses an important point. The writerly identities which Pope and in particular Swift form are by no means narrow. Nor are they necessarily self-interested. It is of course true that the claim of the citizen of the world to be truly disinterested may mask self-interest, but it is difficult to see how Swift can be accused of deception in his claim to serve human liberty. He did not serve merely the liberty of the citizens. On the contrary: he thought it the responsibility of the citizens to serve all. All men are entitled to be free, in the sense that they ought not to be oppressed by others. To flout the freedom of some men in flaunting your own was, for Swift, evil; and if he speaks out with the accents of authority on this matter, as he assuredly does, it is not easy to see how he can then be accused of self-interest.

Swift necessarily opposes the creation and development of certain forms of 'Englishness' as these were occurring during his lifetime. His commitment to what he understood by liberty, immeasurably sharpened by his exile in Dublin, meant that he was both caught up by and bitterly opposed to the imperialist aggressions directed at the Irish nation, just as he was committed to a sustained campaign against the arrogant complacency of the True-Born Englishman. Hence the King of Brobdingnag's famous remark to Gulliver, that Gulliver's boasts have proved 'the Bulk of your Natives, to be the most pernicious Race of little odious Vermin that Nature ever suffered to crawl upon the Surface of the Earth' (*Gulliver's Travels*, Book II, Ch. VI). This is certainly the voice of the citizen of the world, but surely directed with absolute propriety against those who claim special freedoms for themselves.

There is not the space here to pay Swift the attention he deserves. Nevertheless, it has to be said that his is probably the most deliberately unsettling of all the voices which are directed against growing orthodoxies, as the Freeportian tone of the *Modest Proposal* makes clear. As for Pope, his habitual imagery of vermin and insects, derived from the advances of

33

microscopy and intended to invert for ironic purposes the position of humans on the 'great chain' of being, is often pointed against the world of scribblers, less to vindicate himself as darling of the muses than to guard the fabric of the language against the voracious chumbling of the dunces. This directs attention back to language itself, to its construction and preservation.

The German philosopher Fichte thought it impossible to overrate the importance of language in creating cultural nationalism.[2] At the time of the Commonwealth the Levellers had argued that the law should be purged of Latin and French phraseology. Implicit in this was the understandable desire for a legal language that everyone, including Colonel Rainborough's 'poorest he', might use, and as a result of which all men and women could truly belong within their culture. But that particular hope was never realised. The language of the educated, sanctioned by grammar schools, universities and the structures of state power, continued to be deeply indebted to the classical languages. In this sense, as in others, Pope could feel that he was entitled to speak for England; and we have already seen that this is what he intends his poetry to do. But this may involve, if not the silencing of others, at least a readiness to be silent about them which tacitly betrays an uneasy conscience. And if this is so it lends Docherty's case a strength which it lacks when applied to Swift. For such a language may go with an account of England which removes from serious consideration people who speak with other accents, and from other experiences. Here, I am less concerned with Pope's attack on duncery than with his silence about one poet in particular, whom he must surely have wanted to classify as a dunce.

The obvious paradox of the 'Epistle to Arbuthnot' is that on the one hand Pope treats himself as the most private of poets, but on the other the very act of publishing the Epistle is a deliberate intervention in matters of cultural value. He therefore carefully distinguishes himself from the swarms of scribblers, from all those who 'rave, recite, and madden round the land', and whose heat-inflamed dreams of writerly adequacy are a public danger and threaten a general infection. Pope seeks to isolate himself from the possible plague, though he fears he may fail: 'What walls can guard me, or what Shades can hide?/They pierce my thickets, thro' my Grot they glide.' But this image of the beleaguered Horatian poet produces Pope not merely as a centre of attention – that is, as the proper authority on poetry – but as the still point of a cultural maelstrom; and the validity of this is then asserted in the precise way he accounts for the Dunce-Scribes who press in upon him. As the Twickenham editors tell us, the Epistle was put into final shape in August 1734, and August was the month 'of the custom in Juvenal's time of rehearsing poetry'.[3] Pope's wit in 'placing' the dunces makes it possible for him to align himself with a cultural tradition from which they are excluded. Moreover, the very form of the 'Epistle' is testimony to the tradition's vitality: its Horatianism is a studied pose making plausible Pope's implicit claim that the upholding of essential cultural values depends on a few friends.

As I noted in the previous chapter, there is an obvious contradiction in this. Pope makes himself as at once central and marginal: he speaks for and from cultural values which are offered as centrally important, yet he speaks from the seclusion of his house at Twickenham while a new, cultureless, city-led world threatens to overwhelm him. It is a familiar ploy, but one not without some foundation in fact. By 1734 other voices were beginning to be raised, and some of them found listeners. Pope identifies such voices as proceeding from drunken parsons, maudlin poetesses, frantic wives and giddy sons. Put together, they produce a cacophony of untrained, unlearned dunceries. Pope's tactic is to anathematise such voices by an appeal to a body of values, of learning, to which they have no access.

Yet although he compiles a detailed and lengthy catalogue of dunces, he makes no mention of Stephen Duck, whom he might have been expected to put near the top of his list. Nor does he pillory him in *The Dunciad*, and at first glance this seems distinctly odd, given that Duck's *Poems on Several Subjects* had appeared in 1730 and by the end of the year had gone into no fewer than seventeen editions. Duck's immediate celebrity was largely due to the fact that he was a novelty of the season: an untutored poet. As such he would obviously pose a threat to the cultural values Pope endorsed. The explanation for Pope's silence is probably to be found in the activities of Joseph Spence, one of Duck's early champions and a close friend of Pope's. Spence must have feared Pope's reaction to *Poems on Several Subjects*, and so decided to sheathe the poet's claws by telling him that although Duck 'is without anything of what is called Education', he is nevertheless 'grown up into an excellent poet all at once'. Besides, Spence assures Pope

> The Man is yet a common Thresher: plain and modest in his behaviour; but when you come to talk to him, of particular good sense; and of more knowledge than could possibly be expected . . . One sees the struggles of a great Soul in him; much light has he; and much he wants: but there's so much more knowledge in the man than could be expected and so much goodness in this man, that even his Ignorance as he manages it has something even agreeable in it. If you have not yet heard of him, this account I hope wont be impertinent.[4]

On the face of it, it seems that this was the letter which did the trick. A month later Pope was writing to Gay, to tell him that Duck is both 'an honest thresher' and a 'harmless man'.[5] In view of the fact that Pope and Gay had both denounced the kind of pastoral poetry which Duck, as honest thresher and uneducated poet, might be expected to write – and which, to some extent, he *did* write – the letter is highly significant. Spence would have been familiar with Pope's celebrated essay in the *Guardian*, which had satirically applauded Ambrose Philips' pastorals as preferable to Virgil's since

> Virgil hath been thought guilty of too courtly a style: his language is perfectly pure, and he often forgets he is among peasants. . . .Mr Pope hath fallen into the same error with Virgil. His clowns do not converse in all the simplicity proper to the country. His names are borrowed from Theocritus and Virgil. . .whereas Philips, who hath the strictest regard to propriety, makes choice of names peculiar to the country, and more agreeable to a reader of delicacy; such as Hobbinol, Lobbin, Cuddy, and Colin Clout. (*The Guardian*, no 40, 27 April 1713)

Gay's *The Shepherd's Week*, which was published the following year, furthers the satire by including speakers of the pastorals whose names are Lobbin, Cuddy, and Cloddipole.

Pope's letter to Gay is intended to warn him off Duck, as Spence had warned off Pope. Whether Pope actually read Duck's poems is open to doubt, but we do know that Spence offered to send his friend a 'little poem that is good in every way: even in its Design, as well as in the Language, and the Numbers. 'Tis the story of the Shunamite from the book of Kings.' Spence doesn't, however, refer to 'The Thresher's Labour', and with good reason: for this, the finest of Duck's poems, powerfully and painstakingly unpicks the blent vision of *Windsor Forest*, and it therefore threatens – one might almost say demolishes – the politics of Virgilian pastoralism.

> Week after Week, we this dull Task pursue,
> Unless when winn'wing days produce a new:
> A new, indeed, but frequently a worse!
> The Threshal yields but to the Master's Curse.

For Pope, who was the friend of such masters, these lines would have been as difficult to confront as those where Duck speaks of the perpetual dullness of his toil. 'No intermission in the work we know;/The noisy Threshal must for ever go.' Coming upon these lines we are entitled to reflect that if Pope read them his silence about Duck might be explained less as a desire to spare his friend, Spence, than to spare himself. This is the silence of guilt. And such guilt would have been intensified by Duck's description of the look of a place, not from the vantage point of those who profit from it, nor as it could be made into a Virgilian emblem of fruitfulness, but as it appeared to those for whom it held out the promise of unending, backbreaking work: ''Tis all a gloomy melancholy Scene,/Fit only to provoke the Muse's Spleen.'

It depends, of course, whose muse is being provoked. When Thomson first published the full text of *The Seasons* in 1730 (he was constantly to revise it during the rest of his lifetime), he produced an insistently Virgilian image of England:

> Rich is thy soil, and merciful thy skies;
> Thy streams unfailing in the summer's drought;
> Unmatch'd thy guardian-oaks; thy vallies float
> With golden waves; and on thy mountains flocks
> Bleat, numberless; while, roving round their sides,
> Bellow the blackening herds in lusty droves.
> Beneath, thy meadows flame, and rise unquell'd,
> Against the mower's scythe. On every hand,
> Thy villas shine. Thy country teems with wealth;
> And PROPERTY assures it to the swain,
> Pleas'd, and unweary'd, in his certain toil.
>
> *(Summer,* ll. 538–48)

For Thomson 'certain toil' means the guarantee of profitable work for the 'swain'. For Duck, such toil is by no means certain. The only certainty of his life is hardship. In his brief but telling discussion of *The Seasons* in *The Country and the City*, Raymond Williams notes that 'In a revised version, the "certain" toil has become "guarded", but it is in any case the existing social order which guarantees the "scattering of plenty". It is not what any improving agriculturalist ever reported, but it is what most wanted to happen.'[6] Hence the close connection between property and propriety, which, as Philip Corrigan and Derek Sayer point out in *The Great Arch*, are words with the same etymological root. This helped all those who favoured the existing social order to hold onto their belief that 'liberty and property were – simply – *there* for some men: gentry, governors, rulers, regulators; and the rule of propriety takes this natural order for granted'.[7] The connection is further underwritten in Thomson's poem by the insistence that England 'teems' with wealth. In his *Dictionary* Johnson's major definitions concentrate on the word's natural, procreative meaning: 'To be with young'; 'to be pregnant'; 'to be full; to be charged as a breeding animal'. As we saw in Chapter 1, England's abundant fertility is exactly identified with, and is to be explained by, its 'natural' political and social order, although by the time Thomson is writing this order is marked by a constitutional rather than an absolutist monarchy, and there have been other decisive shifts of power. Nothing however is allowed to disturb the confidence of Thomson's vision. Stephen Duck's voice is virtually silenced, and where it cannot be silenced it is easily enough accommodated. The man 'is of particular good sense'. In the orthodox accounts of labour and 'rich industry' as they are being constructed at this time by poets who regard themselves as able to speak for England, the actual, demystifying voice of labour has no place. Whatever is, is natural. Wealth breeds wealth as sheep breed sheep.

Yet here we come upon another matter which requires comment. Thomson's vision is not, strictly speaking, of England, but of a larger space:

Yet here we come upon another matter which requires comment. Thomson's vision is not, strictly speaking, of England, but of a larger space:

> HAPPY BRITANNIA! where the Queen of Arts,
> Inspiring vigour, LIBERTY abroad
> Walks thro' the land of Heroes, unconfin'd
> And scatters plenty with unsparing hand.

1745 is yet to come, but the Act of Union requires Thomson, who was Scottish by birth, to pay lip service to a blest Britain and, as Pope had done, to identify liberty as its peculiar attribute. This identification will be made on future occasions, but by then it will have become more problematic. It was problematic even in 1730, as Stephen Duck could have told Thomson. It is true that foreigners were deeply impressed by the liberty which Englishmen claimed for themselves. Roy Porter quotes Montesquieu's remark of 1729 that 'this nation is passionately fond of liberty. . .every individual is independent'.[8] But this is richly tinted by what Montesquieu knew of his native France, and ignores the individuals he *didn't* see in England – or Scotland. Tonson's vision is similarly limited. He may invoke Britannia in her entirety, but it is essentially England which he addresses, and a very partial version of England at that. A great deal has been made invisible. Just as Thomson's illustrated edition of *Paradise Lost* had the effect of drawing the teeth of Milton's poem, so Thomson's Miltonics have the effect of trying to 'tame' Milton by adapting and accommodating his manner to the Georgic vision of *The Seasons*. Language, subject, form: all *con-form* to this produced image of an England which is focused on the connections between property and propriety. Liberty is the possession of those with both.

The existence of many Georgic poems throughout the first half of the eighteenth century is as well known as are the explanations for them. It is, however, worth noting that they enthusiastically proclaim wealth as the means of securing national well-being. Benevolence as a civic virtue is now largely superseded by the virtue of money-making. Thus Dyer's *The Fleece* (1757) traces the stages by means of which 'Britannia's fleece' is transformed into wool 'and gathered worth'. The poem moves from the Home Counties to Yorkshire, from country to city (especially the port of London), and offers to connect all ranks of society in a vision of a united nation whose harmony is dependent on industry. For Dyer, Britain's influence spreads to foreign countries, as 'happy trade' expands. He admits that the rivalry of France may threaten such influence and (consequent?) happiness, but he does so in a language whose abstractions deny the realities of war and economic aggression. We are asked to see Britain as a land of ideal social relations guaranteed by economic arrangements which benefit everyone, and although the temptations of luxury may pose a threat – like ancient empires Britain could sink into sloth under its allure – the whole tone of the poem is one that ardently endorses the vision it proclaims. And as with Thomson, so Dyer's 'Britannia' is essentially 'England'.

The process and cost of the denials implicit in Thomson's 'Anglicising' poetry are illustrative of that cultural schizophrenia which has been well discussed by David Craig and others, and which is symptomatically present in Hugh Blair, 'the world's first Professor of English Literature', as Robert Crawford has called him. Blair became Professor of Rhetoric and Belles Lettres at Edinburgh University in 1762, and his lectures were entirely indebted to the work of Adam Smith.

> Smith held that 'we in this country are most of us very sensible that the perfection of language is very different from that we commonly speak in', and Blair's ideal style was 'without Scotticisms'. The enterprise of Smith and Blair was to enable the 'provincial' Scots to engage with the culture of England on that culture's own ground. In their Glasgow and Edinburgh lecture rooms Smith and Blair were busy translating their audiences.[9]

This takes for granted the idea of a monolithic culture for England, and Thomson is one of the makers of this culture, a culture, a culture of conformity. What I now want to discuss are some versions of non-conformity.

I I

I am not here principally concerned with non-conformity in its most familiar sense, that is as an expression of religious dissent from the established Church. Although this can hardly be ignored in any account of the period, its existence may be taken for granted, and there is no need to speculate on its growing or declining importance through the eighteenth century. It is enough to remark that its very existence clearly indicates an articulate resistance to the concept of a Church of *England*, and that this tells us less of dissenters' desire for close communion with continental Europe than of a wish to assent, regionally, even locally, to an identity independent of that particular version of England – monarchical, culturally orthodox in the sense already outlined – which is to be known through and identified with its established Church. Nor is it relevant to enquire whether the perception of the establishment was accurate. No doubt the monolithic image was more deeply fissured than appeared either from outside or from within. That doesn't matter. The point at issue is this: the sects which kept their distance from the established orthodoxy did so because they did not wish to owe allegiance to crown, Church or law. Connected with the regional resistance embodied in some versions of sectarianism is the determination of many Welsh, Irish and Scottish people to resist absorption into England/Britannia. It becomes clear that non-conformity, in the sense I use it, implies a sense of belonging, of social identity, that is not to be equated with nor exhausted by the various but coherent and would-be coercive versions of 'Englishness' which were being so assiduously developed at the time. This even applies to Methodism. For although John Wesley was himself a true-blue Anglican, a high Tory with no love of political dissent, those who worked with him in the field were increasingly liable to move beyond his political quietism. For them, liberty of conscience was all. And this brings us to the heart of non-conformity as it developed in the eighteenth century.

It was, it had to be, different from the dreams of the 1640s. Russell E. Richey is probably right when he says that 'By the late seventeenth and early eighteenth centuries . . . the Dissenters had long since disavowed their revolutionary intentions to remake England and repressed entirely their millenarian commitments.' And so, he goes on, given that eighteenth-century dissent typically separated itself from its past even though it kept it in memory, it was bound to have a different view of the significance of liberty.

> Liberty was no longer part of the divine drama for the redemption of the world but a human ideal; it was to be enjoyed as a civil right, not as a prerogative of the community of saints; it was predicated on religious pluralism rather than divine election; it was advocated not so much as the obedient response to a sovereign God but as a human quality; it rested on human ability rather than grace.[10]

This usefully expands on G. R. Cragg's bald statement, in *The Church and the Age of Reason,* that 'It was among the nonconformists that the *cult* of liberty, both in theology and in politics, found fullest scope'[11] (my italics). Like Cragg, however, Richey draws back from identifying religious non-conformity with the development of radical politics, even though, as James Sambrook notes, the Unitarian Joseph Priestley 'shaped and was shaped by the famous Warrington Academy, the cradle of Unitarianism and a centre of radical politics, and academic excellence, which for its brief life from 1757 to 1786 challenged the intellectual leadership of Oxford and Cambridge'.[12]

The connections between liberty, non-conformity and radical politics are a good deal more vital in the middle of the eighteenth century than is sometimes supposed. Nevertheless, I accept the force of Roy Porter's contention that during the century dissent seems to lose, rather than gain, in popularity; and that it was especially hard hit in rural areas. Porter notes, for instance, that in 1729 Hampshire had forty Presbyterian chapels, but that these had been reduced to a mere two by 1812. Dissent did far better in the towns, but there was always pressure on those dissenters who were second-class citizens to convert. Improved financial status could well mean improved social status. 'The Dissenter's second horse carried him to Church.'[13] Yet statistics will not take us very far. They certainly cannot explain the intensity of feeling for radical change that comes in, or back, to life in the 1780s. This may or may not be directly connected with religious non-conformity, but it does suggest that the fires which had apparently been stamped out were all the time smouldering away, waiting for Tom Paine and William Blake, among others, to kick them into flame.

It is not a suggestion I can follow through here. And yet a study primarily concerned with poets can go a good way towards exploring how and why the concept of liberty was so important during the eighteenth century, its meanings so contested, its values so problematic. For this heavily value-laden word is everywhere in poems of the time, and in such taxing ways as to make it evident that large issues are at stake, including that of national identity.

Liberty is the goddess of Britannia. That much was a commonplace by the time Thomson spoke of England as the 'Land of Heroes' where Liberty walked 'unconfined'. We may set beside Montesquieu's discovery of 1729 that England is a nation 'passionately fond of liberty'Günderode's observation that 'The Englishman breathes liberty, and anything that even appears to threaten this is an object of hatred to him and capable of driving him to all lengths.'[14] No doubt this was how it seemed to visitors from the Europe of *ancien régime* autocracies, but not all Englishmen or women enjoyed the liberty which Montesquieu and Günderode found so ubiquitous, and which Thomson and others, drawing on that Greek idea of the free man as responsible citizen, hailed as Britain's peculiar virtue. What exactly *is* liberty: liberty of expression, of conscience, of behaviour, of religion, of politics? Even to put the question is to realise that some men's liberty meant others' tyranny. The view of liberty so enthusiastically endorsed by Thomson becomes inextricably entwined with a developing form of patriotism from which xenophobia is never far removed; and this can then be used to validate the liberty of the East India Company and the liberty of the British (mostly English) armies and navies to behave as they like in Continental Europe. 'Bold, firm, and graceful are thy generous youth,' Thomson writes in *Summer*, 'By hardship sinew'd, and by danger fir'd,/Scattering the nations where they go.' And a little later he enthuses:

> ISLAND of bliss! amid the subject seas,
> That thunder round thy rocky coasts, set up,

> At once the wonder, terror, and delight,
> Of distant nations; whose remotest shore
> Can soon be shaken by thy naval arm . . .

Given this, we should not be surprised that Thomson is also the author of
'Liberty', a long poem about Britannia's commercial prospects, which
speaks in adulation of liberty's role in bringing these prospects nearer
(usually by force); nor that he composed 'Rule Britannia' for Arne's
masque *King Alfred* (1740); nor that the National Anthem should have
been written at this time, with its frank appeal to commercial aggression
backed by military and naval might; nor that Dyer's *The Fleece* should have
been equally frank in its combination of patriotism and commercialism.
Like *The Seasons*, 'Liberty' and *The Fleece* are conformist poems. They
compose, as it were, a flotilla of Georgic vessels which Corrigan and Sayer
correctly report as sailing under a flag of convenience:

> if one side of [this] flag is emblazoned with 'Commerce', the other says
> 'Civilization'. The fabric of the flag is Liberty which if we peer closely at the
> stitching turns out to be Law. The 'market' is *made*, some men must be
> free(d) to constrain other men and almost all women, thereby to construct
> progress.[15]

To repeat, allowing liberty to some means denying it to others, a matter
which the careful abstractions of the term are meant to conceal. To make
an obvious point: Thomson's 'generous youth . . . scattering the nations
where they go', were mostly impressed. And they certainly didn't share in
the 'bliss' of wealth which they often died to produce for others. The
concept of liberty has here shaken quite free of its attachment to the
disinterested citizen and his benevolence. It is now to be identified as the
confident pursuit of self-interest, but with the usual rider that self-interest
is inseparable from national interest. The true patriot is therefore the
upholder of commerce.

There are, however, a number of mid-eighteenth-century poems which
exhibit considerable unease about the patriotic fervour of Thomson and
Dyer. William Collins's 'Ode to Liberty' was written in 1746. Collins
imagines Liberty making her way from ancient Rome until she arrives in
'Albion', where 'Thy shrine in some religious wood,/O soul-enforcing
goddess stood!'

> What hands unknown that fabric raised?
> Even now before his favoured eyes,
> In Gothic pride it seems to rise!
> Yet Graecia's graceful orders join
> Majestic through the mixed design.

Roger Lonsdale points out that the 'progress' poem was a popular genre of
the period.

The reason for the steady progress of the arts to Britain was usually . . . the decline of liberty in the former cultural centres of the world. Only in Britain was true liberty to be found, according to the Augustans, so that the arts had inevitably settled there . . . Nevertheless, by the mid-eighteenth century the patriotic conviction that the classical arts and virtues had not merely been transmitted to Britain but had thrived there as never before was losing some of its confidence.

Lonsdale attributes this new 'sense of inferiority' to the poets' 'sense of the past' as mightier than the present.[16] Surprisingly, he does not consider the possibility that the same poets felt a deep sense of guilt about what was happening to or being done in the name of liberty in mid-eighteenth-century England. He thus makes nothing of the crucial fact that Collins says that Liberty's shrine is hidden from the present time, even though it is somewhere in Albion. And he passes in silence over the poem's concluding lines:

> Ye forms divine, ye laureate band,
> That near her inward altar stand!
> Now soothe her, to her blissful train
> Blithe Concord's social form to gain:
> Concord, whose myrtle wand can steep
> Even Anger's blood-shot eyes in sleep:
> Before whose breathing bosom's balm
> Rage drops his steel and storms grow calm;
> Her let our sires and matrons hoar
> Welcome to Britain's ravaged shore . . .

These lines must be put into their immediate political context if they are to be understood. Why, for example, does Collins switch from talking about *Albion* to talking of *'Britain's* ravaged shore'? The two could certainly be synonymous, but in practice Albion was usually taken to be England, not Britain as a whole. The exchange of terms surely has some connection with the references to 'Anger's blood-shot eyes' and 'Rage's steel', which have made for the 'ravaged shore'. Between them, these phrases compose a reference to some catastrophe which has meant the at least temporary loss of Britannia's liberty and which only the arrival of Concord can make good. Collins must, I think, be referring to the events of 1745, and even more, perhaps, to the terrible massacre of Culloden, which took place on 16 April 1746. Timorous though his poem is, Collins is nevertheless voicing the fear that liberty has been lost and that those who most loudly proclaim it are responsible for its disappearance. This is why in 'Gothic pride it *seems* to rise' (my italics). The Whigs made regular use of the 'Gothic' origins of Britain's constitutional and democratic forms of government. Collins calls that claim into question, or rather he implies that true democracy, true liberty, if it is 'Gothic' in origin, is certainly not to be identified with the brutality of the English against the Scots. The events of Culloden make a mockery of that Act of Union which had been so regularly fêted as an act of concord.

This leads to a further consideration. At about this time, and for reasons that will often be independent of immediate politics, the Gothic becomes associated with those parts of Britain that are not England. But if the constitution is 'Gothic' then England may not assert its liberty against those other parts without ceasing to be true to the source from which such liberty is derived. England is the aggressor against the very liberty it claims to be upholding. In the light of this, certain of Gray's poems become even more interesting than Collins's.

In the 'original argument' to 'The Bard', Gray writes:

> The army of Edward I, as they march through a deep valley, are suddenly stopped by the appearance of a venerable figure seated on the summit of an inaccessible rock, who, with a voice more than human, reproaches the King with all the misery and desolation which he had brought on his country; foretells the misfortunes of the Norman race, and with prophetic spirit declares, that all his cruelty shall never extinguish the noble ardour of poetic genius in this island; and that men shall never be wanting to celebrate true virtue and valour in immortal strains, to expose vice and infamous pleasure, and boldly censure tyranny and oppression. His song ended, he precipitates himself from the mountain, and is swallowed up by the river that rolls at its foot.

In quoting this Lonsdale adds that Gray's friend William Mason believed that Gray found it impossible to persuade himself that the English poets from Spenser to Addison had been preoccupied with celebrating 'true virtue and valour'. Mason remembered that 'The Ode lay unfinished by him for a year or two on this very account.'[17] 'The Bard' was begun in 1755 and completed in 1757. A few years earlier Gray had been engaged on what in some ways feels like a companion poem, 'The Progress of Poesy', although this poem also has important connections with the 'Ode to Liberty'. Like Collins's odde, Gray's iis a 'progress' poem, which conccludes with tthe statementt that the true voice of poetry – 'Thoughts that breathe and words that burn' – is 'heard no more' in England. 'Oh! lyre divine, what daring spirit/Wakes thee now?' To this rhetorical question Gray returns the silent answer, 'none.' Modern poets have failed to be true bards, have failed in their responsibility to utter 'immortal strains' against 'tyranny and oppression'. This reconstruction of Gray's meaning will explain why he had such trouble in finishing 'The Bard'.

For Gray has painted himself into a corner. His poem should be read as a statement against xenophobic, anti-libertarian nationalism. Yet Gray, who was in many ways no radical, found that he had allowed 'The Bard' to point out that the ultimate responsibility of the poet was, if not to radicalism, then to dissent, or non-conformity in the sense in which I am using the term. This was bound to be discomforting. This same Gray had wanted 'mute, inglorious Miltons' to stay mute. The 'Elegy Written in a Country Churchyard' underwrites an almost entirely complacent account of a 'settled' society. It refuses to censure tyranny and oppression. Its recommendation of 'the cool sequestered vale of life' produces an 'innocent' reading of the actual labour and social relations of the vale. On the other hand, the 'Elegy' comes earlier than the other poems of Gray I am discussing here, and I suggest that he progressively moves away from such complacency as he comes to identify poets as bards, that is as oppositional voices. But such identification is bound to be problematic, for what begins as probably no more than a literary-historical interest in the Gothic, the bardic, the druidic, turns out to have political implications. And it is to be doubted whether Gray was much at ease with these implications. Hence, the ending of 'The Bard', which suggests that the true poet cannot exist as the tame singer which Gray in many senses was. Gray, that is, is not one and the same. We can see how and why these difficulties loom if we consider his attitude to Milton.

Milton was bound to be a problem. Of all English poets he most spectacularly celebrated the epic 'true virtue and valour'. He was also the self-proclaimed embodiment of bardic utterance, of 'Thoughts that breathe and words that burn'. He was an inspired poet, who said as much in the opening passage of Book 3 of *Paradise Lost*, and later poets, Gray included, wished to endorse his claim. Inspired poets tell the truth – God's truth. And yet Gray had 'officially' to disregard this, as Mason revealed when he recalled his friend's opinion that the poets between Spenser and Addison had failed to honour their responsibilities. In other words, for all that Gray wants to uphold the poet's right to voice unfettered truths, he finds it difficult to sanction the kinds of truths which Milton uttered. Milton was an unwavering regicide, for whom the promptings of conscience overrode all appeals to that 'common quiet' which Dryden had claimed as 'mankind's concern'. He could not be accommodated to the ideals supposedly embodied in 1688 and the Act of Union. Gray's praise of Milton in 'The Progress of Poesy' is therefore extremely guarded. Milton, he says,

> rode sublime
> Upon the seraph-wings of Ecstasy,
> The secrets of the abyss to spy.
> He passed the flaming bounds of place and time:
> The living throne, the sapphire-blaze,
> Where angels tremble while they gaze,
> He saw; but blasted with excess of light,   .
> Closed his eyes in endless night.

Much later, in 1768, Gray claimed that the source for these last lines was Homer's *Odyssey*, where the minstrel Demodocos has his sight taken away by his muse who, in recompense, 'gave him the power of sweet song'. For reasons which will become clear later, Gray by then felt more confident in aligning himself with the tradition of the blind, inspired poet. (It was, after all, a tradition he had largely helped to rediscover.) But what he has to say about Milton in 'The Progress of Poesy' in no way supports his later gloss. Milton's sight is 'blasted' because he has dared too much, has been found guilty of a kind of Faustian hubris. By comparison, Dryden, who comes next in the Progress, riding a 'less presumptuous car', courses 'Wide o'er the fields of glory'. The political implication is that Dryden, royalist, conservative, produces a more successful poetry than the over-presumptuous epic Milton.

This is why a visit to Cambridge by the blind Welsh harper John Parry made it possible for Gray to complete the stalled 'Progress of Poesy'. Parry was, so Gray told Mason, a musician who 'scratch'd out such ravishing blind Harmony, such tunes of a thousand year old names enough to choak you, as have set all this learned body a dancing'.[18] Parry provided Gray with the way out of his dilemma. The blind musician was both an embodiment of the poet-as-bard-as-minstrel and a living testimony of the ability of primitive communities to nurture poetic genius in a manner to which more sophisticated societies could not aspire. Miltonic aspirations in the modern world could now be seen as potentially dangerous, disruptive but finally unavailing. To put it rather differently: Parry becomes a type of the Miltonic poet, but safely marginalised. He is relevant only as part of a history of poetry whose pathos lurks in the impossibility of contemporary poets intervening as oppositional voices.

Another reason for Gray's dilemma is that he doesn't really know who he is writing for. The bard speaks to 'the people', but Gray's immediate audience was in no sense sympathetic to such radical connections. Between them, 'The Progress of Poesy' and 'The Bard' confusedly admit that true poetry cannot be expected of the poet who writes such poems. This requires further consideration.

'In Yonder grave a Druid lies'. The resonant opening of Collins's 'Ode Occasioned by the Death of Mr Thomson' has caused a good deal of speculation. What exactly did he have in mind? Lonsdale suggests that Collins probably meant 'to allude to [Thomson's] powers as a poet of nature in *The Seasons* and to his celebration of British Liberty in the poem of that name'.[19] In *The Famous Druids*, A. L. Owen remarks that he may have intended to do no more than identify Thomson as a 'poet-philosopher of Nature';[20] and Stuart Piggott, in his study *The Druids*, notes that at the time Collins was writing it was a commonplace to think of the history of Ancient Britain as one in which 'the virtuous British, fired by

Natural Religion [try] to shake off the [Roman] conqueror's threatened yoke in a resistance movement led by the Druids who appear in the apostrophes to liberty by Thomson in 1735 or Collins in 1747, where the anti-Roman British chiefs "Hear their consorted Druids sing/Their Triumphs to th'immortal String'".[21] Piggott helpfully reproduces some illustrations which show that by the 1740s it was a regular practice to connect Druids to Celtic religion and to make them, as Collins does, bards.[22]

This 'new' history, in which a distinctively northern tradition of 'British' emerges in opposition to the Roman, is clearly part of a larger movement to disrupt or replace the cultural continuum which had as its starting point the received idea of the ancients as the source of Western civilisation. The rise of antiquarianism and the researches of William Stukeley, among others, which culminate in his *Stonehenge: a Temple Restored to the Druids* (1740) are of obvious relevance here. So are a number of other matters, including the renewed popularity of Freemasonry (Stukeley was a Mason). Then there is the resurgence of Arthurian lore (not that it was ever far below the surface), and the rapid growth of interest in Celtic history and pre-history. The Dublin Philosophical Society, founded in 1683 by Molyneux and Petty, was mostly popular with antiquarians, which helps explain the fact that several new editions of Sir James Ware's *Antiquities* (concerned with Ireland and first published in 1654) were called for during the middle years of the eighteenth century. All this and much else besides provided the more evident materials out of which it was possible to begin constructing a new image of Britain, one with cultural, historical and, by implication, social and even political consequences.[23] This new image has at its centre the affirmation of northernness. It opposes and is meant to replace the 'classical' spirit of the Augustan cultural configurations.

Given this, it is odd that none of the commentators on Collins's soubriquet for Thomson have mentioned the obvious fact that Thomson's Scottish origins make it especially appropriate for him to be called a Druid. The connection of Druid and Celt was taken for granted, by Gray as by others. It could indeed be argued that Thomson's birthplace is the *only* good reason for calling him a Druid. I have pointed out that his writings about nature and liberty connect him to that tradition of the Georgic which endorses a political, social and cultural vision that can be called conformist. Both Collins and Gray are distinctly uneasy with this vision, even though neither feels confident enough to bring the uneasiness into focus. (It is not so much the subject of certain key poems of theirs as the means whereby the subject itself becomes a problem.) Moreover, their uneasiness becomes most apparent when they write about the poet-as-bard, whose epic voice cannot authentically be raised in praise of a society where freedoms are being stifled (often in the name of liberty), yet whose oppositional voice poses an unacceptable threat. Thomson in this sense is not, and can never be, a Druid. But in the sense that Collins wants to claim him for poetry, as an authentic voice, it is understandable that he should try to identify him as a poet of the people. That is what Druids are and what poets *ought* to be. In short, Collins is in as much of a muddle as Gray.

It may be for this reason that Collins's melancholia developed to the extent that he could no longer write. In 1751 he apparently decided to renounce all books except the Bible. This suggests that he has rejected the world of 'polite learning', whose social and cultural conformity comes under pressure from many directions at this time, often confusedly. Hence, Thomson as 'Druid'. Hence, too, the fact that from the outset of his career Gray seems to have been fascinated by what he and others came to call 'the Gothic', by all things 'Rude and Romantic'.[24] But although this fascination may at first have been containable and have presented itself as a mere matter of taste, 'The Progress of Poesy' and 'The Bard' show a developing commitment to its oppositional, non-conformist implications. I have suggested that in Gray's case this leads his poems into something approaching an irresolvable muddle. At the heart of this lurks Gray's conviction, one Collins seems to have shared, that a poet's function ought to be central to the nation, but that poets who claim such a function are either proposing a cultural-political vision which is a kind of lie (an endorsement of liberty that enslaves others), or embodying an inspirational account of nationhood whose radicalism cannot be contemplated with any comfort. At times, it is true, Gray veers towards this account, but he always withdraws. In the end, therefore, he is left in the paradoxical position of wishing to assert poetry's centrality, but of having nothing much to say beyond how difficult it is to write poetry in the present age.

It would be wrong to underestimate or trivialise the distress this must have caused Gray, but it can be said that by falling silent he saved himself unnecessary pain. I want now to suggest that the tensions about the nature and function of poetry radically affected the lives of other poets.

III

The poets I have in mind include not just Collins but also Christopher Smart, Charles Churchill and William Cowper. Because it is not possible to deal with them all, I will risk a generalisation and say that in the middle of the eighteenth century a number of poets experienced a profound loss of certainty about the culture they had begun by thinking it proper to identify with, and that this loss of certainty led to breakdown and madness. The story of what happened to Christopher Smart is symptomatic. Six years Gray's junior, a revealing mixture of rake and scholar at Cambridge where he was a Fellow until taking off for London in 1749, Smart both irritated the older man by his drunken profligacy and impressed him by his abilities as a writer of wit. Smart had no love for Gray personally – 'Gray *walks* as if he had fouled his small-clothes, and *looks* as if he smelt it,' he is supposed to have remarked – but he was ready to praise him as 'our great Augustan' (in the poem 'The Brocaded Gown and Linen Rag'). The terms of the praise are barely appropriate, but there is no reason to doubt Smart's genuine admiration. Yet, either way, Gray would have been likely to take the compliment as something of a backhander. The poet who wanted to praise bards is identified as very unbardlike. Perhaps unknowingly, Smart points to Gray's dilemma about his poetic identity.

In his own case, Smart literally changed identities. He broke the image of the Cambridge wit and emerged as a wholly different poet. In 1756 his sudden lurch into religious mania became identified as a form of insanity and he was put into an asylum. Thanks to Boswell, Johnson's humane protest at this is well known. 'I did not think he ought to be shut up,' he told Dr Burney. 'His infirmities were not noxious to society. He insisted on people praying with him; and I'd as lief pray with Kit Smart as any one else. Another charge was, that he did not love clean linen; and I have no passion for it.'

Nevertheless, Smart was deeply disturbed. Gray knew about this, knew about Smart's casting off his wife and family, knew about his refusal to see former friends and about the conversion of rakehell into religious devout. He kept a watching brief on Smart's progress in St Luke's asylum, and seems to have helped him financially. In 1763 he was one of the subscribers for Smart's *Psalms of David*.[25] He must therefore have understood the fact and even perhaps the tactic whereby, through this breakdown, the former author of 'polite' Augustan verse became the author of the *Psalms*, became in a word, bardic (*Jubilate Agno* is the most bardic of all Smart's poems). The personal history of Christopher Smart can, then, be read as the most dramatic evidence of the true poet as someone who 'makes' himself, by becoming the voice and indeed the embodiment of oppositional values.

It is appropriate that Smart's breakdown in 1756 should be followed by the completion of 'The Bard' in 1757. This is emphatically not to argue that Gray's poem is about or inspired by Smart. We cannot, however, ignore the implications of Smart's madness as they would have been perceived by Gray. These would, I suggest, include the possibility that the poet, by the very fact of being a poet, must represent and articulate a crisis of identity. For whom did he write, what about, and how? The two events cannot be dissociated from one another, not if we are to understand correctly new formations of cultural consciousness as they emerge in these years, and as they are registered in Gray himself.

For by now Gray was intensely preoccupied with the history of the primitive, barbaric, 'pre-civilised' north. He seems to have begun working on translations of Norse and Welsh poetry in 1753 or thereabouts; and this work, and his commitment to the poet-as-bard, lead him to the conviction that true poetry is not to be found in a highly-developed society, where the poet is divorced from 'the people', or rather where there is no longer a community to and on behalf of whom the poet can uncomplicatedly address his work. Contemporary poets draw on and address themselves to a particular cultural configuration, one that aims at exclusiveness, as Pope had done. Gray would not have put the matter in these terms. But what he *did* say in 1760, when he thought he had discovered the 'true' poetry of Ossian, is of crucial importance. To appreciate this, we need to see it in context.

In 1759 Edward Young published his 'Conjectures on Original Composition', in the course of which he attempts a systematic account of two contrasting kinds of poet. Young identifies these as 'the well accomplished scholar' and 'the divinely-inspired enthusiast'. The first of these, he says, 'is as the bright morning star; the second, as the rising sun'. If Young's similes are to be taken seriously, he must mean that he regards the night-time period of the scholar poets as nearly over. They will fade before the coming glory of the enthusiasts. It may just be that behind such language hovers an appeal to those lines in 'Religio Laici' where Dryden compares the light of reason to the 'wandering beams of moon and stars' which 'fade and dissolve' in the supernatural light of religion. Certainly, the 'divinely-inspired enthusiast' suggests the poet-as-bard-as-prophetic-as-God-ordained; and this reconnects the Milton who had claimed such a role to the new or newly renovated concept of the poet which Young advances in his essay, and which 'mad' Kit Smart also seemed to be claiming for himself. The light within, the 'inspiration' of non-conformist religion, now becomes identified with the true poet. The 'joy' of the religious convert is seen as so closely analogous to the 'joy' of the poet in the act of creating that it becomes possible to identify in both kinds of enthusiast the ungainsayable certainty of 'divine inspiration'.

Young's commitment to the poet-as-enthusiast requires him to undermine the claims for the kinds of cultural centrality associated with Pope, as these are proclaimed in *The Dunciad* and the 'Epistle to Arbuthnot'. The scholar-poet, Young says (although the syntax is slippery),

> makes one of a group, and thinks in wretched unanimity with the throng; incumbered with the notions of others, and impoverished by their abundance, he conceives not the least embryo of new thought; opens not the least vista through the gloom of ordinary writers, into the bright walks of rare imagination, and singular design; while the true genius is crossing all public roads into fresh untrodden ground ...[26]

At this point, and indeed throughout the 'Conjectures', Young is set on dismantling the cultural continuum which Dryden and Pope had laboured so mightily to build. This is why he insists that the divinely-inspired enthusiast will be found breaking into 'fresh untrodden ground'. No matter how metaphoric such language is intended to be, it sanctions the idea of the true poet as de- or pre-civilised: from now on urbanity cannot be the measure of poetic worth. On the contrary. The genuine poet declares himself through what Young, thinking of Milton and contrasting him with Pope, the 'Achilles in petticoats', calls 'the native dignity of heroic song'.[27] It might be a description of Gray's bard. It might equally be a description of Ossian.

The ground is now prepared from which Ossian, as true poet, can spring. To adapt Henry James, *this* was what the years had been making for. Add to the work of Collins and Young James Grainger's 'Solitude: An Ode' (1758), in which Grainger claims that 'Inspiration, Nature's child/Seek[s] the solitary Wild', and it becomes clear that Gray was by no means alone in relishing the disconnection of poetry from values Pope had endorsed. Where Gray stands out is in his belief in and ardent readiness to promote the virtues of the Ossianic fragments which the Reverend James Macpherson foisted on him. Because what the years had been making for was, of course, the invention of precisely that poet and his poetry on whose behalf Gray and his acquaintances had spoken and for which they had yearned. Such poetry couldn't be expected to exist in 'Augustan' England. And insofar as a poet might try to bring it into existence, this was in all likelihood only to be achieved at the cost of his sanity. It could however exist in another place, and at another time. When Gray was first shown some of the fragments, he held onto his scholarly caution. 'I am gone mad about . . . my old Scotch (or rather Irish) poetry,' he wrote to Thomas Wharton in 1760, but added that he was plagued by uncertainty as to whether they were really 'specimens of antiquity'.[28] Three years later the doubts were all dispelled. In a letter to the Reverend James Brown, Gray announced that 'Imagination dwelt many hundred years ago in all her pomp on the cold and barren mountains of Scotland. The truth (I believe) is that without any respect of climates she reigns in all nascent societies of men . . .'[29]

It does not much matter that Gray was mistaken in his belief that the Ossianic fragments were genuine. Forgeries and fakes are made necessary by the historical moment at which they appear, and the Ossianic poems appeared at exactly the right moment. They were an essential ingredient in what gradually develops into a new cultural continuum: concern for the Gothic, the revival of an 'innocent' Spenser (the first significant achievement in this mode was William Shenstone's 'The Schoolmistress' (1737)); the renewed interest in ballad poetry signalled most brightly in Thomas Percy's *Reliques of Ancient English Poetry* (1765): individually and collectively these phenomena manifest a desire to worry at and to reroute the concept of national identity by inspecting or recovering a different history from the one associated with Augustanism.

Inevitably, therefore, the poet-as-bard must be presented as an oppositional voice. When James Beattie provided a preface for his 'The Minstrel; or, The Progress of Genius' (1770), a poem written in Spenserian stanzas, he noted:

> The design was, to trace the progress of a Poetical Genius, born in a rude age, from the first dawning of fancy and reason, till that period at which he may be supposed capable of appearing in the world as a MINSTREL, that is, as an itinerant poet and musician: – a character which, according to the notions of our forefathers, was not only respectable, but sacred.[30]

Of course.

Yet at this point we are bound to sense a problem. Who exactly *are* these 'forefathers'? The answer has to be: Scottish or Irish or Welsh. In other words, the true poet is insistently marginalised, pushed back in time, elbowed away from England. It is as though there is now general agreement that in England poetry cannot flourish and hasn't done so for hundreds of years. Johnson claimed Shakespeare for 'learning' over her 'barbarous foes', and though Shakespeare was won back for 'nature' and 'inspiration', it was obviously going to be difficult, if not impossible, to locate any true poets in the present, given the need to combine poetry with solitude, barbaric societies, bardic inspiration, and so on. Hence Chatterton's invention of the 'Rowlie Ballads'. (But they came too late and weren't good enough to fool the newly sceptical.) Hence, some time later, Burns's invention of himself.

Burns belongs to my narrative because of his witty readiness to make money by presenting himself as a natural genius, a Scottish minstrel. There had, of course, been previous attempts to promote within England 'uneducated poets' (the term is Southey's). Quite apart from Stephen Duck, there were Mary Collier, Anne Yearsley, James Woodhouse, John Lucas ('the Cobler poet') and others. But they counted for little. For one thing, they came a shade too early. For another, they did their best to make themselves acceptable by adopting the language and manners of that cultural orthodoxy to which Duck was recommended. As such, they were vulnerable to Johnson's scorn. 'They had better,' he told Boswell, 'furnish [Woodhouse] with good implements for his trade, than raise a subscription for his poems. He may make an excellent shoemaker, but can never make a good poet.' These 'uneducated poets' are not absorbable into the new tradition I have been outlining, and if they belong anywhere it is with that cult of the tamed 'noble savage' of which Omai is perhaps the most spectacular example.[31]

By comparison, Burns was able to make himself appear as the genuine article. Everything was ready for him (including those stirrings of interest in dialect which testify to an awareness that the language, like the culture and the very land, is becoming rapidly and exclusively enclosed). Burns's Preface to the famous Kilmarnock Edition (1786) is the perfect introduction to poems which, partly because some of them are written in Lallans, could be presented as outflowings of native genius.

> The following trifles are not the production of the Poet, who, with all the advantages of learned art, and perhaps amid the elegancies and idlenesses of upper life, looks down for a rural theme, with an eye to Theocrites or Virgil . . . Unacquainted with the necessary requisites for commencing Poet by rule, he sings the sentiments and manners, he felt and saw in himself and his rustic compeers around him, in his and their native language.

In a sense this is the greatest forgery of them all, a wonderfully witty, tongue-in-cheek performance. And it worked. Burns became famous. His poems sold. But he belongs here only as a poet who made it possible for a 'taste' in 'peasant poetry' to become part of a radical rethinking of the poet, and of the 'England' for which such a poet might speak. And this is a subject that will be developed later. The late date of his *Poems* takes him beyond the limits of the present chapter, for with Burns we move into the period of decisive challenges to, and fracturing of, that version of Englishness which, with various strains, was upheld through the middle years of the century – at least until and including the publication of *The Fleece*.

In this chapter I have been trying to identify the many ways through which radical shifts in thinking about poetry, the poet, and the national identity which poetry addresses, develop. And I have argued that in many ways these shifts happen, if not fortuitously, then often by fortuitous means. For it would be absurd to suggest that Gray, Collins, Young, Smart and others, self-consciously recognised all the implications of those matters in which they became involved. They are troubled by the differing concepts of liberty, they become immersed in ideas of the poet-as-bard, of the poet as spokesman for the people, of poetry as an oppositional voice. Sometimes these matters are developed independently of each other. At other times they suggest connections and possibilities which later, more self-consciously radical poets can draw on. But one poet had a much sharper sense than his contemporaries of what was at issue. He is the subject of the next chapter.

CHAPTER 3

Goldsmith and the Ambiguities of Patriotism

By adoption a Londoner, a friend of Johnson and his circle and a founder member of The Club, Oliver Goldsmith appears to belong with the last attempts to produce a coherent account of Augustan values. Yet although he could play to perfection the part of conformist – not for nothing did Thackeray call him 'the most beloved of English writers' – Goldsmith was also cannily subversive. Above all, he set himself to tease out what was implied by the concept of liberty, and to show how corrupt were likely to be the appeals to it, especially when they were made by that establishment whose values he apparently saluted.

Outsider though he was, Goldsmith did not write like one. His style is consciously 'below refinement and above grossness', as Johnson had said that a permanent style should be. It can even be argued that Goldsmith's style is (very) self-consciously urbane. He writes for those who may be thought to belong to the dry ground of Augustan certainties. He is sure of his audience in a way Gray and Collins were not. But he is also a citizen of the world, in the sense in which I earlier used the term. As a result, coming when he does, what he has to say undermines certainties, discomforts, is intended to produce anxieties. In no sense does Goldsmith uncritically endorse the society he seems to be writing from within and for. Citizen Goldsmith is a tricky customer.

It is possible to argue that what I call subversiveness may amount to no more than an irresponsible evasiveness. Seamus Deane, for example, has been particularly critical of what he considers Goldsmith's refusal to confront the issues he pretends to write about, in particular his most unconvincing attack upon 'Luxury'.

This is Goldsmith's half-hearted way of dealing with the ever-renewable dispute between metropolitan and provincial life, between, say, the Lissoy of his youth and the Vauxhall he patronised in his maturity. In Ireland, the contrast between the world of fashionable Dublin and the rest of the country was especially painful. If Luxury were the cause of it, then Luxury was only another name for colonialism of the most rapacious kind. But, like the rest of his Irish friends, Goldsmith could not quite see Ireland as a colony of England. It had to be, in some fashion, incorporated into English civilization, an integral part of it . . . in effect, Goldsmith's account of the passage from provincial pastoralism to urban frivolity and materialism is futile, because it amounts to little more than an amateur attempt to explain away the Irish-English tension which was at the heart of his experience.[1]

This is subtle and at the same time hard, a good deal harder than John Montague, who has argued that if *The Deserted Village* is in the end unfocused this is less because Goldsmith is trying to explain anything away than because he is trying to explain too much. Auburn can't be both Lissoy *and* an English village.

Donald Davie takes a position different from either Deane or Montague, although agreeing with both that there is something unsatisfactory about Goldsmith's most famous poem. He chooses to direct attention towards *The Traveller*, because in this poem, he claims, Goldsmith's political and social credo is set out with absolute clarity. It is that of the Tory monarchist, very much within 'the English system'.

> *The Deserted Village* prescribes no remedy for the state of affairs it deplores, and therefore puts no reader under obligation to do anything about it. *The Traveller* however *does* prescribe a remedy: enhanced power for George III . . . *The Traveller* is a fervent apologia for the monarchical form of government, taking the time-honoured ground that, since the under-privileged need a power to appeal to above the power of local privilege, the only such power conceivable is the power of the Monarch, elevated above all sectional interests.[2]

The lines to which Davie refers by way of making his case include such key moments as those where Goldsmith speaks about 'contending chiefs' who 'blockade the throne,/Contracting regal power to stretch their own', as a result of which he asks his brother to 'curse with me that baleful hour;/When first ambition struck at regal power.' These lines undoubtedly show Goldsmith in the role of Tory monarchist, and there is any amount of evidence to show that he played the part with some consistency. Boswell records him saying as late as 1773 that 'I'm for the Monarchy to keep us equal,'[3] and in his *History of England* he notes ruefully of the 1760s that 'The strength of the crown was every day declining, while an aristocracy filled up every avenue to the throne, intent only on emoluments, not the duties of office.'[4] This makes him sound like a pre-1688 man, which is what Davie wants us to see him as. Certainly, it is the aristocracy, composed of the 'contending chiefs' who for the most part can be brought together under the familiar title of the Whig supremacy, against which Goldsmith inveighs. His opposition to these people is plain and remarkably consistent: it therefore follows that his Tory monarchism is a deep-rooted and unshakeable conviction.

Or does it? Suppose we put the lines to which Davie refers into context. Goldsmith says that he has been watching with 'Fear, pity, justice, indignation', the chiefs at their work; and he continues:

> 'Till half a patriot, half a coward grown,
> I fly from petty tyrants to the throne.
>
> Yes, brother, curse with me that baleful hour,
> When first ambition struck at regal power;
> And thus polluting honour in its source,
> Gave wealth to sway the mind with double force.
> Have we not seen, round Britain's peopled shore,
> Her useful sons exchanged for useless ore?
> Seen all her triumphs but destruction haste,
> Like flaring tapers brightening as they waste;
> Seen opulence, her grandeur to maintain,
> Lead stern depopulation in her train,
> And over fields where scattered hamlets rose,
> In barren solitary pomp repose?
> Have we not seen at pleasure's lordly call,
> The smiling long-frequented village fall?
> Beheld the duteous son, the sire decayed,
> The modest matron and the blushing maid,
> Forced from their homes, a melancholy train,
> To traverse climes beyond the western main . . .
>
> (ll. 391–410)

Here we have the seed from which *The Deserted Village* will later spring, although Davie and others think the latter poem a deformed growth because it is calculated not to give offence, is too guarded, too bland. By the same token they argue that the vigour of *The Traveller* depends on Goldsmith's readiness to assert that greater power for George III would have prevented the newly enriched aristocracy from furthering their selfish ambitions by enclosing land for their parks and country houses and, in the process, abusing what should have been their social and political responsibilities. In this reading, *The Traveller* can be singled out for its incisive criticisms of that mythic dream of the island of commercially produced and guaranteed bliss, which Thomson invoked and which Dyer and others shared.

I am not convinced. Of course, Goldsmith attacks the (largely Whig) aristocracy. But can we be sure that his poem champions George? 'And thus polluting honour in its source'. Why should we not read this line as implying that the king is part of the problem? I think not only that we can, but that we must. To justify this I need to go back to the first version of *The Traveller*, called *A Prospect of Society*. In this earlier text, when Goldsmith speaks of seeing 'contention hem the throne', it is notable that he feels

I can't forbear; but, half a coward grown,
I wish to shrink from tyrants to the throne.
    Yes, my loved brother, cursed be that hour
When first ambition toil'd for foreign power;
When Britons learnt to swell beyond their shore,
And barter useful men for useless ore . . .
Have we not seen, at pleasure's lordly call,
An hundred villages in ruin fall?

The passage attacks the Whig aristocracy and looks to monarchy to champion the dispossessed. But when it reappears, revised and expanded, in *The Traveller*, matters are less straightforward. For one thing, the original 'half a coward' has now been joined by 'half a patriot', and this is bound to be highly problematic given the way that Goldsmith has used the word 'patriot' earlier in the poem. In lines 73–4 he comments: 'Such is the patriot's boast, where'er we roam,/His first, best country ever is at home.' And a little later: 'Though patriots flatter, still shall wisdom find/An equal portion dealt to all mankind.' In other words patriots suffer, as patriots will, from a blinkered, irrational pride in their own country. Goldsmith would have met many of them in London. When he comes to speak of himself as 'half a patriot' it is inconceivable that he would have forgotten the loaded way in which he had already used the term. Nor would he have expected his readers to have forgotten. The point then is that he is wryly admitting to having almost fallen into the patriotic trap, while retaining enough wit to recognise that it *is* a trap. And this recognition, we must surely reflect, comes readily to a writer who balances, perhaps precariously, between two national identities. A paraphrase of Goldsmith's meaning might run something like this: 'Here I am, having half deluded myself into trying to believe that one big tyrant is better than many small tyrants.' For – and this is the second significant alteration – the original 'tyrants' have now become 'petty tyrants', presumably to contrast with George III, who is therefore the biggest tyrant of them all. Goldsmith would not have been alone in thinking of George in this way. As J. H. Plumb remarks: 'Powers that [George] had every right to exercise seemed despotic when employed by him. It is not remarkable that the grotesque myth that he was aiming at tyranny should have been so widely believed so early in his reign.'[5] Davie could of course argue that although Goldsmith might well have regarded George as a tyrant, it was as an essentially benevolent one, so that we are to see the king, through the poet's eyes at least, as the Good Natured Man and Vicar of Wakefield rolled into one. And as we shall see, Dr Primrose does indeed speak out in favour of the one big tyrant, although in less than flattering terms. But this does not solve the problem about Goldsmith's reference to honour as polluted in its source, which is the third, crucial way in which the text of *The Traveller* differs from *A Prospect*. For in that earlier version Goldsmith had accused ambition of toiling for foreign power, and here we can have no doubt at whom the finger is being pointed: at East and West Indian traders and all those who were bent on prolonging hostilities against France. What we have then to explain is why Goldsmith changed the lines, why, no matter how slyly, he gives the impression that you have to be a bit of a fool – half a patriot – to believe that the monarchy can offer a way out of the mess the country is in, especially since this particular monarch is himself infected by what's rotten in the state. (A reference at line 357 to 'patriot flame' identifies a past when it was possible to feel an untroubled love of one's country, as one now cannot.)

A short explanation for all this is that Goldsmith is probably having fun at the expense of his English friends. If so, he adroitly covers his tracks so that Johnson, say, couldn't openly accuse him of anti-monarchical or anti-English bias – which as far as Johnson was concerned amounted to the same thing. It is, for example, notable that he will not allow the word 'republic' into his *Dictionary*, even though the OED identifies a meaning as dating from 1604: 'a state in which the supreme power rests in the people and their elected representatives or officers, as opp. to one governed by a king or the like; a commonwealth'. Presumably Johnson thought that to offer the word houseroom would be to make its meaning thinkable. His deep distrust of any disturbance to the social order almost certainly explains his violent hostility to the Scots, whose lack of pleasure in the Act of Union was only too apparent, and was not exhausted by the events of 1715 and 1745. (It may also be his way of guarding against guilt at what his nation had done to them. Patriots may *say* 'My country, right or wrong,' but to admit wrongdoing is not easy.)

More seriously, Goldsmith is properly exploiting his double vision, that of an Anglo-Irish writer. He is thus able to open up questions about the kind of patriotism which is rooted in Tory monarchism. This, then, leads me to argue that at a deep level Goldsmith is attempting to come to terms with 'Old Corruption': that is, the state of England as he saw it, which aroused within him a mixture of disquiet and contempt, even though this had occasionally to be hidden under the surface of, and could be compromised by, his role as a 'beloved English writer'. He feels disquiet not merely about George III but about the kinds of arrangements which the 'glorious revolution' had inaugurated, and especially about the concept of liberty and its capturable, exploitable, meanings.

In 1762 Goldsmith published in *Lloyds Evening Post* a short essay called 'The Revolution in Low Life'. The essay, which since its attribution to Goldsmith in 1922 has frequently been referred to as '*The Deserted Village* in prose', tells how the writer had spent the previous summer in 'a little village'. He recalls it as an ideally 'happy community'. But: 'I was informed that a Merchant of immense fortune in London, who had lately purchased the estate on which they lived, intended to lay the whole out as a seat of pleasure for himself.' The community was to be destroyed. 'All the connections of kindred are now irreparably broken; their neat gardens and well cultivated fields were left to desolation.' The tale ends with Goldsmith generalising from his experience: 'I am informed that nothing is at present more common than such realities.' As a result, 'wherever the traveller turns, while he sees one part of the inhabitants of the country becoming immensely rich, he sees the other growing miserably poor . . .' The ultimate cause of this revolution in low life is foreign commerce, which makes governments at length 'Aristocratical; and the immense property, thus necessarily acquired by some, has swallowed up the liberties of all. Venice, Genoa, and Holland are little better at present than retreats for tyrants and prisons for slaves.'

Seamus Deane takes exception to this conclusion. 'Inaccurate or irrelevant', he calls Goldsmith's examples, and adds, 'Ireland, after all, would have prospered a great deal more had the restrictions on its trade been lifted.'[6] I can agree to this while feeling that Deane is being less than fair to Goldsmith. For these three examples turn up again in Chapter 19 of *The Vicar of Wakefield* (most of which was almost certainly written in 1762), where we learn from Dr Primrose that in Holland, Genoa and Venice, 'the laws govern the poor, and the rich govern the law'. This directly anticipates those lines in *The Traveller* where Goldsmith claims that 'Each wanton judge new penal statutes draw,/Laws grind the poor and rich men rule the law.' And here he is talking about England. Thus, if Deane is right to argue that Goldsmith could have focused his case more appropriately by drawing attention to the exploitation of Ireland by the English, it can also be said that by stitching together a number of apparently disparate moments we are able to see how consistently Goldsmith argued against 'Aristocratical' government in England, even though he might not always have made the argument explicit. He is unswervingly hostile to the influence of those whom Plumb terms the 'West Indians, the East Indians, the bankers, the brewers', as well as the 'thickening state of the professional classes' and the 'new industrialists'.[7] In short, he is at odds with all those 'who believed by instinct that England was destined to great wealth if only her opportunities were not scotched by the incompetence of her King and his ministers'; and these newly influential people inevitably included among their ranks members of the Irish nobility, 'gorged with recent plunder . . . buying their way into the English aristocracy'.[8] Goldsmith knew what these people had done to the country he had grown up in, and he would have had little time for their natural spokesman, Pitt, who protested vehemently against the Preliminaries of the Peace of Paris. In Pitt, Plumb remarks, 'the voice of the City spoke. His denunciations were based entirely on commercial strategy.'[9]

Goldsmith's entirely proper and angry contempt for the 'Merchant of immense fortune' is, then, implicitly on behalf of the dispossessed of Ireland as much as it is explicitly on behalf of those of England. This will help to explain why he uses monarchical government as a stick with which to beat the aristocracy, as in Dr Primrose's diatribe against tyrants.

> Now, Sir, for my own part, as I naturally hate the face of a tyrant, the further off he is removed from me, the better pleased I am. The generality of mankind are of my way of thinking, and have unanimously created one king, whose election at once diminishes the number of tyrants . . .
>
> (*The Vicar of Wakefield*, Ch. IV)

Donald Davie insists that Primrose's position is not finally different from Goldsmith's. But to speak of hating the face of a tyrant is hardly an enthusiastic endorsement of George III. And anyway, can we so easily identify Primrose with his creator? Yes, both are against the aristocracy. Yes, both perhaps would like to see in the monarchy a preferable alternative. But there are things Goldsmith knows that Primrose doesn't know, or which at all events he chooses not to know; and it is these which make a commitment to monarchism problematic. They include the fact that benevolence may well equal impotence – as it does for Honeywood and Primrose. That civic virtue Pope had so praised now turns out to be irrelevant to the developing social relations of eighteenth-century England. More important, however, is the reflection that it isn't easy to dissociate the one big tyrant from the many petty ones. To see why this is so we need to turn yet again to the village.

It is 'distant about fifty miles from town, consisting of near an hundred cottages'. This is the village as discussed in *The Revolution in Low Life*, and it isn't very specific. But then neither are the accounts of the 'little neighbourhood' to which Dr Primrose retreats (though that borrows some of its details from the other), nor the 'smiling, long-frequented village' of *The Traveller*. And even Auburn may seem more of a generalised picture than one derived from a real place. Nevertheless, the work of Mavis Batey has made it virtually certain that the village Goldsmith in all cases had in mind was Nuneham Courtenay, in Oxfordshire, which is indeed 'about fifty miles from town'. Between 1760 and 1761 Lord Harcourt began the process of 'improving' his land there. This required the destruction of a church and a village. Parsonage, ale-house, cottages and long-established gardens were wiped out; and the village duckpond was expanded into a lake. The village was removed to the main road some mile and a half away, and new cottages were put up on either side of the road.[10] Only one villager remained behind, and we know about her because she is the subject of a poem by William Whitehead. Some time in the 1760s Whitehead wrote an 'Inscription for a Tree: On the Terrace, at Nuneham, Oxfordshire'. A note to the poem tells us that:

This tree is well-known to the country people by the name of BAB's tree. It was planted by one BARBARA WYAT, who was so much attached to it, that, on the removal of Nuneham, to where it is now built, she earnestly intreated that she might still remain in her old habitation. Her request was complied with, and her cottage not pulled down till after her death.[11]

Whitehead treads carefully. He wants to pay tribute to the woman who might well be called – and who almost certainly was – 'the sad historian of the pensive plain'. On the other hand he has no wish to give offence. He had been Harcourt's tutor and he was still close to him.

But there is perhaps another reason for Whitehead's caution, which is that as Poet Laureate he would need to avoid giving offence to the king, and that would include avoiding criticisms of those close to the king. Harcourt was particularly close. In 1750 he had been appointed governor to the future George III, at that time prince of Wales.[12] Ten years later he acted as an important functionary at George's coronation. The following year he was appointed special ambassador to Mecklenburg-Strelitz, in order to negotiate George's marriage with the princess Elizabeth, whom he accompanied back to England. After the wedding Harcourt became master to the queen's horse, an appointment which he relinquished on being made lord chamberlain of the queen's household. And all this time he was at work on the 'improvement' of Nuneham Courtenay. In his study of Georgian gardens David Jacques claims that Harcourt was 'famous for his republican leanings'.[13] If so, they must have emerged after the period with which I am concerned, or, more likely, Jacques is confusing Harcourt with his son, who continued his father's improving work. At all events, Goldsmith would have been only too aware that this intimate of the king was responsible for the wanton destruction of a village, and that he was thus an example of cumbrous pomp pitted against the peasantry's interests. Small wonder that Goldsmith should find it impossible to make a simple or even workable opposition between king and aristocracy. I shall return to this point, but before I do so I need to call up further evidence that will help to dislodge the conventional view of Goldsmith as an unquestioning Tory monarchist – for this is the view that lies behind Thackeray's praise, just as it lies behind the regular and easy accommodation of Goldsmith as a particular kind of 'Augustan' English writer.[14]

On 23 April 1763, John Wilkes published his famous attack on the king, in no 45 of *The North Briton*. As a result, he was arrested on a charge of seditious libel and at once became a hero for many and a villain for some. Among the latter was the Member of Parliament Martin, secretary to the Treasury and one of Bute's creatures, who challenged Wilkes to a duel and badly wounded the 'champion of liberty'. Wilkes's cause was taken up by Charles Churchill in a poem called 'The Duellist', which hailed liberty as felt, enjoyed and adored, 'far beyond the reach of Kings'. Churchill was already notorious for his attack on the acting profession in *The Rosciad* (1761), a poem the question of whose authorship had let Smollett, one of Goldsmith's mentors, into an undignified squabble with Churchill and his Whig cronies. Here, then, was a perfect opportunity for Goldsmith to speak out for his friends and on behalf of the values of Toryism and throne. Yet he remained silent. John Ginger, in his biography of Goldsmith, is at a loss to know why. Goldsmith 'seemed to have deliberately let slip the chance to add to his income by entering the battle . . . under the command of Smollett'. But to put it this way opens up disturbing implications. Ginger is therefore quick to reassure us. Goldsmith's 'political views were none the less strong and consistent. He was a committed monarchist.'[15] If so, one can only reflect that he had an odd way of showing it. One can also reflect that Goldsmith might well have thought that although Wilkes took his stand on liberty, events had proved there wasn't much in it for him. I have already noted that foreign observers habitually contrasted the state of freedom in England and the independence of its subjects with their own repressive regimes.[16] Goldsmith for one thought such independence 'prized too high'. He coined that phrase for *The Traveller*, with the 'contending chiefs' in mind. But he could hardly have applied it to Wilkes, at least not without an uneasy awareness that the law which was being visited on the champion of liberty was the same law which promoted Harcourt's interests, and that Harcourt was an intimate of the king whom Wilkes had attacked – very mildly, too, be it noted. Liberty no longer speaks with the accents of disinterestedness. The 'contending chiefs' who appeal to it are intent on carving up the kingdom.

After his wounding Wilkes fled to France, where he remained for some four years. But by 1768 he was back in London and again in trouble. His election as an MP for Middlesex led to his arrest and temporary release, 'until such time as a writ of *capias ut legatum* had been served against him'. A week after his arrest, it was. The riots provoked by the law's treatment of Wilkes culminated in what became known as the Massacre of St George's Fields, when at least eleven people were killed by the Foot Guards who had been called up to disperse Wilkes's supporters. Moreover, on the evening of his temporary release from custody, Irish coal-heavers, who had been involved in a strike for higher wages, appeared on the streets of London in a show of support for Wilkes, and as a result of the ensuing violence seven of them 'were sentenced to death at the Old Bailey and hanged at the Sun Tavern Fields in Stepney before a crowd of 50,000, attended by three hundred soldiers and "a prodigious number of peace officers"'.[17]

In *Oliver Goldsmith: His Life and Works*, A. Lytton Sells notes that sometime at the end of the 1760s Goldsmith was approached by a Dr Scott, who tried to hire him to write on behalf of the North government, which was being 'hard-pressed by the opposition in Parliament and by Junius, Wilkes and . . . other political writers'. Goldsmith was apparently 'so absurd as to say – "I can earn as much as will supply my wants without writing for any party; the assistance therefore you offer, is unnecessary to me", and so I left him . . . in his garret'.[18] It goes without saying that Goldsmith was rarely in funds. (At various times he earned a great deal of money, but he spent at a prodigious rate.) Sells can make neither head nor tail of it. Goldsmith would 'have performed a public service by writing in support of the ministry'. In addition, we are assured that Goldsmith disliked Wilkes and in 1773 'actually wrote in support of James Townsend who had put up against Wilkes for election as Lord Mayor of London. Other men of distinction supported North's ministry, including Johnson who had published three pamphlets in its favour.'[19] Sells is therefore left as baffled as John Ginger by this odd failure of Goldsmith's amenability.

In which case it is as well to consider the public service that Goldsmith would have apparently performed if he had written for North and against Wilkes. Seven Irish coal-heavers had been hanged for rioting as part of a demand for better wages, and other people had been cut down by a hail of army gunfire. All were supporters of Wilkes. 'The laws govern the poor, and the rich men govern the law.' Horace Walpole noted with smug satisfaction that Goldsmith 'meddled not with politics', a claim which Davie rightly rejects in his account of *The Traveller*. By attending not merely to what Goldsmith says but to what he doesn't say, we can get a better sense of his political thinking, and it does not lead us to Davie's conclusions. In choosing not to meddle with the politics of party when they are directed against Wilkes, Goldsmith is being properly political. Look at him from the vantage point of the Tory monarchist and his behaviour is a puzzle. Look at him from the vantage point that I suggested as appropriate for *The Traveller* and his silence makes sense. It is at once wily and stubborn. He is not going to be jockeyed into a position that will make him a tame 'English' writer, where that requires him to conform to a version of Englishness which uncompli-catedly endorses the propriety of crown and law.

And there is another point. North was George's Prime Minister and his trusted confidant. I have already referred to Corrigan and Sayer's remark that they are not the first 'to observe that property ("owning, being owned") and propriety ("correctness of behaviour or morals") have the same etymological root. State activities were central to the naturalisation of both.'[20] The principal means of attaining that naturalisation was the law. How far Goldsmith was alert to this we can note if we pause on a couplet which may at first seem remote from such considerations.

> Along the lawn, where scattered hamlets rose,
> Unwieldy wealth and cumbrous pomp repose

There are important social and political implications here. Goldsmith presents the hamlets as natural growths: not so much fashioned in an 'orderly' or 'formal' way as vigorously flourishing because 'scattered'. The term offers a rebuke to the Brownian concept of how to make a landscape look natural, which continually required a 'scattering' of trees. For Goldsmith, it is human activity which in its purposefulness is truly natural, *not* the mimic art of the landscape architect; and it contrasts with all that is 'unwieldy' and 'cumbrous', words which continually point up the uselessness – inutility – of wealth and pomp. Whatever is unwieldy obviously can't be handled, and as for cumbrous, Johnson's various definitions are greatly to the point. 'Troubling; vexatious; disturbing', 'oppressive: burthensome', 'jumbled; obstructing each other'. The word thus plays back with a bitter irony on orthodox connections between property and propriety. What could be less proper than that the land be cumbered with these useless heaps of wealth? Yet pomp monopolises 'the real benefits of nature', as Goldsmith notes elsewhere.[21] It is enabled to do so because 'rich men rule the law'. This, then, emphatically rejects that view of the connection between self-interest and the interests of the nation which Thomson and Dyer had invoked. Self-interest *opposes* national interest.

Goldsmith snaps the argument shut later, in *The Deserted Village*, when he re-introduces pomp.

> Here, while the proud their long-drawn pomps display,
> There the black gibbet glooms beside the way.

At first glance the couplet may seem to provide a violent disjunction – one of those 'odd contrasts' which a certain kind of narrative historian is fond of noting. But we are bound to recognise the causal inter-connectedness between the two displays. Here/There. The monosyllables suggest a vast gap, yet the echoed stresses hint at connection. Very little in eighteenth-century life was attended with greater pomp than the law. As E. P. Thompson in particular has pointed out, law's theatrical, ritualised qualities were a way of insisting that 'the law' was above the law.[22] Enactment of the law developed as a spectacle, and we have seen that one such spectacle was attended by an audience of 50,000. This may seem far removed from another aspect of the eighteenth century: 'the much remarked "civilized" tone of . . . upper-class life – fenced-off parks, elegant mansions with their classical façades and formal gardens'.[23] That it isn't is crucial to Goldsmith's repeated use of the word 'pomp', attached at one point to emparked land, at another to the streets of London where the gibbet glooms, and prompting the reflection that cultural treasures 'have an origin which [the cultural materialist] cannot contemplate without horror. They owe their existence not only to the efforts of the great minds and talents who have created them, but also to the anonymous toil of their contemporaries. There is no document of civilisation which is not at the same time a document of barbarism.'[24] You do not have to claim Goldsmith as a cultural materialist in order to realise that it is by no means absurd to apply Walter Benjamin's famous words to *The Deserted Village*.

This then leads to the all-important question: what exactly is Goldsmith's attitude to his chosen subject. It plainly can't be pinned down by the word 'horror'. Disquiet? Yes, sometimes. Despair? Yes, again. Nostalgic conde-scension – a way of belittling the importance of his subject? Yes, yet again. But to say this is to admit that there may well be something finally evasive about the tone of *The Deserted Village*, and Raymond Williams probably has this in mind when he remarks that as soon as Goldsmith's feelings for his villagers are 'extended to memory and imagination . . . what takes over . . . is a different pressure: the social history of the writer'.[25] As we have seen, that social history is a complex matter and it exposes Goldsmith to contradic-tions that the very nature of his subject is bound to exacerbate, and which he may try to evade by the attack on 'luxury' which Deane finds so inaccurate. John Montague puts the case more forgivingly when he speaks of Goldsmith's 'skilful alternation between images of original innocence and malignant destruction',[26] and John Barrell takes this further by suggesting that the most radical element in the poem is Goldsmith's appeal, not so much on behalf of the industrious poor, as on behalf of leisure: his interest is in the periods 'when toil remitting lent its turn to play':

> But this concentration on leisure may have been precisely the point, a point confirmed by that feature of the village before its destruction which, in the description which opens the poem, is most conspicuous by its absence – the hall. For the bold peasantry of England, thought Goldsmith, the lightest labour would easily secure the necessities of life, if as freeholders once again they were obliged neither to pay rent, nor to work for money wages. Goldsmith disengaged the labourer from his 'proper' and 'natural' identity as a labourer, as a man born to toil, and suggested that he could be as free to dispose of his time as other poets agreed only the rich man or the shepherd was free to do.[27]

Barrell's argument is especially useful because it enables us to see that the Adamic 'soft primitive' state of leisure Goldsmith invokes can hardly be consonant with that more feudalistic vision which, be it never so 'innocent', is part and parcel of the fervent and uncomplicated Tory monarchism Davie wishes onto him, and which certainly depends on the presence of the hall, to whose absence from the pre-deserted village Barrell rightly draws attention. (Whereas such a hall, together with its estate, is part of the habitation to which the Vicar of Wakefield retreats; and that this should in no way cloud Dr Primrose's golden view of society is one reason among many why it will hardly do to identify him with Goldsmith.)

There is no denying the passion of Goldsmith's attack on Whig wealth and pomp. Such pomp evidences the allure of luxury against which Dyer had warned, although his warning, faint at best, is more or less blotted out by his enthusiastic vision of the wealth for all apparently promised by Britannia's golden fleece. It is a vision which Goldsmith demolishes in his own 'vision of decay consequent upon imperial expansion and excessive trade', and this makes for some of the poem's greatest moments.

> Kingdoms, by thee to sickly greatness grown,
> Boast of a florid vigour not their own.
> At every draught more large and large they grow,
> A bloated mass of rank unwieldy woe;
> Till sapped their strength and every part unsound,
> Down, down they sink, and spread a ruin round.

(ll. 389–394)

In these lines England becomes a Rowlandson-like parody of gluttonous excess and a grotesque vision of overblown fruitfulness, a garden whose original, Adamic, 'florid vigour' has turned into an overrun park. The wit is formidable, the lines packed with vivid awareness of how this wealth-congested England has become a weed-infested 'unwieldy' chaos. (The word comes into play again with stunning effect.) This is the fruit of the private, competitive spirit, unforgettably laid before us.

The passage may also seem at first to bring comfort for all those wishing to claim Goldsmith as that true patriot, the Tory monarchist. For there is no difficulty in identifying the Whig sympathies of most of the new men of wealth, nor in listing their acquisitions of land and property. Among them are to be found the very grandest: Pitt, Earl of Chatham, and Robert, Lord Clive, both of whom employed Capability Brown to carry out improvements on their land; Chatham in 1765, Clive in 1769. What this entailed has been often enough spelt out by historians of landscape architecture, who have had to note that the great scale of Brown's gardens could not have been achieved without the help of enclosure acts. No wonder, then, that the host of improvers should earn Goldsmith's scorn. By contrast he could be free to admire Shenstone's garden at Leasowe's because it was on a small scale, and therefore reared with no man's ruin, no man's groan. (Except, that is, Shenstone's: he spent so much on it that it beggared him and his heirs had to sell it off in order to settle the debts he left.)

But it won't do. I have already remarked on the fact that at the time Harcourt began his work of improvement he was an intimate of the king. It is an example which can be almost endlessly multiplied, so that even if we chose to resist the identification of Auburn with Nuneham Courtenay we would have finally to admit that 'improvement' was by no means left to Whig aristocrats. No less a man than Bute was among the improvers. When George's first Prime Minister and most trusted ally left office in 1763, he set about landscaping his properties at Luton Hoo and Highcliffe; and he appointed Capability Brown to plan and supervise the work. Goldsmith would have known about that, just as he would have known that in 1764 George had appointed Brown to be Royal Surveyor of Gardens and Waters. If we need an explanation of why the text of *A Prospect of Society* was rewritten for *The Traveller* this will do as well as any. Of course it is true that Brown was especially friendly with leading Whigs. He was bound to be. They had a great deal of money and were bent on acquiring land. They therefore guaranteed him important commissions. But he had no objection to being friendly with Tories, and they had no objection to being friendly with him. Luxury, pomp, law: these constituents of Old Corruption are not simply a function of any one party, and if Goldsmith began by thinking or hoping that this was the case he was bound to become disillusioned. The disillusionment must have grown the more he travelled around England, as he did during the 1760s. It is this growing disillusionment and the occasional struggle to contain or suppress it which accounts for those contradictions one finds in some of his reported comments, most of his work, and above all in *The Deserted Village*.

For on the one hand we have a poem which is recognisably Augustan in its nostalgic placing of 'The swain mistrustless of his smutted face', and which is the work of an amenable poet, one who knows on which side his bread is buttered. 'The Drama's Laws the Drama's Patrons give,/For we that live to please, must please to live.' Goldsmith would have sighed a heartfelt amen to Johnson's words. He knew all about being a professional man of letters in eighteenth-century London, and it is the professional who is to the fore when it comes to the presentation of village life in terms of a lost idyll. Davie has this aspect of the poem in mind when he says that it prescribes 'no remedy for the state of affairs it deplores'. How could it? The pastoral poem as picturesque exercise rests on the assumption that loss, however regrettable, is inevitable. It comes about through a 'principle of change'.[28] Regret or sadness can then be easily indulged, the more easily the more the idyll is placed in the past. Besides, which of Goldsmith's readers would wish to be a smutty-faced swain, or for that matter to share the Vicar of Wakefield's retreat, or be part of the happy community described in *The Revolution in Low Life*? 'They were merry at Christmas and mournful in Lent, got drunk on St George's day, and religiously cracked nuts on Michaelmas-eve.' This way of writing is a way of writing down and therefore writing off. It allows for – indeed, it ensures – an evasion of proper interest in its own subject. It assuages where it should hurt. You can find such writing in *The Deserted Village*, and for some readers at least this fatally compromises the poem's worth.

Yet in the dedication to Reynolds – 'all my views and enquiries have led me to believe those miseries real, which I here attempt to display' – and elsewhere in the poem, Goldsmith insists on identifying the causes of the state of affairs he deplores. And these have nothing to do with the so-called 'principle of change'. On the contrary, they are social actualities. To ignore this element and the force it has in the poem is to refuse to see the troubled, radical wit that takes Goldsmith well beyond an amateur indictment of luxury as the root of the village's – and England's – evils, and which leads him to a formidably suggestive account of how such luxury, or more accurately 'pomp', operates through specific social agencies. There is here no room for evasion and compromise. At the heart of the matter is law, functioning in the name of the Crown. And in more than name. For it was not Whig aristocrats alone who profited from the connection of law with pomp. The monarchy, George III and his cronies, are an integral part of Old Corruption. 'In England,' Tom Paine wrote in *Common Sense*, two years after Goldsmith's death, 'a king hath little more to do than to make war and to give away places; which in plain terms, is to impoverish the nation and set it together by the ears.' I do not suggest that Goldsmith would have assented to the truth of Paine's words. I do, however, suggest that Paine could have looked to elements in *The Deserted Village* to vindicate his argument. This will then help to explain why Blake could note in his Marginalia to Reynolds's *Discourses* that 'Such Men as Goldsmith ought not to have been Acquainted with such Men as Reynolds.'

Goldsmith's position is both valuable and instructive. His is the most considered attempt to hold the middle ground. He speaks from a certain cultural position, much of which had been prepared for him by the work of those great writers I have already discussed but which is beginning to break up, as such positions must. Goldsmith is more sharply aware of this than is normally assumed. This is why his strategies can appear evasive. But, sympathetically viewed, they can be taken as a series of audacious, imaginative interventions in what he sensed was no less than a cultural crisis.

One way of identifying this crisis is by registering what was happening to the idea of the poet, and this I attempted to do in the previous chapter, as I there touched on the difficult matter of ideas of liberty, through which a gathering crisis can also be detected. We need also to note what was happening to language and ideas of language. In the Preface to his edition of Shakespeare, Johnson remarked that:

> If there be, what I believe there is, in every nation, a stile which never becomes obsolete, a certain mode of phraseology so consonant and congenial to the analogy and principles of its respective language as to remain settled and unaltered; this stile is to be sought in the common intercourse of life, among those who speak only to be understood, without the ambition of elegance . . . there is a conversation above grossness and below refinement, where propriety resides.[29]

Above grossness and below refinement. Is this the language of a new 'middle' class? In his *Dictionary* Johnson announces that he will give no room to words which can be thought of as either 'cant' or 'low terms'. They are banished along with 'the diction of the laborious and mercantile part of the people [which] is in great measure casual and mutable'.[30] Such people lack propriety as they lack property. Only certain people can speak for England, and although they are a larger number than Pope could have envisaged – new forms of liberty have seen to that – the language is nevertheless enclosed against many others.

But against this, the notional emergence of the divinely-inspired enthusiast, who will speak very differently, and with a different sense of 'common intercourse' in mind, indicates why Johnson's hopes for a stable language must prove unrealistic. Goldsmith's major poems offer what is perhaps the most serious, sustained attempt in the middle of the eighteenth century to realise such a language, to honour a commitment to cultural stability. Yet given that he can speak *to* 'Lettered Pomp', but only *for* 'a bold peasantry', *The Deserted Village* enacts a breakdown of common intercourse as Johnson understood it. Its 'stile', far from binding the nation together, bears witness to the fact of separations. At the end of the poem Goldsmith imagines poetry as deserting England, because it cannot belong 'in these degenerate times of shame'. It flies from the 'sensual joys' which the poet envisages a future England as being swamped by. This is not the same as Pope's 'Great Anarch'. To be sure, the dunces had threatened the survival of poetry. But Goldsmith's politics require him to acknowledge the awareness that poetry can no longer speak for an England which banishes the true liberty by which alone poetry is nourished. True liberty must be for those who do not necessarily have either property or propriety. This is a very new meaning for 'liberty'. And so, from afar, poetry must

> let thy voice, prevailing over time,
> Redress the rigours of the inclement clime;
> Aid slighted truth; with thy persuasive strain
> Teach erring man to spurn the rage of gain . . .

> (ll. 421–424)

It is a call to action, in a sense reminiscent of Gray's 'The Bard' and 'The Progress of Poesy', and of Collins's 'Ode to Liberty'. But it more powerfully and self-consciously articulates the distress which had in muted fashion stirred in their poems. Goldsmith knows that future poets and poetry will have to be very unlike their predecessors. They will need to be voices of opposition. Or, if they are to forge a 'common intercourse' it will have to be in markedly different terms from those created by Dryden and Pope. Goldsmith comes to the conclusion Gray and Collins evaded. True poetry, like true liberty, is no longer to be confidently expected in England. The three terms require to be redefined if they are to co-exist.

CHAPTER 4

The Wanderer in the City: William Blake

I

'To rove: to ramble here and there; to go, without any certain course. It has always an ill sense.' These are Johnson's glosses on the verb 'to wander'. As for 'wandering', it is: '1) Uncertain peregrination; 2) Aberration: mistaken way; 3) Incertainty: want of being fixed.' Gypsies, whose pariah-like wanderings pose a threat to orderliness and stability, are outcasts. So are wandering thoughts. Johnson appeals to Locke here in order to banish from sympathetic consideration such aberrant ways. Clearly, wandering has always an ill sense.

Some twenty years or so after the publication of the *Dictionary*, friends of the young William Blake printed his collection of *Poetical Sketches*. It includes 'To the Muses', a lamentation for the death of poetry – and specifically English poetry – now that the muses have left it to 'wander fair' about, above and below the world:

> Whether on crystal rocks ye rove,
>   Beneath the bosom of the sea
> Wandering in many a coral grove,
>   Fair Nine, forsaking poetry!
>
> How have you left the ancient love
>   That bards of old enjoyed in you!
> The languid strings do scarcely move,
>   The sound is forced, the notes are few.[1]

The poem in effect says that the fears of Gray, Collins and Goldsmith have been realised. Poetry no longer flourishes in England. That the muses wander the wide world implies that they have broken free of those rules by which they had become trammelled; they have escaped from what Blake came to call 'the great cage' of the Augustan couplet. They have left behind them a poetry which will languish until they return to rescue it from its near-deathly condition: 'The sound is forced, the notes are few.' Given that for Blake, as for those older contemporaries discussed in Chapter 2, poetry is prophecy, is 'inspired' truth, it seems reasonable to conclude that 'To the Muses' is at one level a threnody for the loss of poetry's true voice.

And yet the poem obviously marks the arrival of an authentically new voice. It has been the custom ever since F. R. Leavis's account of Blake in *The Common Pursuit* to call his voice essentially English. There are, so Leavis insisted, vital connections and continuities between Blake's lyric mode and the characteristic achievements of Shakespeare. In both may be found a vivid enactment of the language's metaphoric possibilities, a rich particularity of cadence and word, a reaching for and rejoicing in the proverbial speech of 'the people', which is crucial to their achievement and in a sense *is* that achievement. Hence, Leavis's eager endorsement of the reasons Keats gave for stopping work on *Hyperion*. It had too many Miltonic inversions. 'English,' Keats admonishes himself, 'ought to be kept up.'

There is, however, a world of difference between Miltonic 'effects' and the truly liberating example that Milton both embodies in himself and offered to others, of thinking through and voicing an unappeasable political awareness, one that was intrinsic to being a poet.[2] I have already suggested that in the eighteenth century the sedulous aping of the effects could go hand in hand with a rejection of Milton's radicalism. Blake, however, is an intensely radical poet; and he had no doubt that Milton was his true precursor. When Blake speaks of, to, and for England, he does not ape Milton, but he certainly assumes the right and responsibility to speak from the deep heart of that unappeasable conscience which is for him, as it had been for Milton, the everlasting gospel. In Blake, poetry recovers epic ambitions and epic virtues.

There will be more to say about this, and especially about the reception of Milton at the end of the eighteenth century. But for the moment I need to add to my remarks about 'To the Muses', in order to underline a very obvious point: that in its mode of utterance the poem, brief and apparently lightweight though it may seem to be, denies the claim that it is ostensibly making. Poetry, English poetry, is alive again. The poem's confident lyric impulse testifies to new beginnings. Blake's use of common measure links his poem to ballad and to hymn, and is therefore of great strategic importance. It ushers in a way of speaking that lies beyond the great cage. For all its modesty it is a declaration of independence. And this is true of the *Poetical Sketches* as a whole. Certain connections are renounced, others are esstablished. Hence, the significant placing of 'To Spring' at the head of the volume:

> O thou with dewy locks, who lookest down
> Through the clear windows of the morning, turn
> Thine angel eyes upon our western isle,
> Which in full choir hails thy approach, O Spring!
>
> The hills tell each other, and the listening
> Valleys hear; all our longing eyes are turned
> Up to thy bright pavilions. Issue forth,
> And let thy holy feet visit our clime.

Come o'er the eastern hills, and let our winds
Kiss thy perfumed garments; let us taste
Thy morn and evening breath; scatter thy pearls
Upon our love-sick land that mourns for thee.

O deck her forth with thy fair fingers. Pour
Thy soft kisses on her bosom, and put
Thy golden crown upon her languished head,
Whose modest tresses were bound up for thee.

It might almost come from the psalms of David. And yet, as W. H. Stevenson points out, although much of the language is 'biblical', it is Blake's own and 'not derived directly from any passage in the Bible'. The poem does, however, borrow some key words and phrases from Milton; and if these two stylistic elements are put together we can have some sense of Blake's early attempt to reroute poetry, through traditions which are basically *popular* ('vulgar; plebian'; 'suited to the common people' – Johnson). For the Bible and Milton were common property, as Dryden and Pope, and their models, could never be. And it is worth remarking that throughout much of the eighteenth and earlier part of the nineteenth centuries, the metrical psalms were familiar parts of Anglican ceremonies.[3] No matter how loosely these elements are threaded together, they constitute a kind of language which people shared. Blake, the artisan and city dweller, takes over, or (re)invents, a language with which certain readers can confidently identify. It is one they know, not in the sense that they speak it (although they certainly sang it), but in the more important sense that they go to it as their source for truths. It is the language not merely of the Bible and Milton but of Bunyan; and it has or is taken to have the kind of authority that is in no sense Augustan-orthodox. It enables an audience, also artisan and city dwelling, which had been excluded from the procedures of eighteenth-century literary orthodoxy, to feel at ease with this poetry, to take it as *their* poetry; and by that token this poetry inevitably excludes or places at a serious disadvantage readers who wish to identify with the Johnsonian version of 'common intercourse'.

As I have already noted, the question of audience was bound to be a troubling one for eighteenth-century poets, because in one sense the audience was ready chosen, while in another, new developments in thinking about poetry left it out of account, or challenged the assumptions out of which it had been created. Stephen Duck both made himself and was assisted into making himself acceptable to Pope's circle of free men, of citizens. His reward was to be given the post of librarian, custodian and guide to the nonsensical Merlin's Cave which was constructed at Richmond for Queen Caroline. Later, he confirmed his new-found status by being accepted into holy orders. Chauncy Tinker is probably right to say that Duck's mind 'gave way as a result of his attempts to acquire the airs of a courtier and live up to the reputation which Caroline had thrust upon him'.[4] Certainly, his suicide can be considered to have been brought about by irresolvable tensions, much as the madness of a later and greater poet, John Clare, cannot be dissociated from tensions at work within him, tensions which become the matter of his poetry, as they never do with Duck. For once Duck had achieved respectability there would be no more 'Thresher's Labour'. Christopher Smart, moving in the reverse direction, broke away from the society of university wits, chose the disreputable alternative of 'mania', and transformed himself into an 'inspired' poet.

Blake's tactics are every bit as self-conscious as those of Duck or Smart. Unlike them, however, he has a sure sense of audience (it doesn't matter whether that sense was greater than the reality). It develops out of his experiences as a London-born artisan and son of radical dissenting parents. The man who wrote 'To Spring' also wrote 'Rome & Greece swept Art into their maws & destroy'd it . . . Grecian is Mathematical Form: Gothic is Living Form.'[5] Gothic here operates as a synonym for whatever lies beyond those expressions of cultural orthodoxy which have been discussed in previous chapters. The social and political implications of Blake's preference for Gothic over Greek are plain.

There is a further point. The unrhymed stanzas of 'To Spring' alert us to that radical approval of Milton's blank verse which Edward Young had voiced when he said that 'what we mean by blank verse, is, verse unfallen, uncurst, verse reclaimed, reinthroned in the true llanguage oof the Gods'. Rhyme is the token of a fallen state. 'I wish the nature of our language could bear its entire expulsion, but our lesser poetry stands in need of a toleration for it; it raises that, but sinks the great.'[6] Young's statements are made from within the radical tradition for which Milton is the source and the great spokesman: it is a commonplace of this tradition that rhyme is dangerously conformist in its solacing sweetness and in its readiness to foreclose on or to improperly resolve issues which the true poet must wish to keep open. Moreover, as Milton himself had noted in his introductory remarks to *Paradise Lost*: 'This neglect then of rhyme so little is to be taken for a defect, though it may seem so perhaps to vulgar readers, that it is rather to be esteemed an example set, the first in English, of ancient liberty recovered to heroic poem from the troublesome and modern bondage of rhyming.'

The ambition of the poet who puts 'To Spring' at the head of his first volume of poems is, then, to reconnect an English poetry which has more or less died of inanition to a tradition of ancient liberty which Milton commends. And, as we shall see, this is part of a larger ambition of Blake's. The radical poet is called upon to break open those rule-forg'd manacles by which poetry has become bound. Poetry must wander free of its prison. Spring itself is an embodiment of true poetry returning to England. Blake's poem echoes the allegorical playfulness of Collins's 'Ode on the Poetical

Character', although the ardency of its cadences and diction take it well beyond mere pastiche. The returning spirit of poetry is connected to an abundant revival of energies. Collins's ode picks up Spenser's account of Phoebus, who 'Fresh as brydgroome to his mate/Came dancing forth shaking his dewie hayre,/And hurld his glistring beams through gloomy ayre'. Blake's 'love-sick land' lies in waiting for those renewed sexual energies which are at once literal and metaphoric of recovered political and social energies; the figure of Spring is connected in Blake's imagination to the figure of Orc, and Orc, as Northrop Frye has observed, is a direct descendant of Collins's '"rich-hair'd youth of morn", associated with the sun-god, like the Greek Apollo, a prophet and visionary of whom the last exemplar was Milton'.[7]

To say all this may make Blake's poem look not much more than a ravelled skein of arbitrarily-chosen traditions. Far from it. His 'visionary energy', his linking of the poetical character to Milton, to Orc, to Glad Day, also requires us to notice that the title to this, the most famous of all his engravings and colour-prints, is more properly 'Albion Rose', or 'The Dance of Albion'. The image may well have been first used in 1780.[8] This early in his career, Blake is identifying poetry with that revolutionary impulse which Milton had embodied, or was taken to have embodied. For the recovery of radical Milton comes about at the moment when radical possibilities begin once more to stir under the wintry surface of late-eighteenth-century life. It is, then, significant that in 1780, the year of no-Popery riots, Blake, 'chancing to meet the rioters, was swept down to Newgate in the front rank. There he saw the prison burnt, and the prisoners released.'[9] This is not to say that he would have been in sympathy with those particular rioters. But the event was symptomatic. Moreover, as David Erdman has shown, the republicanism of Blake's early historical paintings and poetry, from which he never wavered, needs to be linked to his intense admiration for Tom Paine, who, Blake said, was able 'to overthrow all the armies of Europe with a small pamphlet'.[10]

In the previous chapter I quoted a relevant passage from *Common Sense*, Paine's devastating attack on the arguments for monarchy. Here, I need add only that Paine's pamphlet is written in that 'plain', vigorous style which is deliberately aimed at a readership markedly different from the one Edmund Burke addressed. It can therefore be read as one more sign of spring's approach.[11] The promise of rebirth is the promise of an England radical, republican, anti-Church, an England that will release and honour 'genius' in so far as that is ordained by powers other than the power of liberty associated with orthodox education, money, social position. The concern with 'natural genius' now becomes a good deal more vivid than it had been at the time Young was speaking of the divinely-inspired enthusiast; and it will explain the mythicising process whereby, for example, Burns and Chatter-

ton are turned into types of such genius. Milton's radical republicanism is
thus reconstituted and rewritten. In particular his hierarchical ordering of
the sexes – 'He for God only, she for the God in him' – is overset by the
democratic requirements of 'the lineaments of gratified desire'; and the
rights of man are met by the rights of women. There are other rewritings, all
of them opposed to the structures which orthodoxy has been assembling:
hence the new dictionaries, grammars, even new typographic conventions,
which take away the right of monarchs to have their names printed in upper
case.[12] Hence, the interest in dialect and in ballad. Hence, too, the visions of
new societies, and encouragement derived from the American revolution.

I inevitably foreshorten. But the evidence abounds and has been finely
marshalled by Olivia Smith and others.[13] The point to be made is familiar
and simple; it is that from 1780 onwards there are various expressions of a
rebirth of England; that such a rebirth may be expressed through and in
large part *as* poetry; and that it is impossible to separate this expression from
an exuberant conviction that new voices, or voices long suppressed, are now
ready to speak for *their* vision of England. The fragmentary 'King Edward
III', from *Poetical Sketches*, ironises the vision of imperial liberty which
Thomson and others had so blandly championed. England's history – that
is, the 'patriotic' history of Trojan Brutus – is one that celebrates the
destruction of other nations. Brutus tells his troops that

> 'Our sons shall rise from thrones in joy,
> Each one buckling on his armour. Morning
> Shall be prevented by their swords gleaming,
> And evening hear their song of victory.
> Their towers shall be built upon the rocks,
> Their daughters shall sing, surrounded with shining spears.
> Liberty shall stand upon the cliffs of Albion . . .'

> (Scene vi, ll. 49–55)

But this is 'perfide Albion', as the French came to call it, a bullying, imperial
force (it is worth recalling just *how* bloodthirsty, aggressive and brutal
eighteenth-century England was), a nation which Blake sees as 'Rolling
dark clouds o'er France, muffling the sun/In sickly darkness like a dim
eclipse,/Threatening as the red brow of storms, as fire/Burning up nations
in [its] wrath and fury' (Scene vi, ll. 3–6). True joy lies elsewhere, with those
who can find their lives uttered through the risen Albion. And this, then,
leads to the 'Songs of Innocence and Experience', and to the visions they
generate.

I I

Most commentators agree that the date of the appearance of *Songs of
Innocence*, in 1789, is not without its significance. Surprisingly few, however,

are prepared to admit how politically radical the poems are. This may be because such key songs as 'Little Boy Lost', 'Nurse's Song' and 'Holy Thursday' first appeared in *An Island in the Moon* in 1784, when Blake was supposedly not yet a fully radical poet. Yet this will hardly do. Blake's radicalism begins early – at least as early as 1780; and given his parents' dissenting radicalism it is reasonable to assume that from his earliest years he was aware of and immersed in radical politics. At all events, radical politics are deeply embedded within *Songs of Innocence*. Of course it is true, as John Holloway among others has usefully indicated, that many of these songs *of* innocence challenge those many eighteenth-century collections of hymns by Watts, Barbauld, Smart and others that were addressed to or on behalf of innocence. Blake's songs speak not to the condition of innocence, but from and of it. But it is important to emphasise that such speaking includes, as of right, and at its centre, the vision of Glad Day which in its exuberance bursts the shackles of law, of subservience; and that it is quite likely to do this through language which specifically echoes biblical language, especially moments in the Testaments which are prophetic of revolutionary change, of the overthrow of oppressors. Here again, Blake is reconnecting poetry to its radical, Miltonic past, and he does it in such a way as to assert and make apparent its present vitality. Breaking chains, bursting out of shackles – these are the epic virtues by means of which a new nationhood can be formed.

It is the confidence of the songs that is so remarkable. 'Holy Thursday', for example, could hardly be more unlike Smart's 'Pray Remember the Poor', which at first glance has a very similar subject – the need to remember charity children. But where Smart's hymn offers an entirely paternalistic view of charity, the 'harmonious thunderings' of Blake's children innocently, and even rapturously, threaten – the oxymoron is *that* challenging – a society which is identified through totemic, containing structures: in this instance Anglicanism and beadledom. These charity children, the 'flowers of London town', are instinct with an irresistible vitality which speaks through their colours, red and blue and green, the fact that they 'flow' into St Paul's like the Thames, and, most resonantly, through their song: the 'hum of multitudes . . . multitudes of lambs'. The children are an incarnation of spring, of new possibilities. Blake and his readers would have known where to look to find the source of that hum of multitudes: 'The noise of a multitude in the mountains, like as of a great people; a tumultuous noise of the kingdoms of nations gathered together: the Lord of hosts mustereth the host of the battle' (Isaiah 13:4). The song the children raise is like a 'mighty wind', and the biblical echoes of that are equally powerful, whether we turn to Kings, where Elijah witnesses the 'Lord [passing] by, and a great and strong wind rent the mountains' (1 Kings, 19:11) or whether we concentrate on the song's 'harmonious thunderings', in which case we shall turn to Revelation 14, where 'the voice of many waters, and . . . the voice of a great thunder' accompany the fall of Babylon. Either way, the innocence of the children is inseparable from the unqualified rightness of their revolutionary energies, that 'radiance all their own'.

And we can go further. 'Thousands of little boys and girls raising their innocent hands'. The line feels like a great, exultant acclamation, the voice thrilling on the discovery of those thousands, the septennary bursting out from the confines of the five-stress line, the mixed metre shouldering aside iambic restraint, the rhyme of 'lambs/hands' gleefully approximate rather than slavishly exact. The raised hands also remind us of that exultant stepping out from the frame of his picture of the youth of Glad Day: and the children then provide another evocation of the dance of Albion, of Albion rising. Not to register this, not to see how 'Holy Thursday' pulses with the joy of such energy, is to deny its politics and thus to denature the poem.

The same is true of 'The Chimney Sweeper'. In this song, the narrator, who is an older, more experienced sweeper than those for whom he offers to speak, tells us that 'little Tom Dacre' while sleeping 'had such a sight':

> That thousands of sweepers, Dick, Joe, Ned, and Jack,
> Were all of them locked up in coffins of black;
>
> And by came an angel, who had a bright key,
> And he opened the coffins and set them all free;
> Then down a green plain leaping, laughing they run,
> And wash in a river and shine in the sun.

The narrator interprets this 'sight' in a manner which is, I think, problematic, and may even involve a deep, conformist misunderstanding of what it implies. 'So if all do their duty they need not fear harm'. This may well be the voice of defeat, the utterance of one who has resigned himself to accommodation within a system that very certainly does him harm. Yet the 'sight' itself is truly liberating – and Blake's deliberate use of this word surely insists on the unmediated truth of vision: it cannot be fobbed off as a 'mere' dream, an unrealisable fantasy of Cockayne, especially once we note that the Angel comes from the Book of Revelation, where he shows John 'a new heaven and a new earth', and 'a pure river of water of life' (Revelation 21:1 and 22:1).

I do not intend to comment here on the tangled and largely unprofitable question of Blake's specific religious affiliations. Whether he was more for Swedenborg or Boehme is unimportant compared to the fact that we misunderstand a vital element in the *Songs of Innocence* if we fail to recognise that their use of biblical allusion is intrinsic to their radicalism. Above all, perhaps, the songs testify to the 'everlasting gospel' of revelation. They speak out of – and for – a passionately non-conformist and in all senses radical rejection of those Anglican pieties whose politics are deferential, hierarchical, monarchical, and which then are inevitably to be identified with 'duty', with submission, and with warning against the follies and dangers of the explosive exuberance which characterise the innocent children of Albion. The language of the songs, their multi-layered biblical allusions and echoes which are offered in the full knowledge of how the Book of the People could be and was read by those people in revolutionary terms, or terms that reject institutionalised order – this is truly Miltonic. It is also a way of wresting poetry away from the dead hand of institutional powers and returning it to the people. And this is made further or equally possible because such poetry is 'song': is shared, its anapaestic metres, stanza forms, rhyme schemes knowable, familiar, 'owned' by those who are excluded from the society of the great cage. It hardly needs saying that the rhymes of Blake's songs are acceptable within the radical tradition because that tradition is precisely one of song, of shared, collective utterance.

But then this great gaiety of enterprise begins to curdle. *Songs of Experience* may be part of a schematic presentation of the 'Two Contrary States of the Human Soul', but the later songs very significantly emerge from the prolonged moment when the grand, opening vistas of *Songs of Innocence* are being closed down. There is, then, a bitter paradox in the first stanza of 'London'.

> I wander through each chartered street
> Near where the chartered Thames does flow,
> And mark in every face I meet
> Marks of weakness, marks of woe.

The children flowing into St Paul's were a cleansing, irruptive force. Here, the poet's listless wandering is matched by the river's 'chartered' flow: a charter may be intended to provide liberties, but all too clearly such liberties have been denied to the 'marked' citizens of London, among whom is the poet himself, his present wandering no more than an inert echo of that glad wandering of the muses, or of the spirit of Spring. E. P. Thompson has drawn attention to Paine's demolition in *The Rights of Man* of the pretence that charters conferred rights. On the contrary 'charters, by annulling these rights in the majority, leave the right by exclusion in the hands of the few . . .'[14] In this darkened city, its 'midnight streets' the polar opposite of glad day, all are marked. As Heather Glen has acutely noted:

The essential strategy of this society is, very exactly, one of *marking*: blackening, daubing with blood, blighting with plague. And the speaker's mode of experience is the same: isolated and at a remove from real human warmth and reciprocity, yet imprinting its own damning stamp on everything . . . There seems to be no other way for human beings to conceive of or relate to one another in this society, and the poet is no exception.[15]

It does not even greatly help to add that the biblical echoes of 'marking' would have alerted Blake's few readers to his use of Ezekiel: 'And the Lord said to him, Go through the midst of the city . . . and set a mark upon the foreheads of the men that sigh and that cry for all the abominations that be done in the midst thereof' (Ezekiel 9:4). For what could be done to oppose or challenge such abominations? Britain was at war with France, and the threats to civil liberties and to free speech had become so great as to silence or send into exile most of those who had responded with such joy to the events of 1789. Habeas Corpus was suspended in 1794. A Seditious Meetings Act followed the attack on George III's carriage when, in October of that year, he drove to Westminster to open parliament; there were prosecutions of men suspected of any revolutionary activities (for 'activities' read 'possible tendencies'); and so on. But listing the forms that state suppression and oppression took in these years does not fully account for the deep, tragic disillusionment of the *Songs of Experience*.

In the notebooks of Blake which Stevenson dates to *c*.1791–2, there is a four-liner called 'An Ancient Proverb'.

> Remove away that blackening church,
> Remove away that marriage hearse,
> Remove away that — of blood –
> You'll quite remove the ancient curse.

Other drafts of this have for the blank in the third line 'that man of blood' and 'that place of blood'. The reference is to George III or to London – or conceivably England. They are anyway a form of metonymy, the proof of the king's power. Remove the instruments and instances of this power, the proverb says, and you will remove the ancient curse. Blake, it is clear, rejects a conventional Christian view of the curse as the fall of man. Men have fashioned their own overthrow, have constructed the systems by which they have become enslaved. But as the incomplete line implies, this is so far from being easy to reverse as to suggest an almost insuperable problem. (I assume Blake sardonically drew the blank as a form of self-censorship. Better that than a charge of seditious libel.) The man and place of blood have so much power that their opponents daren't even name them. And if this is so, there is little hope that they can be removed. The 'proverb' is obviously a starting point for those stanzas in 'London' where Blake speaks of

> How the chimney-sweeper's cry
> Every blackening church appalls,
> And the hapless soldier's sigh
> Runs in blood down palace walls;
>
> But most through midnight streets I hear
> How the youthful harlot's curse

> Blasts the new-born infant's tear
> And blights with plagues the marriage hearse.

In those lines of *Windsor Forest* where Pope had welcomed in a new era of peace, London had been imaged as a kind of earthly celestial city: its harmonious achievements were guaranteed by the existence of palace, Church and parliament (backed by law). In Blake's poem the same structures of power combine to produce a society distinguished by its cries, sighs and curses. London is now a hell on earth, its citizens endlessly condemned to suffering. For their cries are in no sense like the 'harmonious thunderings' of the innocent children of 'Holy Thursday'. These later cries may appal, but they cannot sound an irresistible threat to the system that makes them hapless. The harlot's curse may have a terrible potency in that, as gonorrhea, it will destroy her destroyer and others who come within his power (the partner of his marriage hearse and their infant). But as an 'appeal to a supernatural power for harm to come to a specific person, group etc.' it echoes like the other cries through the midnight streets, telling of repeated cycles of defeat and death, of hatred and the loss of communality. That is why the street cries of this London cannot be harmonious.

It is also why, wherever you look in the *Songs of Experience*, you find a denial of mutuality. The mind-forged manacles lock people into private miseries, deny them the chance of growth or of connection with others. The second and concluding stanza of 'Nurse's Song' is among the most eloquently grieving, saddening statements of this:

> Then come home, my children, the sun is gone down
> And the dews of night arise;
> Your spring and your day are wasted in play,
> And your winter and night in disguise.

In the fractured syntax of the last line the nurse comes as near as possible to admitting the deceptions and waste of her life. This indeed is the voice of experience. But it means that Blake himself has to voice the more generous, releasing, experience of anger, as he does in 'The Garden of Love'. For typically this voice is absent from the poems, and anyway it can never be combined with others to form harmonious thunderings. *Songs of Experience* is a diagnostic collection of verse which tries to affirm sociality, but which repeatedly finds the possibilities for sociality thwarted. And the explanation for this lies not merely in the system, of Church, law, throne, but also in those mind-forged manacles which may conceivably testify to a more ancient curse.

In order to get the measure of Blake's radicalism it is worth comparing *Songs of Innocence* with the work of his older contemporary, Erasmus Darwin. Darwin (1731–1802) is very much a figure of the English Enlightenment. A medical practitioner and writer, he also made important contributions to current debates on education and agriculture, and as a member of the Lunar Society he was keenly aware of developments in science and especially those that bore on industry. Maureen McNeil has shown that Darwin was by no means an uncritical neo-Newtonian. He was alertly sympathetic to hostile accounts of Lockeian and Newtonian epistemology as altogether too ready to accept the passivity of the mind in relation to the physical world. Blake admired some of Darwin's work. He engraved *The Botanic Garden*, and Desmond King-Hele has noted a number of possible verbal and imagistic links between the two poets. King-Hele goes so far as to say that 'Darwin had an important influence on Blake in his most creative years'.[16] Nevertheless, Darwin is a long way from sharing Blake's perception of the fact and consequences of mind-forged manacles. He had, for example, a largely unqualified enthusiasm for scientific and technological advances which are seen entirely from the standpoint of the interested observer (a kind of scientific brother to the student of the picturesque); or as studied through the eyes of the inventor or factory owner. His accounts of these advances thus obliterate the role of the labourer.

In her essay on Darwin, Maureen McNeil makes good use of Marx's account of the phase of capitalism in which Darwin lived, where, as Marx notes, 'the entire production process appears as not subsumed under the direct skilfulness of the worker, but rather as the technological application of science'; and she links this to her own account of Darwin's work in which the labourer becomes by and large invisible. This, too, Marx can explain.

> The special skill of each individual machine-operator, who has now been deprived of all significance, vanishes as an infinite quantity in the face of the science, the gigantic natural forces, and the mass of social labour, embodied in the system of machinery, which, together with these three forces, constitute the power of the 'master'.

In the light of this, McNeil is right to say that 'while Darwin acknowledged the technical domination of nature realised by industrialists, he was largely silent about their social domination over their workers'.[17]

But the point that must especially concern us is that Darwin's endorsement of man's triumph over nature makes it appear that this is an achievement of all men, is, indeed, a kind of national triumph. For although he never quite goes so far as to identify industrialism and nation through a patriotic trope, it is certainly the case that the achievement of science and technology are presented as though they go with an endless annealment of interests; they represent a victory for social cohesion. And in this he sustains the kind of Whig reading of social relations that we saw was characteristic of Thomson and Dyer, among others. Nature, if not the enemy, is a force to be subdued and put to work. That there may be other – human – forces, similarly subdued, also put to work, is not a matter Darwin is prepared to confront. Admittedly, he takes a Malthusian line on population: 'war and pestilence, disease and death,/Sweep the superfluous myriads from the earth, (*The Temple of Nature*, Canto ivxs, ll. 373–4). Here, nature triumphs over man – war is as 'natural' as pestilence, but only in so far as after it man may resume his onward march over nature. And the march is directed towards and through industry. Again and again, therefore, Darwin detaches labour from the activities and exploitation of men and attaches it to machines.

> So Arkwright taught from Cotton-pods to cull,
> And stretch in lines the vegetable wool;
> With teeth of steel its fibre-knots unfurl'd,
> And thus with silver tissue clothed the world.
>
> (*The Temple of Nature*, Canto iv, ll. 261–4)

As McNeil remarks, the verb 'taught' has no object. *Whom* did Arkwright teach? The syntax makes it seem that he taught machines, not men, and that the machines, not men, then learned to clothe the world. Given this, it is significant that by the time *The Temple of Nature* appeared, in 1803, the men who clothed the world were often incapable of clothing themselves, and that the triumph of the cotton industry was one that involved the exploitation of thousands of labouring men and women. Not only are these facts missing from Darwin's work, they are, it seems fair to say, evidently suppressed. Sir Thomas Bernard's *Reports of the Society for Bettering the Condition and Increasing the Comforts of the Poor*, which appeared in two volumes in 1805, was by no means the first or the only document to spell out what was going on in the factories which clothed the world. We have, then, to see Darwin's work as self-consciously projecting an account of 'natural' human relations from which all tensions and contradictory interests are removed. Men do not exploit men, they subdue nature. As a result, machines labour. Men do not.

By contrast, Blake's tragic recognition of what the dark Satanic mills of England actually signify has about it great political, imaginative, wisdom. And where Darwin mutely appeals to national interests and speaks from a perspective that in its suppressions cancels all signs of strain, it is the strains which Blake insists on – although the word is too weak to do justice to the radical greatness of his understanding of what was happening in the England of his times.

Thus in *Jerusalem* (written and etched 1804–20), he writes of how the sons of Urizen negotiate successive phases of national history, from masonry ('the hammer & the chisel') through punitive wars and then into that prolonged moment in which he finds himself, of an aggressively industrialising nation where 'all the Arts of life they chang'd into the Arts of Death in Albion', and

> intricate wheels invented, wheel without wheel,
> To perplex youth in their outgoings & to bind to labours in Albion
> Or day & night the myriads of eternity: that they may grind
> And polish brass & iron hour after hour, laborious task,
> Kept ignorant of its use, that they might spend the days of wisdom
> In sorrowful drudgery to obtain a scanty pittance of bread,
> In ignorance to view a small portion & think that All . . .

This is the generous outrage of a writer who, as a manual worker (and Blake remained one all his life), refuses to acknowledge the propriety of those abstractions by means of which Erasmus Darwin could endorse the inventions of Arkwright and others. The insights of *Jerusalem* provide for the first time a profound, critical understanding of what was actually happening to those English men and women who were being newly defined in a language that exemplified their experience of self-division, self-alienation: hands, operatives. This is more familiar to us in Ruskin's classic formulation, that 'you can either make a tool of the creature, or a man of him' ('The Nature of Gothic', in *The Stones of Venice*, Part 2). But it is Blake, living through the experience as it actually impinged upon him, who first fully grasped its terrible implications.

This is not to say that Blake abandoned his revolutionary hopes. He remained committed to the Friends of Liberty and to the men of the London Corresponding Society. And David Erdman has shown, definitively, how he never wavered from his self-appointed role as prophet against empire. In addition, we have to take as fully serious to his enterprise that moment which occurred sometime before September 1800, when, bending to tie his sandal, he felt himself invaded by Milton's spirit.

> And I became one man with him, arising in my strength;
> 'Twas too late now to recede. Los had entered my soul;
> His terrors now possessed me whole. I arose in fury and strength.
>
> (*Milton*, 1st Book, 22, 12–14)

Nevertheless, and as these very lines make plain, Blake's prophecies are now mostly contained within those Ossianic poems which are essentially a kind of arcanum. They may be intended for 'The Young Men of the New Age', and they may also be meant as a 'Gothic' poetry: that is, a 'living form' which can be offered as truly epic, as the word of the people. But the sad reality is that these poems are at best a form of *samizdat*. As indeed they had to be. Blake was sufficiently alarmed by state powers to decide on almost secret printings of his work. As a result, he was forced underground. Not that there was anything new in that. The history of radical literature in England has nearly always been the history of 'underground' or unofficial printing presses.[18] But it does seem that from the mid-1790s onwards Blake began to lose a sense of that community which he had evoked and assumed in *Songs of Innocence*. There were very few readers for the *Songs of Experience* or for the Prophetic Books. It is not then surprising that the *Memoranda* of 1807 includes an entry for 20 January: 'Between Two and Seven in the Evening – Despair.'

Of course, this is by no means the whole story. Blake still wants to build Jerusalem in England's green and pleasant land, and in *Jerusalem* itself he begs Albion to

> return!
> Thy brethren call thee, and thy fathers and thy sons,
> Thy nurses and thy mothers, thy sisters and thy daughters
> Weep at thy soul's disease, and the Divine Vision is darken'd . . .

But the abstract language of this suggests all too clearly what difficulties lie in the way of animating the vision without which the act of building cannot be begun. It is as though Blake is going through the motions. So that although he seems never to have wavered in his desire to work for the new Albion (his personal life is as instructive here as his creative work), it increasingly feels as though, lacking both a sense of community and a language by means of which to speak to and for it (and they are essentially aspects of the same thing), he comes at least in part to doubt the reality of that vision which had been so eagerly grasped in the early songs. The Prophetic Books endlessly rehearse *possible* histories, but their accounts of confused battles and of the building and destruction of cities are speculative in a manner that suggests dream rather than a shareable vision, and the manner is a matter of style, of that 'Gothicry' which is at once assuaging and self-deceiving.

I do not believe that it is enough to dismiss as merely a mistaken tactic Blake's almost complete reliance after the *Songs of Experience* on the would-be epic style of the Prophetic Books. True, he had produced such work earlier, and it testifies to his unflagging concern to be a latter-day Milton. But the Prophetic Books quite lack an answerable style. You could not perhaps expect Blake to realise that it was too late in history for the kind of epic at which he laboured. It was, after all, a preoccupation for all the Romantics. (Typically, Byron was the only one to realise that a poet could best hope to succeed through scaling the subject matter and style down to the everyday. But then *Don Juan* is not merely an anti-epic, it is well on the way to being a novel in verse, and of course the true epics – the books of the people – of the nineteenth century were, as they had to be, novels.) But Blake's problem goes deeper. It might be said, and indeed it *has* been said, that in the Prophetic Books he turns his back on history in the belief that history has turned its back on him, that the revolutionary hopes of risen Albion have foundered on the rocky reality of England's entry into war against France, on the successful governmental suppression of all forms of

dissent – those mind-forged manacles again; and on Napoleon's transformation from Glad Day to Urizen. There is some truth in all of this, but to
offer it as the complete explanation for what happened to Blake after 1794
would be merely glib. The passage from 1789 to 1794 is a tragic one, but in
Songs of Experience Blake takes the weight of this tragedy. Having done that,
he is left convinced of his isolation. Hence, the increased private 'system', of
an alternative history in an alternate style, of the Prophetic Books.

Blake's dilemma is familiar in English radical experience. Given the rare
moments of victory and the longer episodes of defeat, or setback, it would be
surprising were this not to be so, especially since such defeats, such
setbacks, are often accompanied by, expressed through, the defection of
allies – mind-forged manacles yet again – which signal the collapse of
community. This will then explain why Blake increasingly turns away from
the present to the future, to 'the Young Men of the New Age' who cannot
yet be expected, and for whom the Prophetic Books are intended. Blake has
no present readers. Moreover, his vision is necessarily utopian, in the sense
that he cannot imagine the transition from present to future, well though he
understands the movement from successive pasts to present. It may also be
the case that his antinomianism aligns him more with a habit of thinking that
was itself on the point of exhaustion than with others, more securely
grounded, which characterise radical movements of the nineteenth century.
And if this is so, it gives added point to A. L. Morton's suggestion that
Blake's 'Everlasting Gospel', simple and apparently accessible though it is
in its mode of expression, owes much to the millenarial thought of Ranters
and Muggletonians. Although he admits that 'It is not possible to prove that
Blake borrowed directly from any of these', Morton insists that 'he and they
shared a body of ideas and expressed those ideas in a common language'. In
addition:

> many of the sects of the seventeenth century, Quakers, Muggletonians and
> Traskites, for example, did survive in London till Blake's time. And it is
> certain that they persisted most strongly, as they had sprung up originally,
> among the artisans and petty tradesmen of the thickly-peopled working-class
> quarters. These were exactly the social circles and the geographical areas in
> which Blake was born and in which his whole life was passed.[19]

Blake's utopianism may then be compared to that of the Commonwealth
Ranter Abiezer Coppe. Coppe's extraordinary work, *The Fiery Flying Roll*,
asserts that Jerusalem is built out of the harrowing of hell/Babylon. The
new world of the Everlasting Gospel can come only out of agony and
conflict. This is what Blake seems to say, both in 'The Everlasting Gospel'
and in *Jerusalem*. But however this may be, the great value of the post-1789
work has to do with its radical understanding of what the Urizenic world of
experience amounts to, how it does not and cannot offer anything like

fullness of being to those Englishmen it binds up in mind-forged manacles.

It is in this context, then, that we may take note of the illustration of 1808, of Adam and Eve leaving Paradise, their eyes downcast, staring at the serpent and thorns and thistles of the world they now enter. Their 'wandering steps and slow' bring them to the midnight streets of the world's fallen city, from which there can be no escape. And yet a year earlier, in a version produced for the Reverend J. J. Thomas, Adam and Eve look up, and the expressions on their faces combine quick eagerness with something that approaches joy. This version is closer to the one produced by Francis Hayman for Bishop Newton's great edition of Milton (1749), and this is very important because Hayman was the first to keep close to Milton's actual words. For although Hayman does not show Adam and Eve hand in hand, their wrists are only lightly held by the Angel who leads them out from Paradise; and instead of moving across the picture plane in those various postures of unutterable grief which all previous illustrators from Aldrich on had accepted, Hayman deliberately has them stepping towards us, the spectators. Here, then, 'wandering' can imply a sense of freedom, as it does in Blake's 1807 version.

The dates could be reversed and it wouldn't matter. What does matter is Blake's dark recognition that wandering may now not be a sign of freedom but of aimlessness, of lack, or anyway loss, of purpose. And it is not, I think, to play fast and loose with words to suggest that his later career suggests a wandering off into the writing of self-marginalised poems where communication – reciprocity – becomes impossible to imagine or sustain. Yet against this, always, is the belief that he has Miltonic responsibilities so that despite his collapsed hopes and the terrible defeats which the 1790s ushered in, he must go on.

The site of this continuing battle was the city. Blake's democratic, republican vision is always focused on it. It is in the city that freedoms must be asserted. Men have made the city, men must be responsible for it. Blake knew what was wrong with the city, understood the implications and consequences of its being charted and chartered, knew about the dark Satanic mills, knew why it was the great wen. Nevertheless, the children who flow into St Paul's are 'flowers of London town'. This is not a pastoral image, not anyway as I use the term in this book. It does not try to fix the children as an element in a hierarchical structure of relationships. If anything, Blake inverts this structure. The wise guardians of the poor sit beneath the children. But this is less important than his sense that the heavenly city on earth is where all are free to wander as they will: to flow unconstrainedly.

Blake called his imagined heavenly city Golgonooza, and he derived it from the London in which he lived and worked. London was where you could be free. (The only time he was threatened with prison came when he was staying in the country.) Golgonooza is Los's city of art and manufacture. It consists of the bodies of men and women and it encompasses an entire imaginative universe. 'It is the spiritual fourfold/London, (*Jerusalem*, Ch. 3, ll. 18–19).[20] Blake was the first writer of modern times to grasp the fact that if you cannot define nationhood in terms that include the city, and for that matter give it real primacy, then you cannot define it at all. This is not to say that the definition has to be uncritical. The poet who wrote 'London' obviously didn't think that. But it is to say that poets who try to write the city out of their accounts of nationhood are unlikely to produce an image of 'England' or 'Englishness' which can carry authority, even though they may claim such authority for themselves.

This is a consideration we shall need to keep in mind when thinking about Wordsworth.

CHAPTER 5

The Country Dweller: William Wordsworth

I

More even than Blake, Wordsworth was a wanderer. He might almost be called a drifter, so determined was he not to be determined. There is about the early Wordsworth an almost calculated directionlessness. This is not to say that he lacked seriousness of purpose. When he was left the small amount of money that made him financially independent and so enabled him to concentrate on a career as poet, Wordsworth remarked that his benefactor, Raisley Calvert, had told him that he had 'a confidence on his part that I had powers and attainments which might be of use to mankind'.[1] The point is that Wordsworth realised that to become a poet of worth – and what other kind of poet would do? – he needed to find his own way. To be of use to mankind entailed a responsibility towards poetry that couldn't be squared with contemporary orthodoxies, because very obviously they *weren't* of use.

In the light of this it may be suggested that Wordsworth's criticism of eighteenth-century poetic diction, which has often enough been attacked for its incautious generalisations, makes the best sense if it is seen not as a considered critique of that diction, but as a considered statement about his own sense of poetry and the poet, which will include the matter of usefulness. Wordsworth, that is, offers himself as a version of Young's divinely-inspired enthusiast, wanting to cross public paths into fresh, untrodden ground: it is there that England will be found, both literally and figuratively: in place and utterance. His rejection of eighteenth-century poetics is perhaps less fully thought-through than Blake's, but it leaves him free to wander where he chooses so that he may find those connections which will be of most use to him (they of course include Milton). Like Blake, he wants to redefine poetic continuity, in the interest of establishing his identity as an *English* poet.

A great many strands of those theories about poetry and images of the poet which we have seen developing through the second half of the eighteenth century come together in Wordsworth. They do not arrive all at once, any more than they compose an image he can ever be fully at ease with, but they are nevertheless crucial to his gradual, often tentative efforts at forging an identity he can accept. It is essential to put the matter this way, because otherwise we impute to Wordsworth a hardness, a certainty, to which he may have made pretence but which is different from the reality. He was never entirely sure of how to achieve usefulness, of how to be a poet. As V. G. Kiernan says, during the early 1790s Wordsworth's views 'were very radical indeed: he thought, though reluctantly, that things might soon become so bad as to make even that terrible event of a revolution in England welcome; not agitation, but a villainous Government, was driving the country towards it'.[2] By this time Wordsworth had wandered across a great deal of England and so seen for himself much that was wrong. He had also wandered across France and seen the 'golden hours' of 1789 and famously, so he says, identified with human nature being born again. This is universal human nature. Like Blake, the young Wordsworth is in no sense a narrow patriot. Not England *against* the rest of Europe, but *with* it. What counts for most about the radicalism of this moment is its contempt for xenophobia, its delighted recognition of the human possibilities that democratic republicanism could release (the storming of the Bastille symbolises more than the opening of the gates of any one prison) and its *European* sense of affiliative love and comradeship.

And yet there is always something theoretical, speculative, about Wordsworth's vision of a radically regenerated society. This is emphatically not to question the ardour with which he expressed his feelings, his hopes. 'Throw aside your books of Chemistry,' he is supposed to have advised a student, 'and read Godwin on necessity.' But it is impossible, I find, to read the poems of this period, when he is apparently most radical, without being aware of the fact that such works as 'Guilt and Sorrow' and *The Borderers*, while they owe their theoretical positions to Godwin, are always most interesting when he begins to brood upon that suffering which, unlike transitory action, is 'permanent, obscure and dark,/And has the nature of infinity' (*The Borderers*, ll. 1543–4). Many commentators have remarked that Wordsworth turns away from the tragic, and this is true; but they have not sufficiently focused on that preoccupation with suffering which, while it is by no means the mere misery which Lawrence wonderfully said tragedy should be a great kick against, is nevertheless often present in his consciousness as 'permanent' – as though it is beyond challenge, somehow an ultimate truth. And this then brings us to the crucial point, which is that the suffering to which Wordsworth most repeatedly attends is, after all, understandable in social-political terms, that it *can* therefore be challenged and *isn't* necessarily permanent. In short, its causes are not to be found in that mystificatory 'nature of infinity' but in 'what man hath made of man'. But Paine rather than Godwin is the definitive analyst of this. Wordsworth's trust in Godwin means that when he comes to distrust him he is the more easily enabled to renounce his radical youth as a time of incautious reliance on speculative theory.

It would clearly be impertinent to enquire into why Wordsworth so persistently identified suffering with the nature of infinity, or why he should have seen it as a kind of 'Destiny'. But it is surely proper to suggest that there are occasions when this move represents a readiness to retreat into a passivity which is perhaps less aptly called wise or principled than merely desired. And this desire, a desire for withdrawal, seems at least as strong as the desire to establish those connections which a loosening of or indifference to the ties of orthodoxy made possible; and in both, contrary, impulses wandering becomes a key concept. For if you wander in search of new connections you can just as easily wander away from them. When, at the very end of *The Borderers*, Marmaduke says 'a wanderer *must I* go/ . . . A Man by pain and thought compelled to live', he might in some circumstances be speaking for his author. And we have then to note that unlike Blake Wordsworth was neither of nor for the city, and that Godwinian theory is remarkably indifferent to certain actualities which the city testifies to and which Paine could and did address.

But there are other circumstances in which Wordsworth ardently wishes to establish connections. Hence his claim that a poet is a man speaking to men. His desire to keep dialect alive may in this context be read as a sign of his wanting the 'real language of men' to issue as a challenge to the developing standardisation of pronunciation, of 'polite speech', which is a much-remarked feature of that society Johnson had in mind when he spoke on behalf of the propriety of 'common intercourse'. This is why Wordsworth rejects the conventions of the picturesque, for these combine to impose a conformity of visual language, of style. And this is the driving force behind his contribution to the *Lyrical Ballads*.

The very phrase 'a man speaking to men' implies a dialogue in which no one is granted superiority. But Wordsworth also claims that the poet is

> the rock of defence of human nature; an upholder and preserver, carrying everywhere with him relationship and love. In spite of difference of soil and climate, of 'language and manners, of laws and customs, in spite of things silently gone out of mind and things violently destroyed, the Poet binds together by passion and knowledge the vast empire of human society, as it is spread over the whole earth, and over all time.

Wordsworth is saying that the poet is a medium through which men can speak to other men. It isn't so much that the poet writes about the vast empire of human society, as that in entering into dialogue with particular 'men', remote from the knowledge or experience of other 'men', he creates the opportunity for further dialogue. As Wordsworth makes clear, the audience for his lyrical ballads is composed of the 'gentle' or polite reader. What this reader will be made to discover is Wordsworth in the act of addressing other, very different, kinds of people: Simon Lee, for example, or the old man travelling. And by giving these their voices and hence individuality he rebukes the polite reader's generalisations about 'difference', and compels him to acknowledge the incontestable, highly individual reality of lives from which social arrangements – 'language and manners, laws and customs' – have made this reader remote. Only 'The Complaint of a forsaken Indian Woman' can be adduced as evidence for the largest claims of 'the vast empire of human society' the poet will bind together, but this poem may at all events remind us of how wide are Wordsworth's democratic vistas, as they are employed both in the preface and contents and in the strategy of *Lyrical Ballads*.

It is a strategy which Heather Glen has well described when she remarks that the ballads 'question the unarticulated moral assumptions of the polite reader: most centrally, that paternalistic diminution of the other which insidiously structured later eighteenth-century social thinking, even in its consciously radical manifestation'.[3] This is true, although I want to add that what gives especial power to such poems as 'Simon Lee' and 'Old Man Travelling' is that the gentle reader is led, by their titles and by Wordsworth's apparent stance towards his material, to expect a series of exercises in the picturesque convention, only to have these expectations broken in on and entirely disrupted.

It is, after all, an important feature of the picturesque that the viewer or reader isn't morally, socially or politically implicated in what he/she sees or reads. To go in search of the picturesque is to go in search of merely aesthetic experiences, and as Martin Price has said in his invaluable essay 'The Picturesque Moment', the 'typical picturesque object or scene – the aged man, the old house, the road with cart-wheel tracks – carries within it the principle of change. All of them imply the passage of time and the slow working of its change upon them.'[4] William Gilpin positively opposed the introduction of what he called 'peasants engaged in their several professions' into picturesque paintings.[5] If beggars and aged men were to appear it should be in a manner that allowed them to be aesthetically absorbed into the scene so that the spectator could indulge thoughts of pleasing melancholy. The favourite time of day for the picturesque was evening, and picturesque properties – ruins, travelling beggars, aged men – all spoke of the 'principle of change'.

'Old Man Travelling: Animal Tranquillity and Decay: A Sketch' is, as its title announces, perfect material for the picturesque. The picturesque, Price remarks, 'turns to the sketch, which precedes formal perfection', and the informality of Wordsworth's sketch is such that it even begins with a half-line: 'The little hedge-row birds'. Moreover, the fact that this old man is travelling and is subdued to a state of animal tranquillity and decay makes it evident that he can be painlessly absorbed into the picturesque aesthetic. Until, that is, he speaks. For when he is given his own voice he entirely fractures the rapt, contemplative calm of the poet-as-spectator. The stubborn prosaicism of his words cannot be accommodated to the enclosed interpretation of him which the title announces and which the poem seeks to sustain through the poet's controlling vision. If the old man is an instance of 'apt admonishment', he is so not merely for the poet, but for the poem's inevitably gentle readers. (What other readers could Wordsworth expect to have?) Much the same may be said of 'Simon Lee', whose title and opening prepare the polite reader for a comic ballad of which Cowper's 'Diverting History of John Gilpin' may stand as one of the more familiar – and better – examples. Yet by the end of the poem, Simon Lee has become, if not unknowable, then certainly not comfortably 'placeable' in the categories of the picturesque, or indeed anywhere else.

In her account of these poems Heather Glen concludes that 'there is no imaginative sense of what positive interaction with the other – in all his difference and uniqueness – might be like'; and she suggests that the very awkwardness of the poems 'seems to bespeak less a consistent, coherent challenge to established attitudes than a confusion of imaginative impulse – a confusion which springs from Wordsworth's deeply felt uncertainty as to his own proper relation to his subject-matter'.[6] This is persuasive, yet her account, which she puts forward as criticism, works better as description. Wordsworth is of course quite capable of deliberately confusing his gentle reader (and in this respect it may be worth recalling Hazlitt's description of that 'convulsive inclination to laughter' about Wordsworth's mouth); but what he most valuably registers in the ballads are less confusions than discomposures, which, at least strategically, are his every bit as much as they have to be those of his gentle reader. This may not be to carry everywhere 'relationship and love' in a way that Pecksniff would understand; but it is to admit the inadequacies of any one view (the reader's, Wordsworth's, Enlightenment philosophy) which seeks to impose on, or derive from, those encounters which the ballads explore, a confident, authoritative account of human identity.

But then it is precisely such an account that in later years Wordsworth begins to move towards. As a result, he alters the ballads and is himself altered to the extent that he can be fitted into the Arnoldian view of poetry's authority which depends absolutely on resolving all feelings of contradiction – or of confusion – or of discomposure. And it is *this* Wordsworth whom Arnold allows to 'speak for England'. So, too, do others. Rewritten and smoothed down, 'Simon Lee the Old Huntsman' takes its place in Palgrave's *The Golden Treasury of the Best Songs and Lyrical Poems in the English Language* (1861). There it appears in Book Four, 'Poems of the

93

Modern Period', which as Palgrave says in his prefatory note to the book is one of lavish wealth in poetry.

> Exhaustive reasons can hardly be given for the strangely sudden appearance of individual genius: but none, in the Editor's judgement, can be less adequate than that which assigns the splendid national achievements of our recent poetry to an impulse from the frantic follies and criminal wars that at that time disgraced the least essentially civilised of our foreign neighbours.

Palgrave was the son of the liberal historian Sir Francis Palgrave, whose *Rise and Progress of the English Commonwealth* (1837) discerns a kind of seamless continuity of English history brought about through endless reconciliations of apparently conflicting interests: very unlike the home life of 'the least essentially civilised of our foreign neighbours', in other words. It may be unfair to place much stress on Arnold's praise for 'Mr Palgrave's fine and skilfully chosen specimens of Wordsworth',[7] but we should not pass by without comment the fact that in *The Golden Treasury* 'Simon Lee the Old Huntsman' (shorn of the rest of his title) appears between Charles Wolfe's 'The Burial of Sir John Moore at Corunna' and Charles Lamb's 'The Old Familiar Faces'.

> I have had playmates, I have had companions
> In my days of childhood, in my joyful school-days;
> All, all, are gone, the old familiar faces.

'Simon Lee' is now absorbed into the world of pathos – of the principle of change – and made part of a tongue-and-groove account of English society: together with Sir John Moore and Lamb's companions he can be blended into a unitary image of England. This *is* love and relationship in the Pecksniffian mode.

It could be argued that Palgrave has captured the poem, and in so doing has wilfully misrepresented it. Yet it has to be admitted that Wordsworth has made Palgrave's task simpler by reworking the poem of 1798 so that now Simon Lee can become an object of pitying condescension. The old huntsman is tidied up: and so in his final metamorphosis of 1845 his 'poor old ancles' have become merely 'weak', and the reference to his having 'but one eye left' has been cancelled. Commenting in 1853 on a painting by Murillo of child beggars, Ruskin said

> Do you feel moved with any charity towards children as you look at these repulsive and wicked beggars. Are we the least bit more likely to take an interest in ragged schools, or help the next pauper child that comes in our way, because the painter has shown us a cunning beggar eating greedily.[8]

Helping Simon Lee at his task becomes a good deal easier once he doesn't look so ridiculous; and 'the gratitude of men' can then be seen as a proper cause for mourning if only because it belongs within a world of pathos, of 'the principle of change', the loss of old familiar faces.

Something similar happens with 'Old Man Travelling'. When he came to revise the poem, Wordsworth lopped off the man's actual words. He denied him the irreducible otherness which had made the original poem so radically disturbing. In his book *The Making of the Reader*, David Trotter says of the revised version of the poem: 'We know [the old man] at the same time as figure in the landscape and ritual function . . .' And, identifying the old man as a 'liminal entity', Trotter adds that when Wordsworth uses the generalising phrases 'he is one by whom/All effort seems forgotten; one to whom/Long patience hath such mild composure given,/That patience now doth seem a thing of which/He hath no need', '"One" refers to a category whose definition lies beyond the scope of the poem. We know that it means "a person", but it doesn't refer to an occurrence of the word "person" anywhere in the text. *We* supply from our own experience or imagination, the definition of the category referred to . . . We co-operate by identifying something the poem itself declines to identify.'[9] It is undoubtedly true that by taking away the old man's words Wordsworth makes it simpler for us to supply 'from our own experience or imagination' what the poem now doesn't supply. But an essential part of the meaning of the original poem was that it showed how nothing in the experience or imagination of gentle readers *could have* prepared them for what the old man says. 'We' therefore find it much easier to absorb – or discover words for – a man who is himself denied them. And this is made even easier because, despite Trotter's disclaimer, Wordsworth *does* define the category of 'one'. In its revised, truncated, version – the one Trotter uses – the poem is simply called 'Animal Tranquillity and Decay'. Such a title invites us, even requires us, to consider the old man as an object of pathos, a being subject to 'the principle of change'.

At this point it may help to quote Mikhail Bakhtin's remark that

> every utterance participates in the 'unitary language' (in its centripetal forces and tendencies) and at the same time partakes of social and historical heteroglossia (in the centrifugal, stratifying forces) . . .
>
> The authentic environment of an utterance, the environment in which it lives and takes shape, is dialogised heteroglossia, anonymous and social as a language, but simultaneously concrete, filled with specific content and accented as an individual utterance.[10]

Bakhtin's point can be usefully brought to bear especially on the poet's questioning the man as to where he is bound and what is the object of his journey, and the man's reply:

> "Sir! I am going many miles to take
> A Last leave of my son, a mariner,

> Who from a sea-fight has been brought to Falmouth,
> And there is dying in an hospital."

'Sir' is fenced off from the following words by an exclamation mark. Such emphasis reveals that the old man regards the poet, whatever the poet's own inclinations or wishes, as a gentleman, someone socially apart from the old man himself. 'Sir' also identifies the poet as 'one' of a kind, the kind you call 'Sir'. In other words 'Sir!' both individualises the old man, who to the poet has been a type, and typifies the poet, puts him into the generalised category of gentleman.

This is chastening enough, especially since the brooding quality of the poem's opening lines have highlighted the poet's sense of his own, very specialised, sensibility. But there is worse to come. For gentlemen were by and large on the side of England's war effort against Napoleon. Wordsworth himself was, however reluctantly, coming round to that side. In order to continue the war large numbers of non-gentlemen had to be press-ganged, or made to do the fighting which gentlemen thought desirable, but which by and large they escaped. Having registered the old man's utterance, and rethinking the force of 'Sir', we can now, as gentle readers, recognise how it carries the possibility of an unstated rebuke. 'Thanks to your kind, sir, my son is dying.' And it then follows that what is accented as an individual utterance is liable deeply to discompose the gentleman poet who up to this point had found it possible to objectify the old man, to accommodate him to the kind of generalisation which allowed soothing thoughts to spring out of human – well, perhaps not suffering, but certainly out of 'the principle of change':

> He is by nature led
> To peace so perfect, that the young behold
> With envy, what the old man hardly feels.

This is not meant to imply that by having the old man's words break in on his apparently contained and certainly consolatory meditation Wordsworth invites the gentle reader to consider the possibility that there may be blood on his hands. (For all we can know to the contrary, the softening substitution of 'lying in an hospital' of 1800 for 1798's 'dying in an hospital' may have been a printer's error: at all events, 'dying' was restored in the text of 1802.) Nevertheless, in getting rid of specific content and individual utterance from the finally revised version of the poem – that is, by cancelling both the poet's gentlemanly questions and the old man's answer – Wordsworth leaves the poem 'anonymous and social', to twist Bakhtin's words a little. For now we have a series of impersonal-seeming observations for which, it must appear, nobody is responsible. The poem is, in Arnold's formulation, 'inevitable'. Yet what Arnold characterises as being produced by the hand of nature can more properly be regarded as a product of a student of the picturesque; and this student can choose to be anonymous because, in looking down on his subject from a commanding height, he identifies with that crucial element in picturesque theory which stresses its 'dissociation of visual, pictorial or generally aesthetic elements from other values in contemplating a scene'.[11] It is this which allows Wordsworth the now unchallenged generalisations about the old man as 'one' who is led to 'peace so perfect'; generalisations which are of course ultimately authoritarian and coercive. Even the statement that the man is 'insensibly subdued to settled quiet' feels deeply condescending, the more so when he is denied words, because insensibility implies that the man is somehow less than fully human. Johnson defined the word as meaning 'inability to perceive; stupidity; dullness of mental perception; torpor, dullness of corporal sense'. And if we then add in the more recent connection between sensibility and capacity for feeling it is clear that the observing poet, from a class position, looks down on the man in a way which, were it not for the difference in tone, might be said to anticipate Steerforth on the Peggottys.

These words may seem unduly harsh, but it must be remembered that some time before Wordsworth began work on the *Lyrical Ballads* he had abandoned the experiment of living in London. We should note that in the opening lines of *The Prelude*, lines that were written after 1799, Wordsworth speaks with relief of having broken out of the prison of the city, where he has been 'a captive' in 'bondage . . . long immured'. The allusion to Exodus, 'out from Egypt', 'out of the house of bondage', suggests that Wordsworth sees the city as alien to himself, or himself as a foreigner in the city. The city is therefore somehow not England, and here of course we have the beginnings of that formulation which becomes increasingly familiar throughout the following two centuries: the heart of England is to be found in rural circumstance. As it develops, this trope will gather different political meanings, but from its outset – and *The Prelude* is a key starting point – it embodies a rejection of the multifariousness of the crowd on which the experience of the city is predicated.

The crowd comes to seem a threat to selfhood. Lost in the crowd. Anonymous. The connections and interdependence of these terms are obvious enough. What is at stake then, is less the authenticating of others than of the self. But self in separation *from* others can hardly make possible a valid communication *with* them, still less a justifiable manner of speaking *for* them. 'They' have therefore to become themselves anonymous, undifferentiated. Only then can they be confidently spoken for, or contemplated, as Wordsworth contemplated the old man (or, I will note in passing, as Godwin contemplated political justice). Of course it is true, as Wordsworth himself remarked, that from boyhood he had constantly to be reminded of the world 'out there'; and this has often enough been referred to in justification of his almost Dantean treatment of people as spectres. But the early version of 'Old Man Travelling' deliberately brings forward the otherness of the old man: his words make him irreducibly 'out there'. By cancelling those words Wordsworth doesn't so much confirm his own Dante-esque imagination as make a politic decision to distance himself from the man. And this cannot finally be treated as separate from his decision to distance himself from the city.

Wordsworth, as Coleridge was the first to remark, was the 'observer *ab extra*'. You can turn this to Wordsworth's discredit, but to do so is probably unfair. In *The Making of a Tory Humanist: William Wordsworth and the Idea of Community*, Michael Friedman says that:

> Even if his travels had not separated Wordsworth from the dalesmen whom he observed, his adult consciousness of his class status would surely have done so. He was not, as he may have been in childhood or may have wished to believe he was after his return, a fellow with the dalesmen in the fellowship of nature. He was a gentleman. The shepherds and the dalesmen were not. His awareness of and his desire to maintain his gentleness [I take it Friedman means gentlemanliness] created a gulf between him and the common folk he observed.[12]

This may be so, but part of the radical greatness of the original *Lyrical Ballads* depends on Wordsworth's readiness to acknowledge this gulf, and what Friedman rather crudely defines as Wordsworth's desire to maintain his gentlemanliness is no more than the poet's recognition of inevitable forces at work within the social process, ones that make for separation, for unbinding of communality.

And yet Friedman has some right on his side. His argument becomes stronger the more we consider the ways in which Wordsworth revised the poems already discussed. Moreover, one of the greatest of all Wordsworth's poems calls into question the precise ways in which he wants, as a poet, to be of use to mankind. It was with 'Michael' especially in mind that Arnold spoke of the inevitability of Wordsworth's greatest poetry. In her discussion of the poem Heather Glen also identifies a feeling of inevitability, although for her what is inevitable has much to do with Wordsworth's deep-seated apprehension of 'the necessary end of all maturity: human life is seen less as action and choice than as an unwilled progression to [distress and failure]'.[13] I agree, the poem does have about it the feeling of inevitability, but this is puzzling if only because the misfortunes that come to Michael are set off by a chance happening. It isn't inevitable that 'unforeseen misfortunes' should press upon that brother's son for whom Michael has stood surety; it isn't inevitable that Luke should have to leave home; and it isn't inevitable that, having done so, 'ignominy and shame' should fall on him. Why then does it seem that whatever happens to happen *has* to happen?

Everyone who comments on the poem goes straight for the story itself. In other words, they ignore the opening:

> If from the public way you turn your steps
> Up the tumultuous brook of Green-head Gill,
> You will suppose that with an upright path
> Your feet must struggle; in such bold ascent
> The pastoral Mountains front you, face to face.

The tone, courteous and levelly helpful, takes for granted that 'you' are a stranger. This is a Guide to the Lakes, of the kind that made their appearance in vast numbers towards the end of the eighteenth century. 'You', the town-traveller, most probably in search of the picturesque whose occurrence the guides existed to pinpoint, do not know how to read or interpret the landscape. This particular guide pauses on an apparently unremarkable object: 'which you might pass by,/Might see and notice not. Beside the brook/There is a straggling heap of unhewn stones!' In a picturesque scene such a heap would take its place as a composed effect only if it was part of a mouldering ruin, in which case it would testify to the 'principle of change'. We eventually discover that the straggling heap of unhewn stones *does* seem to testify to such a principle, such inevitability; and yet at the same time our guide tells us that a story 'ungarnish'd with events' belongs to the place of stones, one which he will relate

> For the delight of a few natural hearts,
> And with yet fonder feeling, for the sake
> Of youthful Poets, who among these hills
> Will be my second self when I am gone.

The rebuff implicit in these last lines is obviously an important element in the poem's strategy. It is as much as to say that 'you' aren't really the audience for this tale. At best 'you' are an accidental auditor, excluded from the deepest feelings of community implied in the 'few natural hearts' and 'youthful poets . . . among these hills'. To put it rather differently: as in the tale itself Wordsworth takes for granted the harmful effects of the 'dissolute city' and its absolute opposition to the worth of values identified with the hills and fields of Michael's habitation, so at the conclusion of the poem's prefatory lines 'you' are suddenly made to feel part of that dissoluteness, or at the very least guiltily implicated in events whose significance 'you' can't be expected to understand. 'You', journeying about the England which, then, feels as though it is yours because you and your kind own much of it, are convicted of an ultimate ignorance about it and its inhabitants.

This is made clear in the opening of the story itself. 'Upon the Forest-side in Grasmere Vale/There dwelt a Shepherd, Michael was his name.' This sets the tale firmly in the past, and the word 'dwelt' identifies a mode of existence very different from any 'you' may know about. For to 'dwell' implies occupation as well as abode. The word had a deep, almost talismanic power for Wordsworth. Indeed dwelling *is* a kind of talisman, 'having magical or protective powers'. Lucy

> dwelt among th'untrodden ways
> Beside the springs of Dove,
> A Maid whom there were none to praise
> And very few to love.

Here, dwelling is a protection against intrusive humanity, as it is for Poor Susan: 'a single small cottage, a nest like a dove's,/The only one dwelling on earth that she loves'. In the last, subsequently cancelled stanza of this poem, Susan is urged to return from the city to her dwelling:

> Poor Outcast! return – to receive thee once more
> The house of thy Father will open its door,
> And thou once again, in thy plain russet gown,
> May'st hear the thrush sing from a tree of its own.

Wordsworth probably struck out this stanza because Lamb told him that to call the girl 'poor outcast' was to suggest that she was a prostitute. It is unlikely that the poet had intended to imply this, but 'dwelling' undoubtedly offers a protective alternative to the 'shiftless' life of the 'dissolute city'. In the last analysis, this kind of dwelling is very different from that summoned up at the conclusion of 'To Penshurst', where Jonson opposes Sidney's house to 'proud, ambitious heaps', for 'their lords have built, but thy lord dwells'. Coming at the end of a poem which has been about community and social relationship, Jonson uses 'dwells' to signal a nexus of such relationships, such responsibilities. In Wordsworth, although the word doesn't perhaps imply a denial of social relationships, it undoubtedly suggests itself as an alternative to community. And this being so it follows that whatever is beyond the immediate 'dwelling' can come to seem a threat, one moreover which will – inevitably – triumph.

Yet against this triumph stands the dream of freedom which, no matter how paradoxical it may appear, is expressed through dwelling. At the very opening of *The Prelude*, Wordsworth writes:

> O welcome friend!
> A captive greets thee, coming from a house
> Of bondage, from yon City's walls set free,
> A prison where he hath been long immured.
> Now I am free, enfranchis'd and at large,
> May fix my habitation where I will.
> What dwelling shall receive me? In what Vale
> Shall be my harbour? Underneath what grove
> Shall I take up my home, and what sweet stream
> Shall with its murmur lull me to my rest?
> The earth is all before me . . .

Here, the deliberate echo of the ending of *Paradise Lost* ('The world was all before them') implies, as I have already noted, that Wordsworth sees himself as freed only in so far as he can escape from the city. Milton's terms are inverted. Adam and Eve, thrust out from Paradise, must choose to confront the world. Wordsworth, thrust out from the world, may choose to enter Paradise. Hell, then, is other people, or other people in the mass. The city as community is a prison. It is as though civic life embodies a threat to that which Wordsworth considers or unconsciously reveals as being the most intimate, most reassuring of all relationships: that of mother and child. For vale and grove adumbrate a womb-like enclosing, or at the very least a nurturing, protective care which is further underwritten by the 'sweet' stream which 'with its murmurs lulls me to my rest'. The social pressures beyond such feminine sweetness will then appear as masculine, sternly paternal forces – like that minatory 'huge cliff . . . with power instinct' – from whose 'civil' authority the poet must seek refuge, a dwelling. But this is to reify power, to take for granted its authority. It is also to blur distinctions between the kind of dweller for whom occupation and abode are necessary, as they are for Michael, and the kind who is free to choose, as Wordsworth is.

What then is the threat to Michael's dwelling? It is in trying to answer this question that the gap between contingent action and feelings of inevitability troublingly opens up. In his account of the poem, Geoffrey Hartman says that 'Industrialization is causing great changes, changes affecting also the minds of men; and Wordsworth, writing towards the beginning of this epoch, is not less than prophetic. The Industrial Revolution, in his eyes, is divorcing man from the earth . . . He sees that what is happening is indeed a revolution, cutting men off from their past . . .'[14] I accept the force of this, and in a sense Wordsworth dramatises the way in which the gentle city reader is cut off from the past by placing himself between 'you' and an already legendary Michael: 'I have convers'd with more than one who well/Remember the Old Man . . .' This distances Michael from us by emphasising the 'fact' that his way of life belongs to the now irrecoverable past and that he has fallen victim – according to Hartman – to the Industrial Revolution. Yet as soon as it is put like that the argument is bound to look silly. In his own defence, however, Hartman could point to the famous letter to Charles James Fox which Wordsworth sent together with a copy of the *Lyrical Ballads*, and in which he particularly drew the great man's attention to 'The Brothers' and 'Michael'. For, Wordsworth tells him:

> It appears to me that the most calamitous effect, which has followed the measures which have lately been pursued in this country, is a rapid decay in the domestic affections among the lower orders of society. This effect the present Rulers of this country are not conscious of, or they disregard it . . . recently by the spreading of manufactures through every part of the country, by the heavy taxes upon postage, by workhouses, Houses of Industry, and the invention of Soup-shops &c. &c. superadded to the encreasing disproportion

between the price of labour and that of the necessaries of life, the bonds of domestic feeling among the poor, as far as the influences of these things has extended, have been weakened, and in innumerable instances entirely destroyed.[15]

There is something slightly odd about this. I have no wish to question Wordsworth's concern for 'the bonds of domestic feeling' which – expressed at their most intense through 'dwelling' – are explored and testified to in a manner which has much to do with what is most compelling about the poem. Yet it is surely very strange that the 'measures' of which he speaks so passionately in his letter make no appearance in the poem. Luke doesn't leave the land because of 'the spreading of manufactures through every part of the country', but because of the financial failure of Michael's nephew. In terms of social history this may be plausible enough – by the end of the eighteenth century many people in the Lake District were involved directly or indirectly in commercial ventures, often at great risk[16] – but it isn't what the letter leads us to expect, and I am not at all sure how Fox could have been expected to find in the poem what the letter seems to be preparing him for.

Of course, Wordsworth was right in the sense that the measures of which he speaks were having the effect he claimed. G. E. Mingay has the Lake District in mind when he says that 'the growth of modern industry and the development of urban society drew the countryman from the land and from his ancient trades; the cottage loom was silenced'. This, he adds, brought about a landscape marked by 'abandoned cottages, fallen into ruin and the neglected states of those still inhabited'.[17] Compare the ending of 'Michael':

> the estate
> Was sold, and went into a Stranger's hand.
> The Cottage which was nam'd the Evening Star
> Is gone, the ploughshare has been through the ground
> On which it stood; great changes have been wrought
> In all the neighbourhood . . .

'The cottage loom was silenced'. That passive construction finds its counterpart in the closing paragraph of Wordsworth's poem where, as Heather Glen says, 'The series of passive verbs suggests a process removed from any identifiable human agency, a process which can neither be controlled or resisted.'[18]

Yet the letter to Fox *does* speak of resistance. Fox is praised for the 'illustrious efforts which you have made to stem this and other evils with which the country is labouring'. Perhaps then we would do best to read 'Michael' as an admonitory tale, an effort to warn 'you', the gentle reader, of the loss of values embodied in the domestic feelings of these small landed proprietors, who, as Wordsworth says in the letter and exemplifies in the poem, are identified with the tract of land: 'a tablet upon which they are written which makes them objects of memory in a thousand instances when they would otherwise be forgotten'.[19] Here, it is true, the phrase 'objects of memory' implies the residual evidence of community to which I have argued Wordsworth seems customarily opposed or indifferent. Memory speaks for continuity among a community made up of these 'small independent proprietors of land here called statesmen, men of respectable education who daily labour on their own little properties'. They are, Wordsworth says, 'now almost confined to the North of England'. 'You' are given fair warning: to allow certain 'measures' to continue is to guarantee the final, irredeemable loss of a particular way of English life, and the values inherent in it. In this context, then, Wordsworth mediates between two kinds of English experience, one which – broadly speaking – governs, and one which is governed and is in danger of being not merely exploited but exterminated. Putting the matter in these terms may seem hysterical, but then the issues with which Wordsworth is engaged invite extreme language.

This is not how it strikes everybody. In *Politics and the Poet: A Study of Wordsworth*, F. M. Todd argues that the letter to Fox

> makes clear Wordsworth's new preoccupation with spiritual and personal rather than political and public reform, and to that extent it confirms the implications of his poetry. While it is plain, if only from the name of the addressee, that he was still a liberal in politics, it is equally clear that he now sees the political question as but one aspect, and possibly a minor one, of a larger aspiration.[20]

But how can you separate one from the other? If the land is to remain Michael's – 'land as old and free as the hills' in Hartman's revealingly inexact formulation, or, more properly, the 'private property' of H. A. Mason's account[21] – then it has to be protected not from the kind of accident that exceptionally befalls Michael, but from other measures which typically affect the proprietors of whom Michael is offered as an example. Yet given that the feeling and language of the poem also imply the inevitability of what happens, it seems that such protection cannot be hoped for. The proprietors, 'now almost confined to the North of England', are doomed to follow into extinction those who have already been wiped from memory, from continuity, who typify 'things silently gone out of mind and things violently destroyed', and for whom the poet can be no more than the elegist.

At this point, it needs to be remarked that the 'measures' which Wordsworth itemises in his letter to Fox cannot be dissociated from other processes to which Mingay draws attention.

The big rise in agricultural prices which marked the fifty years between the early 1760s and the early 1810s made it attractive to landowners to invest substantial sums in converting scattered open-field holdings into compact farms, and in bringing overstocked commons and unproductive wasteland into the cultivated acreage. Between 1793 and 1815, the era of exceptionally high wartime prices, there were some 200 private Acts of Parliament authorising the enclosure of a rather greater number of parishes, and in the hundred years after 1750 about six million acres, perhaps a quarter of the farm acreage, was affected. After 1815 the number of enclosures dropped away, mainly because there were by then relatively few parishes left to enclose, and most of the subsequent enclosures affected remote and little-used hill pastures and rough grazing.[22]

We should also note Kiernan's remark that

> Neither in the 'pastoral poems' nor in the letter to Fox did [Wordsworth] speak of the vices of an archaic tenurial law in this old border country, still burdened with 'numerous and strong remains of vassalage', covered with customary manors demanding heriots, boon services, and worst of all those arbitrary *fines* on succession which did as much as anything to make it hard for families to cling to their little holdings.

Kiernan helpfully refers to K. MacLean's *Agrarian Age: A Background for Wordsworth*, in which MacLean draws attention to Wordsworth's neglect of 'the part the landlords and improvers had in creating disasters in the counties affected by the Agricultural Revolution'.[23]

We can supplement these accounts by noting that in 1801 Parliament passed the General Act of Enclosure, which made it a great deal easier to drive squatters from village ground and marginal freeholders and copy-holders from their holdings. A bill to make this law was to be put before Parliament at the time Wordsworth was writing 'Michael'; and there can be little doubt that this is what he has in mind when he refers in his letter to the proprietors 'now almost confined to the North of England'. But he perhaps thought he should use some discretion when writing to Fox. Fox, the people's friend, was also a good friend of the reforming, enclosing, Mr Coke of Holkham Hall (later Lord Leicester), and, more famously, of the Devonshires, a family whose land-grabbing proclivities were second to none.

Yet this will still not explain why the poem presents the unfolding history of Michael as irreversible and inevitable. What will then? We have to recognise that the poem's authority – its powerful presentation of what must be – is meant to conceal feelings of contradiction, or discomposure, which cannot be brought into the open because Wordsworth is much more deeply implicated in elements of the social process than he can bring himself to admit, and which his commitment to 'dwelling' is meant to conceal. This is why Todd is in a sense right to feel that in the letter to Fox, as well as in the poem itself, Wordsworth wishes to see 'the political question as but one aspect ... of a larger aspiration'. The aspiration is to speak as the memorialist for values which he cherishes and which, as he presents them to the gentle reader, will endorse his entitlement to be a 'rock of defence of human nature; an upholder and preserver, carrying everywhere with him relationship and love': in short, to be a poet who can speak for *all* Englishmen. The problem is that other aspirations confuse this entitlement.

In the spring of 1806 Wordsworth was in London for an eight-week stay. There he met Fox, a few months before the statesman's death. According to Mary Moorman the meeting took place at one of the great Whig houses. Wordsworth was introduced by Samuel Rogers, 'who went everywhere and knew everyone'. It is not possible to know whether Southey witnessed the meeting, but we do know that he was in London at the time and that he saw Wordsworth on other occasions during the visit. 'No man,' he wrote then, 'is more flattered by the attentions of the great, and no man would be more offended to be told so.'[24] It could be argued that Southey is an unreliable witness, and that anyway much had happened between the writing of 'Michael' and 1806. Yet by 1800 Wordsworth was doing his best to distance himself from certain 'men' and to ingratiate himself with certain others. It may be this which explains his anxious recommendation to Fox of the proprietors on the grounds that they are men of 'respectable education'; but it has also to be noted that in the Preface of 1800 Wordsworth altered a phrase from the Advertisement of the 1798 edition of the *Lyrical Ballads*. There, he had said that the poems 'were written chiefly with a view to ascertain how far the language of conversation in the middle and lower classes of society is adapted to the purposes of poetic pleasure'. In 1800 this becomes:

> it [the volume] was published as an experiment which, I hoped, might be of some use to ascertain how far, by fitting to metrical arrangements a selection of the real language of men in a state of vivid sensation, that sort of pleasure and that quantity of pleasure might be imparted, which a poet may rationally endeavour to impart.[25]

To replace 'the conversation in the middle and lower classes of society' by 'a selection of the real language of men' is not to imply a more inclusive intention. For 'a selection of the real language of men' is so imprecise as to evade any particularity of social or political commitment. On the contrary: the phrase is grandly vague in its authoritative claim to speak for all men, and explains how, two years later, Wordsworth could come to write that series of sonnets which so embarrass most of his modern admirers that they forget to mention them. (Although they didn't at all embarrass Palgrave. He put several of them into his *Treasury*.) It can hardly be an accident that in one of those sonnets Wordsworth should write:

> Thou art free
> My Country! and 'tis joy enough and pride
> For one hour's perfect bliss, to tread the grass
> Of England once again . . .
>
> ('Composed in the Valley near Dover')

Tell that to the old man or to Michael. Freedom here is a notably abstract term, one that can easily be evoked as part of the kind of routine patriotism that offers to speak with authority 'for England', in the pretence that 'England' can justly compose a unitary image, even though the ballads at their greatest have shown this to be an illusion.

In 1803 Wordsworth met Sir George Beaumont, who was to become his friend as well as patron. Almost immediately, Beaumont gave Wordsworth an estate in Applethwaite, with which he never parted and which he never attempted to restore, though he did write a very bad sonnet about it. In a letter to his brother Richard, Wordsworth commented:

> Sir George Beaumont made me a present . . . of a few old houses with two small fields attached to them in the Vale of Keswick . . . it was for me to patch up a house there if I liked to be near Mr Coleridge. But this I decline, though he insists on my keeping the land, so you see I am a freeholder of the County of Cumberland.[26]

But hardly a freeholder in the sense that Michael yearned to be one. The 'inevitability' of the social process has made possible Wordsworth's acquisition. He is now free to be a dweller.

Beaumont himself was a large, wealthy landowner, although much of his money came from the coal which was mined close to his estate, Coleorton, in Leicestershire. Guests at the house were spared the sight of workers and workings. Beaumont so landscaped the estate as to screen off the colliery. He was helped in this by Wordsworth.[27]

I have been paying particularly close attention to the gap in 'Michael' between 'inevitability' and accident because it is important to trace the process whereby Wordsworth turns away from his 'useful' ambition of being a man speaking to men, out of guilt, or out of an awareness that he has become committed to and identified with a social structuring that is ultimately exploitative. He has become a 'dweller', conceivably at the expense of others. And it is then worth recalling that if the verb 'to dwell' does, as I suggest, operate talismanically in Wordsworth's imagination, it may be because at a very deep level he hopes to preserve kinds of life – dwellers – which he also knows to be doomed, and that their fate is in some measure sealed by his own commitments. For whatever his emotional connections, these commitments align him with elements in the social-economic process by means of which dwellers are evicted, uprooted, denied their occupation and abode.

I I

From these irresolvable and undoubtedly grievous tensions, Wordsworth's reactionary Toryism will develop as a mode of rationalising and justifying his acquired position. But before that happens, his acute sense of predicament forces him into writing a number of poems which are of great significance because they so deeply try to make sense of tensions at work within him, and which exactly focus on what it is to be a poet. The greatest of these poems is 'Resolution and Independence', and since it has often been misunderstood, even when praised, it is worth spending a little time on trying to show why it is so crucial a poem, not merely in Wordsworth's *œuvre*, but for the whole enterprise that is called Romanticism.

It begins with the 'thoughtless' yet privileged wandering of the poet about the moors. The absorbed intensity of his regard for the life he finds here, for the hare 'that raced about with joy', an emotional vivacity that is internalised, provides for a perfect congruence between poet and outer world. This is a familiar enough construct: the poet *as* poet is distinguished by that joy whose ultimate source is God. The poet is chosen.[28] This may then seem to justify his being a man apart. And so:

> The pleasant season did my heart employ:
> My old remembrances went from me wholly;
> And all the ways of men, so vain and melancholy.[29]

But from that moment of absolute apartness, of utter self-absorption, Wordsworth begins to move in a different direction: towards the very melancholy which he had pronounced himself free of. It is as though by naming it he has given it a life which consumes all other thoughts.

> And fears, and fancies, thick upon me came;
> Dim sadness, blind thoughts I knew not nor could name.

Yet he does try to name them, and as he does so they begin to focus precisely on that apartness which had been the source of his joy. In other words, a link is established between the ways of men, 'so vain and melancholy', and fears and fancies; and in the very act of saying that his mind is empty of thinking of those ways he admits that he cannot entirely expunge them from his consciousness. 'Blind thoughts', then, emerge indirectly from the apparently cancelled 'ways of men'; and they lead to the poet's frank and perhaps frankly guilty acknowledgement that 'Far from the world I walk, and from all care'. From this he moves to the question as to whether

> He [can] expect that others should
> Build for him, sow for him, and at his call
> Love him, who for himself will take no heed at all?

What does Wordsworth mean? Who are these others? They cannot be merely those immediate members of his family whose domestic care helped him to get on with his poetry. (Building and sowing – not sewing – must indicate a wider circle of responsibilities.) I shall return to this, but before I do so it is worth commenting that Wordsworth has slipped from first to the third person: 'He' not 'I'. It seems to be this slippage that makes possible the famous stanza on Chatterton and Burns. For here Wordsworth is both generalising his condition – it is that of the poet – and in a very deep way admitting that 'I is another'. That is, he begins to recognise and explore a fissure between himself as self-validating poet and himself as a man.

> I thought of Chatterton, the marvellous Boy,
> The sleepless Soul that perish'd in its pride;
> Of Him who walk'd in glory and in joy
> Behind his plough, upon the mountain-side:
> By our own spirits are we deified;
> We Poets in our youth begin in gladness;
> But thereof comes in the end despondency and madness.

Chatterton and Burns are offered as enigmas: if they were poets, how could it be that they died in 'despondency and madness'? Are these the spirits that have deified them? The questions cannot confidently be answered, but it *can* be suggested that in some ways poets make their own lives, are responsible for how they live; and that they seem to fail this responsibility. Hence, 'despondency and madness'. Wordsworth knew about Smart, just as he knew about Cowper and Collins. But he does not try to seek refuge in what later in the century and elsewhere, will become a kind of orthodoxy: the self-pitying identification of poet with necessary suffering. Except, that is, in one respect; and this the poem is about to expose. For he has asked that odd question how he can expect others to look after him when he 'for himself will take no heed at all'. And this is odd because the logic of the question ought surely to lead him to ask not whether he will take heed for himself but whether he will take heed for others? ('I had powers and attainments which might be of use to mankind'.) If we try to paraphrase the question the stanza seems to be requiring, we might then come up with something like: how can I expect others to care for me, if I won't care for them. And we can then recognise that the slide from first to third person, although it makes possible the generalisation that will lead to a troubled assessment of 'We poets', originates in a kind of self-deception, or in an unwillingness to confront the real issue, which is precisely the matter of being of use, that is, of responsibility, of being a man speaking to men.

It now becomes clear that the poet who speaks the opening stanzas of 'Resolution and Independence' is not speaking to men: hence, 'My old remembrances went from me wholly'. And if we then attempt to decide what those remembrances were, we will be likely to conclude that they have to do with the radical, democratic ways of thought which characterise the *Lyrical Ballads*. It is these remembrances which have apparently been shed, which nevertheless return as dim sadness and blind thoughts, which in their turn lead to the troubled contemplation of 'poets', and from which Wordsworth is awoken by his awareness of 'a Man before me unawares'. For at this critical juncture he is brought face to face with an embodiment of what those old remembrances signified.

In his factual obduracy, the leech-gatherer is very similar to the old man travelling. Critics who complain that in the dialogue between the poet and the leech-gatherer the poem 'descends' to the prosaic utterly miss the point. The prosaic is essential to the poem's meaning. Heather Glen's definitive account of the meeting between Wordsworth and the blind beggar which occurs in Book 8 of *The Prelude* allows her to generalise about a strategy which is typical of his procedure:

> In poem after poem the shocked recognition of another's real, inassimilable existence forces [Wordsworth] to question a whole previous way of feeling. And in doing so he is not merely becoming conscious of personal guilt, but criticising and transcending a central strategy of the imaginative tradition of his culture: the egocentric, dehumanising 'distancing' which lies equally behind the aesthetic contemplation of disturbing situations, and paternalistic attitudes towards the poor.[30]

This is very well said, but I want to add to Glen's account. In 'Resolution and Independence' Wordsworth questions the old man about the work he does. The questions come from one who has already admitted that he expects others to work for him: 'Build for him, sow for him'. And, to repeat, this cannot possibly mean Dorothy and Mary alone. If he walks 'Far from the world . . . and from all care', it is because others enable him to do so; and his reflection on a possible future of 'Solitude, pain of heart, distress, and poverty' makes little sense unless we move away from the literal meaning of poverty or unless we acknowledge that Wordsworth is in a dark or muffled sense wondering about a world of work and whether he ought not perhaps to work himself.

But then we come to the crucial question, is poetry work? This may seem impossibly naive. Certainly, the question is not one that the poem ever asks, if only because as a poet Wordsworth is, so he says, 'a happy Child of earth'. We might interpret this as implying that the function of being a poet allows for a completely purposeful sense of activity: that poetic labour is, to put it starkly, non-alienated labour. But the question is implicit, and if we look at the letter in which Wordsworth explained much about his poem we can see even more clearly why 'dim sadness and blind thoughts' are tantamount to a confession of guilt. Everyone who cites the letter refers to Wordsworth's account of the old man who *was*: 'not *stood*, nor *sat*, but *was*'. Very few bother to note that Wordsworth then goes on to speak of how the old man carried with him 'the necessities which an unjust state of society has laid upon him'.[31] The poem doesn't confront that unjust state, but – and this is the key point – 'Resolution and Independence' cannot fully be understood unless we are aware that the poet is unable to shake off the consciousness that it is such a state which nevertheless allows him to be a poet.

In a typically incisive essay on 'Culture', his contribution to *Marx: The First Hundred Years*, Raymond Williams discusses the development of those divisions in labour which resulted in 'mental labour' being privileged over 'manual labour', especially as the former is restricted to a certain class.

> The effect is not only the undervaluation of manual labour . . . on [which] in fact the maintenance of human life still absolutely depends. The effect is also on the character of 'mental labour' itself. In its separation from the basic processes of assuring human existence it is inherently more likely to develop false conceptions of both general and specific human conditions, since it is not as a matter of necessary practice exposed to and tested by human activity in general. Even more, since the fact of the division of labour, in this basic classic sense, is not just a matter of different kinds of work but of social relations which determine greater rewards and greater respect for 'mental labour', and of these relations as established in and protected by a specifically exploiting and unequal social order, the operations of 'mental labour' cannot be assumed in advance to be exclusively devoted to 'higher' or 'the highest' human concerns, but are in many or perhaps all cases likely to be bound up, in greater or lesser degree, with propagation, ratification, defence, apologia, naturalisation of that exploiting and unequal social order itself.[32]

It might almost have been written with 'Resolution and Independence' in mind. And yet we have immediately to qualify the remark. For Wordsworth does not so much try to ratify and defend the unequal social order as to confront the fact of its inequality, and this is essential to the poem's meaning and to its significance.

But then again, the confrontation is muted, not merely by the suppression of that 'unjust state of society', but by the odd deflections from heed of others to heed for self, and this is also significant because, great as the poem undoubtedly is in its attempt to come to terms with the privileged status of poet, and hard though it works to unpick the mystificatory process whereby 'the poet' is produced as a special type, in the last resort Wordsworth cannot bear to let go of that type. If we want further evidence of this we can look at the altogether more comic account he produces of himself as poet in 'Stanzas Written in My Pocket Copy of Thomson's "Castle of Indolence"', which was composed at exactly the time he was working on 'Resolution and Independence'. This poem also speaks of the poet – that is, Wordsworth himself – in the third person; and it makes him altogether 'unfathomably' mysterious:

> Some thought he was a lover, and did woo:
> Some thought far worse of him, and judged him wrong;
> But verse was what he had been wedded to;
> And his own mind did like a tempest strong
> Come to him thus, and drove the weary Wight along.

Given that this was not published until 1815, it may be that we should not place great weight upon it. Yet it claims that the poet is somehow the passive instrument of poetry – is driven, chosen, 'inspired' (the terms fall into place). It therefore suggests a man struggling to justify his wandering 'far from the world', even though that same man had earlier wished to justify poetry as the act of a man speaking to men. And *that* man, by refusing to endorse the 'egocentric dehumanising distancing' which Heather Glen identifies as central to his culture, had hoped that *as poet* he would be of real use.

I I I

Yet no matter how far he might wander, Wordsworth could not wander from himself. At his truest, this meant discovering in himself those elements, qualities, feelings, which he had in common with others. In 'Resolution and Independence' the leech-gatherer provides the opportunity, or the enforced occasion, for such a discovery. He seems, Wordsworth says, 'like a Man from some far region sent;/To give me human strength, and strong admonishment'. This was later changed to 'To give me human strength by apt admonishment', which perhaps unfortunately implies that the old man is a figure of almost comically stern reproof. But it is more important to note how often in Wordsworth's poems the word 'human' turns up in challenging, difficult contexts. At the beginning of 'Michael' Wordsworth speaks of how as a young man he had been led to feel

> For passions that were not my own, and think
> At random and imperfectly indeed
> On Man; the heart of man and human life.

At the end of the great Immortality Ode he gives 'Thanks to the human heart by which we live,/Thanks to its tenderness, its joys, its fears'. In the 'Elegiac Stanzas Suggested by a Picture of Peele Castle, in a Storm', he says that 'A deep distress hath humaniz'd my Soul'; and in the third of the Lucy poems he writes:

> A slumber did my spirit seal,
> I had no human fears:
> She seem'd a thing that could not feel
> The touch of earthly years.

In all these cases, to be human is to be caught up in, or at the very least made aware of, suffering, of fears which have to be met and – somehow – accommodated in any adequate living. To be human is to be moved out of that 'sealed' infancy, that delighted, unclouded vision which is unapprehensive of the tragic possibilities attached to 'human life'.

The most sensitively acute account of this movement is to be found in Keats's famous letter to his friend John Reynolds, in which he speaks of the chamber of maiden thought and the inevitability of going beyond it, through

> sharpening one's Vision into the heart and nature of Man – of convincing one's nerves that the world is full of Misery and Heartbreak, Pain, Sickness and oppression – whereby this Chamber of Maiden Thought becomes gradually darkened, and at the same time, on all sides of it, many doors are set open – but all dark – all leading to dark passages. We see not the balance of good and evil; we are in a mist . . . To this point was Wordsworth come, as far as I can conceive, when he wrote 'Tintern Abbey,' and it seems to me that his genius is explorative of those dark passages.[33]

'The heart and nature of Man' – the phrase might almost be Wordsworth's. But Keats does not, I think, acknowledge the yearning in Wordsworth to be able to 'seal' the dark passages, so that the Lucy poems, for example, hope against hope for the continuation or recovery of what, in 'Elegiac Stanzas' is called 'A power' which, gone now, 'nothing can restore'. Many of the great poems are about this: they confront the loss of precisely that power whose glory has somehow prohibited or hidden the dark passages. It is even possible to read 'Old Man Travelling' as being about the need to endorse the vision of them and himself as 'sealed' against suffering: by being 'insensibly subdued/To settled quiet' and because he is 'by nature led/To peace so perfect', the old man is without 'human fears'. But then he speaks.

The leech-gatherer, the old man, the blind beggar: in their different ways they can all be seen as admonishers. But I suggest that Wordsworth became incapable of enduring their endurance, of bearing the admonishment. It not only connected him too painfully to the 'human heart', it required him to acknowledge that the connection denied him his authority as poet and as representative of certain class aspirations. In the end, therefore, the wanderer away from the world won, and the poet, as opposed to the 'poet' lost. This is the real meaning of the egotistical sublime. Autobiography becomes the means of securing selfhood, although the greatness of *The Prelude* has much to do with Wordsworth's awareness of how the world breaks in upon him, how, in other words, the self cannot be constructed apart from history.

Yet the counter movement, which Coleridge encouraged, towards the construction of the 'private' self in opposition to those 'out there', announced in the poem's opening lines, is very recognisable. It is both an element in Wordsworth's poetry, and a feature of the period. Raymond Williams has noted that such a movement anticipates a crisis in modern literature, which he explains as

> the division of experience into social and personal categories. It is now much more than an emphasis. It is a rooted division, into which the flow of experience is directed, and from which, with their own kinds of vigour, the separated kinds of life flow.[34]

Coleridge lived this division in particularly acute ways. He begins as a political radical, typically enough for an intellectual of his period, and from the early collaborative work with Southey he moves onto the great enterprise of the *Lyrical Ballads*. He and Wordsworth are to re-unite divergent strains of poetry: of lyric (the personal) and ballad (the social). Yet from the outset of his career, Coleridge exhibits grave doubts and insecurities leading to a posture, a way of thinking and feeling, which seems very like paranoia. (A term which enters the language at about this time.) 'Others' represent a threat to the sense of selfhood so painfully constructed and so deeply doubted. And in Coleridge's case, this self is, of course, 'the poet'. Coleridge, we may say, almost needs to think of himself as 'a poet', where the term can be held to define a complex of given characteristics (given by Coleridge though derived from concepts we saw being linked together in Chapter 2: 'imagination', 'joy', 'inspiration'). These are then taken to be self-validating. They are also held to separate the poet from others, who in the 'Dejection' ode are lumped together as 'the poor loveless, ever-anxious crowd', and who pose a threat because they may not see the poet as he wants to see himself and to be seen. As a result, the personal and social cannot be reconciled or connected in a knowable community unless the social – whatever is 'out there' – is theorised as potentially destructive and thus requiring to be brought under control.

Whatever else *The Rime of the Ancient Mariner* is about, it is about this fear of others. As W. H. Auden pointed out, the individualised mariner is contrasted with the sailors *en masse*, who behave as an undifferentiated crowd. They live together, they die together:

> Four times fifty living men,
> (And I heard nor sigh nor groan)
> With heavy thump, a lifeless lump,
> They dropped down one by one.

The collective pronoun works here as it does in Edward Lear's limericks: 'They' signify the irresponsible but threatening crowd and as such 'they' are close to Wordsworth's presentation of the city crowd in *The Prelude*:

> The slaves unrespited of low pursuits,
> Living amid the same perpetual flow
> Of trivial objects, melted and reduced
> To one identity, by differences
> That have no law, no meaning, and no end.
>
> (Book 7, ll. 700–4)

Wordsworth at his greatest works to combat this reductivism. Coleridge, I think, never does. His theoretic early radicalism is always threatened by the habit of thought which later becomes frankly reactionary/Burkean in its contempt for 'the crowd'. Auden quotes Kierkegaard to the effect that

> A public is neither a nation, nor a generation, nor a community . . . no single person who belongs to the public makes a real commitment; . . . a public is a kind of gigantic something, an abstract and deserted void which is everything and nothing.[35]

It is true that in 'This Lime Tree Bower My Prison' Coleridge struggles free of the prison of self so that the poem may end with him voicing his love for friends, and specifically for Charles Lamb, 'my gentle-hearted Charles'; and it is possible to make connections between this movement from imprisoned, internalised brooding towards social, affiliative love, and the movement of the mariner from *his* paranoid certainties to his 'blessing' the sea-creatures. It is further possible to note that in the beautiful 'Frost at Midnight' Coleridge's mind turns outward from 'Abstruser musings' to musings over his 'cradled infant'. In all these cases there is a movement from self-absorption towards that which is beyond the self. But what is beyond is not confronted as it is in Wordsworth. Vague blessings take the place of that painful, detailed encounter with the unfamiliar which distinguishes Wordsworth's radically great work. Coleridge's doubts and fears, on the other hand, are no doubt the motive power for his wanting Wordsworth to write that philosophical poem which would justify the act of poetry, of the *individual* imagination. This will explain why he complained of his friend's

> undue predilection for the *dramatic* form in certain poems, from which one or other of two evils result. Either the thoughts and diction are different from that of the poet, and then there arises an incongruity of style; or they are the

same and indistinguishable, and then it presents a species of ventriloquism, where two are represented as talking, while in truth only one speaks.[36]

To *complain* of the incongruity of styles is of course what gives Coleridge away. He refuses to acknowledge that such incongruity is the point. No wonder that he should have remarked to Crabb Robinson that Wordsworth 'unreasonably attached himself to the low'.[37] Fear of others now becomes a justification of separation from others, especially those who may be separated by class considerations. A consequence of all this is that the political and social commentator has to be brought into line with the literary theorist, and the result is that the many facets of Coleridge's thought are melded together by a conservatism which is affirmed as somehow 'natural'. Thus Coleridge can complain in a letter of 1809 of 'the present illogical age, which has in imitation of the French rejected all the *cements* of language', just as he can assert that the ideal statesman must not

> delude the uninstructed into the belief that their shortest way of obtaining the good things of this life is to commence busy politicians, instead of remaining industrious labourers. He knows, and acts on the knowledge, that it is the duty of the enlightened philanthropist to plead *for* the poor and ignorant, not *to* them.[38]

These unargued assertions show how far Coleridge has moved from his early radicalism towards the reactionary position into which he later hardened. And although not all aspects of his thought move at the same pace or with the same intensity, those that don't are pushed to the margins. This is why, as Paul Hamilton has excellently observed, there is an irreconcilable split between Coleridge's radical theory of the need for poetic language to be *constructive*, and that political and social conservatism which eventually means that he 'removes the conclusions of his radical philosophy to an isolated, immediate domain whenever they threaten his conservative interests in existing institutions'.[39]

That this does not make Coleridge pause to wonder whether he is entitled to speak 'for England' is evidence only of his typicality in believing that the isolated intellectual, like the poet, is properly privileged, or sanctioned, precisely because he is 'above' the crowd. Coleridge naturalises a socially constructed image of poet/intellectual in a manner that is familiar to us through the assumptions of his disciple, Matthew Arnold. This is the very opposite of that embattled commitment which other Romantic poets recognised in Milton; and it is typical of Coleridge that when he does make use of Milton it is to the Milton of *Samson Agonistes* he turns. In the 'Dejection' ode, Coleridge echoes words which the despairing Samson had addressed to his father, Manoa. Samson tells Manoa that he feels 'My genial spirits droop'. Coleridge says that he feels his own 'genial spirits fail'. The echo, whether conscious or not, is of great significance. The ode is about Coleridge's feeling himself to be no longer a 'chosen' poet. He traces the cause of his rejection to God's displeasure at his guilty relationship with Sarah Hutchinson. (I put the matter baldly, but this is what it comes to.) Joy has been withdrawn from him. Milton's Samson similarly feels himself to be no longer a 'chosen' vessel of God. Coleridge is constructing an idea of the poet which derives from those half-developed concepts of inspiration and the sacred calling which will allow him to say something about the 'shaping spirit of imagination'. It is meant to be a contribution to, even a correction of, Wordsworth's brooding about the failure of such imagination. And this is quite deliberate.

One starting point for Coleridge's poem is the 'Immortality' ode, or as much of it as Wordsworth had written when Coleridge happened upon it at the beginning of April 1802. The relationship between the two poems is as complicated as was the relationship between the two poets.[40] But we know it was partly as a result of reading Coleridge's poem that Wordsworth wrote 'Resolution and Independence'. Wordsworth's poem is, among other things, a rebuke to that 'naturalised' and mystificatory image of the poet which his friend tried to substantiate in his 'Dejection' ode.

I draw attention to this for two reasons. First, it shows that the great Wordsworth was not prepared to rest content with Coleridge's idealist concept of the poet. Second, the other side to the coin is that Wordsworth was more affected by Coleridge's theory than might at first seem clear, or than is admitted by those who want to pretend that the poet of 'Resolution and Independence' isn't the poet of 'Sonnets Dedicated to Liberty'. And yet, here again matters are far from simple. Against the routine patriotism of 'On Returning to Dover' there is, for example, the sonnet on Toussaint L'Ouverture, whose terrible fate, although not completed by the time Wordsworth wrote his sonnet in August 1802 (Toussaint died in a French prison in 1803), is nevertheless emblematic of the reversal of events from the great days of the French Revolution. In 1801 Napoleon had reinstated in the French colonies the slavery which the Republic had abolished in 1794, and had brought to France the man who had freed the slaves of San Domingo. One can therefore understand why Wordsworth should now look to England as the land of liberty and why the cadences of many of the sonnets in this sequence should be derived from Milton, just as one can understand Landor's remark about France in 1802, when he heard of Napoleon's assuming the title of First Consul for life, that 'as to the cause of liberty, this cursed nation has ruined it for ever'.

The problem, however, is that unlike the Blake of *Poetical Sketches* and the *Songs*, Wordsworth has no way of going on from Milton. The ending of the sonnet to Toussaint, which tells him that 'thou hast great allies;/Thy friends are exultations, agonies,/And love, and Man's unconquerable mind' may be touching, but is spoken in conquered accents. These are the accents of Milton's sonnets to Fairfax and Cromwell, and 'On the Late Massacre in Piedmont', which we know that Wordsworth deeply admired. Thus the despairing 'Milton! thou shouldst be living at this hour' can do no more than ape 'Miltonics' in its account of England as 'a fen/Of stagnant waters'. In short, these are not the poems of a man speaking to men. They are more the work of a man putting on – not airs, that would be quite wrong, but putting on borrowed robes.

I would suggest that at this period Wordsworth faced an acute crisis. He hated what had happened to the French Revolution, and felt England had no option but to renew war in 1803 (he even offered his services, should they be needed). But he had lost the ability to find a poetic voice which would connect him to the radical concerns which had sustained his earlier work. The Miltonics are, then, part of a lapse into nostalgia which allows him to speak of the 'Great men [who] have been among us' as a way of writing off the present. The dilemmas of the moment left Wordsworth with insuperable difficulties when it came to finding a poetic strategy – a language – that would be equal to the occasion. The sonnets do what he rightly condemned Paley and Godwin for doing, fitting things to words rather than words to things. They are 'powerless in regulating our judgements concerning the value of men & things. They contain no picture of human life: they *describe* nothing'.[41] They are, in short, 'poetry'. From here it is a short step to the fantasising that shows through 'Rob Roy's Grave' (1803).

> And, if the word had been fulfill'd,
> As *might* have been, then, thought of joy!
> France would have had her present Boast;
> And we our brave Rob Roy!

The word that might have been was Rob Roy's boast that 'kingdoms shall shift about, like clouds,/Obedient to my breath'. The implausibility of this is only slightly less than the poem's soft-focus hero-worship; and this, in its anti-democratic individualism, makes possible that stance of apartness from the world whose variant expression can be aloofness: of being above the crowd. As Kiernan remarks, Wordsworth increasingly came to 'think of the mind's contact with other minds in social life as cramping and strangling, instead of moulding and fertilising'.[42] Speaking 'for' England means insisting on an unopposable authority which denies the possibility of speaking *to* or *with* those men and women who are both within Wordsworth's greatest poetry and who provide a possible constituency for its reception.

Blake, never seeking to appease a readership, ends without one. Wordsworth, seeking appeasement, ends as Poet Laureate. Blake's visions of England are liberating and tragically truthful. Wordsworth's are increasingly false. Wordsworth, of course, does what becomes accepted as orthodox and proper. He retreats to higher ground – that ground which Arnold thought all true prophets and commentators should occupy if they were to avoid being blackened by the smoke of the market place. From this prospect he can comment, in 'Miltonic' style, upon that vast and empty abstraction, 'England', while at the same time claiming the right to be a private poet.

But it is a false division. For 'private' turns out to mean identification with certain forces, interests, which between them compose a social and cultural orthodoxy. This is to be a lost leader. Nor will it do to say that Wordsworth moves towards the kind of Horatianism which Pope adopted in his later years. Too much has happened in between times for that to be possible. The choices are different and indeed became so from the moment when Wordsworth announced that a poet was a man speaking to men. The grandeur of that claim and the ambition to make it good are hardly to be denied. But Wordsworth finds it too painful to sustain them. Instead, he tries to cover over the fact that he is someone who, both as man and as poet, is implicated in the social process in ways that make for separation and thus impede the connections which a man speaking to men must wish to establish. Of course, the impediments could have become a proper part of speech, could indeed have been what that speech, that poetry, was *about*. But for that to have been so would have required Wordsworth to have stripped away what was meant by 'poet', and this he would not or could not bring himself to do. The result is that he has to mystify his role just as he has to mystify as 'inevitable' particular processes by means of which he is separated from the 'men' whom he hopes to address in communality. And it then follows that 'poet' and historical 'inevitability' are alike constructions which are used to make legitimate a withdrawal onto what is asserted as a more authoritative plane of utterance.

From his 'free' place, or 'dwelling', among the Lakes, remote from the city, the poet poses as a man speaking *for* men, and particularly for Englishmen and England. This is the ultimate, deeply conservative, ambition of pastoral. It falsifies the actual relationships of non-city communities just as much and for the same reason that it falsifies city communities. 'Merry England' stands at the opposite end of a vision of nationhood from Blake's Golgonooza. And as we have seen, neither old men travelling nor city crowds may be allowed their own voices, for these might disturb and even undermine the poet's authority. 'England' now becomes a vacant site, its custodian the poet who claims for himself the right *as poet* to interpret it in a way that denies all other interpretations. Everything now becomes mysterious.

CHAPTER 6

Shelley and the Men of England

I

The publication of *Ecclesiastical Sonnets* in 1822 marks Wordsworth's full retreat into an essentially anti-democratic monarchism. In tracing the history of Christianity in England, which is the sonnets' purpose, he pauses on 'Troubles of Charles the First', where 'some fierce maniac' is said to usurp piety's name. He then laments William Laud's treatment at the hands of 'madding faction', rejoices in the return of Charles II, and greets the accession of William III as the moment when England is truly liberated. In this history there can be no place for Milton. And this implies a new orthodoxy. As we shall see in a later chapter, Milton, who had been a problem for eighteenth-century poets, remains a problem for those nineteenth-century poets who hoped to reconcile their commitment to him with a newly-affirmed assertion of patriotic monarchism. For such monarchism to be at all convincing there has to be some show of support for the two Charleses. The result is that support for Milton becomes very difficult, except where he can be regarded as a master of style alone, his politics ignored.

Wordsworth's sonnets were mostly composed in 1821, by which time he had become a political Tory. This involves him in endlessly invoking the good past – all of it – as an idealised feudalistic set of relations. Thus, in a letter of 1817, he tells Daniel Stuart that

> farmers used formerly to be attached to their landlords, and labourers to their farmers who employed them. All that kind of feeling has vanished – in like manner, the connection between the trading and landed interests of county towns undergoes no modification whatever from personal feeling, whereas in my memory it was almost wholly governed by it.[1]

This may seem intolerably sentimental, until we recall that very similar statements are made by a poet as differently positioned as John Clare. Clearly, Wordsworth and Clare were both responding to the active presence of social forces about whose nature they rightly felt the deepest doubts. Their awareness of separative processes at work upon them and the registering of relationship are, then, more important than their assertions that they can bear witness to a so-different, unified, past, although it undoubtedly does much to explain the intensity of that assertion.

In Wordsworth's case, however, the decisive move towards political and social reaction means that he becomes contained by those cultural properties – forms, modes of utterance, habits of thought – which his great poetry had repeatedly broken open in order to show that they *were* containments. Wordsworth's England becomes a sealed-off vision, with little purchase upon the complicating actualities which the work of his great decade had repeatedly discovered and addressed. In a sonnet of 1833, he asks, can

> This face of rural beauty be a mask
> For discontent, and poverty, and crime;
> These spreading towns a cloak for lawless will?

'Forbid it, Heaven,' he begs, 'And MERRY ENGLAND still/Shall be thy rightful name, in prose and rhyme!' But this bundling together of undifferentiated 'ills' is merely a way of writing them off, or at the very least an admission that there is nothing the poet-as-sonneteer can do to discriminate between them, account for them, confront them. The appeal to Merry England is entirely escapist, a way of keeping apart from spreading towns and crowds of men. This is the Wordsworth who was in favour of further suspension of Habeas Corpus, who actively supported the 'landed interest' of Lord Lonsdale, and who shared his titled friends' loathing of the rebellions in Italy.

Given that the Italian rebellions occurred in 1821, the *Ecclesiastical Sonnets* may owe something to the threat Wordsworth assumed them to pose. But the sonnets' candidly monarchist stance also reminds us of the fact that in April of that year Southey, who had been Poet Laureate since 1813, published his fatuous elegy for George III, *A Vision of Judgement*. Like Wordsworth, Southey had retreated from the flaming republicanism of his youth, which had been marked by such headily radical works as *Joan of Arc* (1793) and *Wat Tyler* (1794). *A Vision of Judgement* imagines George III as pausing before ascending to Heaven, 'so deeply the care of his country/Lay in that royal soul repos'd'. However, he need not fear. 'Firm hath he proved and wise', Southey says of the Prince Regent. *A Vision of Judgement* is a dreary and ridiculous piece of time-serving, made the more absurd by its preface, in which Southey famously speaks of the 'Satanic school' of Byron and Shelley (although he does not name them). The school is 'characterised by a Satanic spirit of pride and audacious impiety . . . [which] is political as well as moral'.[2] This school houses the spirit of internationalism, of democratic radicalism, and above all, of republicanism.

Byron's definitive retort is among the greatest of all acts of literary demolition. Moreover, his well-mannered republicanism means that he can find a place in Heaven even for George. 'And when the tumult dwindled to a calm,/I left him practising the hundredth psalm'. This particular psalm is

'A Psalm of Praise', and by implication it deflates the vanity of kings. 'Know ye that the Lord He is God: it is He that hath made us, and not we ourselves; we are His people, and the sheep of His pasture.' Byron's show of magnanimous wit is such that he allows George the place in Heaven which Southey had denied to Shelley and himself while at the same time making George disavow his own special status. This is altogether more 'civilised' than the huffing of Byron's opponent, for all that Southey wishes to speak with the authority of the Laureate. While it is commonly remarked that in finding this tone of voice Byron owes much to Pope, it should also be remarked that he does not suffer in the comparison. His great strength is his tone. Free as it must seem of rancour or party spirit, it offers itself as truly reasonable. It will be heard later in the century, in the poetry of Arthur Clough.

Such a tone is difficult to sustain. More characteristic of the period is the anger of Hazlitt and Cobbett. This, too, is a voice not easy to accommodate in poetry, and it indicates the difficulty of pointing to *any* voice, *any* mode of utterance, which may be said to have unchallengeable or plausible authority. For the 'poise' which is so often recommended as the equivalent or embodiment of truly civilised values is, customarily, an inflection of class, against which other 'unbalanced' voices will seem less than 'civilised'. But then 'balance', 'poise', 'civility' are self-referential qualities whose accomplishment has the effect of averting the force of hostile enquiry, of blunting the sharp edge of questions which seek an answer to what such civility is *for*.

Byron turns this to his own advantage. The kind of voice he self-consciously adopts allows him a posture of disinterestedness: through it he speaks satirically, in detestation of 'cant political, cant poetical, cant religious, cant moral'. His man-of-the-worldliness is professedly even-handed. In the very act of demolishing Southey's pretentious and incompetent hexameters ('not one of whose gouty feet would stir') he can confess to an occasional inadequacy in his own writing ('I am doubtful of the grammar/Of that last phrase, which makes the stanza stammer'). This disarms criticism by getting in first with such panache that any further comment would be inept. Not surprisingly, Paul Hamilton describes Byron's 'search for a sufficient language' in company with other poets of the second generation of Romantics, as yielding 'the more capable language of a new maturity, confidently combining high and low styles without political anxiety'.[3] If we use this as a guide to the nature of Byron's achievement we will be led to note that his genial contempt for the praise Southey heaps on George III is voiced through Satan. The Devil pleads his case for having George consigned to Hell. It is one which even allows the late king's virtues:

> I know he was a constant consort; own
> He was a decent sire and middling lord.
> All this is much, and most upon a throne;

As temperance, if at Apicius's board,
Is more than at an anchorite's supper shown.
I grant him all the kindest can accord;
And this was well for him, but not for those
Millions who found him what oppression chose.

(Stanza XLVI)

The voice that swings round the ending of the penultimate line and then, after a considered pause, drops emphatically onto 'Millions' presents its hearers with the overwhelming fact of what oppressive monarchy entails. Nor is it hyperbole. Byron covers a great deal of the history of George's reign: his war against the American states (a matter which Southey ridiculously fudges); his refusal of Catholic emancipation; the endorsement of laws which acted as a means to deny natural justice. As Satan says: 'Nations as men, home subjects, foreign foes,/So that they utter'd the word "liberty!"/Found George the Third their first opponent.' In managing this tone of voice so unerringly throughout *A Vision of Judgement* Byron succeeds magnificently in exposing cant – as he did in his great speech to the House of Lords about the frame-breaker's Bill of 1812, and as he would do in his stanzas in *Don Juan* on the Duke of Wellington.

But this brings us to what some may wish to regard as a limitation. Byron, we know, held 'strong views on particular issues'.[4] Yet it would be very difficult to assemble a coherent political vision from his writings. In the preface to 'Julian and Maddalo' Shelley noted of Count Maddalo, who is based on Byron, that

> He is a person of the most consummate genius, and capable, if he would direct his energies to such an end, of becoming the redeemer of his degraded country. But it is his weakness to be proud: he derives, from a comparison of his own extraordinary mind with the dwarfish intellects that surround him, an intense apprehension of the nothingness of human life.[5]

If this reveals some incaution on Shelley's part – no one man can be a redeemer – it also indicates a shrewd understanding of Byron's temperament and of its flaws. He recognises that Byron as the noble lord allows a habit of self-willed detachment to dominate his thinking and ways of being, in the mistaken belief that this is the same thing as disinterest, and in this he anticipates Carlyle's complaint that Byron was too much of a lord to be a committed poet. Marx was probably wrong to say that had Shelley and Byron lived to see 1848 Shelley would have been on the side of the people, Byron on the side of the governors, but his remark points to Byron's insecure sense of where and with whom he belonged. If this can be welcomed as a readiness not to rush to judgement it must also be seen as nurturing that kind of cynicism which, although it passes for detestation of cant, may on occasions become altogether more negative and demeaning. The road from Byron to Eugene Wrayburn is a winding one, but it runs without visible break.

It was, I suspect, Byron's recognition of this flaw in his pose, the flaw that *was* his pose, that made him so determined after Shelley's death to commit himself to the cause of Greek liberation. His outbursts on behalf of Shelley are remarkable, both for their violence and the terms in which he chooses to praise his friend. 'As to poor Shelley,' he wrote to Thomas Moore on 4 March 1822, 'who is another bugbear to you and the world, he is, to my knowledge the *least* selfish and the mildest of men – a man who has made more sacrifices of his fortunes and feelings than any I ever heard of.' Then comes the qualification. 'With his speculative opinion I have nothing in common, nor desire to have.'[6]

But in a letter to the same friend written in August, a month after Shelley's death, the qualifications have disappeared. 'There is thus another man gone, about whom the world was ill-naturedly, and ignorantly, and brutally mistaken. It will, perhaps, do him justice *now*, when he can be no better for it.'[7] Byron's own death at Missolonghi is not far distant.

Nevertheless, it would be wrong to play down the great differences between the two poets. In the end, Shelley is not only more of a political idealist, he is much more of an English patriot. Byron might echo Cowper's 'England, with all thy faults I love thee still', but as the stanzas in *Beppo* which this introduces make plain, his commitment to England was of a piece with his other commitments. He could take it or leave it. Shelley, on the other hand, though he left England, took it with him. His republicanism is of a different order from Byron's. For example, while it is never quite clear whether Byron is any more than the scourge of particular monarchs, Shelley is an avowed king-hater. And if it seems strange to us that an avowed atheist and republican should also or indeed *therefore* be a patriot, we need to remember that at the end of the twentieth century we are living in that prolonged phase of England's history when republicanism has been forced on the defensive, to the extent that it can confidently be labelled *anti-English*; whereas Shelley had no reason to believe that victory would finally go to the monarchists. As Linda Colley remarks, 'The libertarian, anti-imperialist mode of patriotism was very far from dead in Britain by 1820.'[8] The enemy Southey was trying to line up in his blurred, shaking sights was a real one; and it could look very like a British version of that French radicalism which had so altered the rest of Europe. In defending the monarchy, Southey – and Wordsworth and Coleridge – are identifying with forces of reaction that inhibit any movement towards democracy. This is the England which they emerge to champion. The democratic Shelley was *necessarily* anti-monarchical, and his detestation of the institution of the monarchy was based on something far more substantial than personal dislike of the king's or regent's characteristic modes of behaviour: of lunacy and lechery. Hence his 'Sonnet: England in 1819'.

> An old, mad, blind, despised, and dying king, –
> Princes, the dregs of their dull race, who flow
> Through public scorn, – mud from a muddy spring, –
> Rulers who neither see, nor feel, nor know,
> But leech-like to their fainting country cling,
> Till they drop, blind in blood, without a blow, –
> A people starved and stabbed in the untilled field, –
> An army, which liberticide and prey
> Makes as a two-edged sword to all who wield, –
> Golden and sanguine laws which tempt and slay;
> Religion Christless, Godless – a book sealed;
> A Senate, – Time's worst statute unrepealed, –
> Are graves, from which a glorious Phantom may
> Burst, to illumine our tempestuous day.

This is formally unlike any sonnet of Wordsworth's. In fact, it is unlike *any* English sonnet. Quite apart from the unfamiliar rhyme scheme, it is made up of one sentence, whose clauses seem to be strung together at random rather than causally or formally connected. (If there is a connection it appears to depend on the use throughout the sonnet of a continuous present tense.) What 'Sonnet: England in 1819' offers is the haphazard itemising of a permanent hellishness. This permanence is challenged by the last two lines and the possibilities released by 'may/Burst'. But the energy of 'Burst' is qualified by the hesitancies of 'may', which refuses innocently to prophesy a liberating revolution of the kind many Englishmen, including the older generation of Romantic poets, were by then dreading. Both words are heavily stressed: they operate in perilous balance. This is speculative opinion intently dramatised.

That speculation, however, is derived from contemporary events. The political possibilities exist within history. The poem was written after the Peterloo massacre, an event which Jerome McGann suggests may have influenced Keats's 'To Autumn', requiring us to read the ode in the bitter knowledge that for thousands of English people the dystopic late summer of 1819 was emphatically not a time of mellow fruitfulness.[9] I am sceptical of the implications of McGann's account, but Shelley certainly confronts those issues from which a glorious Phantom may burst. It is also worth remarking that critics who take for granted the propriety of Keats's criticism of Shelley's gestural rhetoric – of lines unloaded with ore – would have difficulty in sustaining the charge here. The rulers who drop 'blind in blood', for example, make for a vivid repudiation of the medical orthodoxy whose cure was customarily worse than the diseases it pretended to diagnose. The phrase re-animates the cliché about the body politic and directs attention not merely to Peterloo but to the selfish absorption and bloodletting of successive Liverpool ministries. It has about it a public, polemical vigour which is to some extent reminiscent of Dryden ('And popularly prosecute the plot'), but which also has much of the oratorical strength of Cobbett. This public voice both expresses a precise anger over actual events and is directed towards their perpetrators on behalf of those who suffer. You have only to compare 'Sonnet: England in 1819' with any of the sonnets about the condition of England which Wordsworth was writing in 1802–3 in order to see how much better Shelley's poem is (e.g. 'England! the time is come when thou shouldst wean/Thy heart from its emasculating food').

In its synchronic, virtually paratactic mode of utterance, Shelley's sonnet brings together incidents and conditions in a manner which invites speculation about their being the causal preconditions of revolution. This enables the release of the last two lines and the gesture – it can be no more than that – towards a conceivable utopia. The glorious Phantom is an ideal person, an imago which bursts from its chrysalis. It is the corrective vision of all that is deformed in the image of Frankenstein's monster. The monster must be read as the botched modern Prometheus, a construct of Enlightenment science and philosophy, the possible explanations for whose disfigurements I touched on in Chapter 4 in my brief discussion of Erasmus Darwin. Mary Shelley's scientist 'dabbled among the unhallowed damps of the grave'. But this Burke-and-Hare activity is beside the point in Shelley's poem, for if his Phantom is to burst from the grave it will be on its own account. Revolutionary energy is self-generating; and although I do not know exactly how Shelley wants us to take the word 'Phantom', it certainly combines form and energy in an electrical discharge which will enable it to 'illumine our tempestuous day'. We should also note that it is androgynous.

This has obvious connections with the 'Ode to the West Wind', in which the speaker also reads the advent of a new order into the coming storm:

> O Wild West Wind, thou breath of Autumn's being,
> Thou, from whose unseen presence the leaves dead
> Are driven, like ghosts from an enchanter fleeing . . .

This, too, is the autumn of 1819, and the west wind presumably blows from America, the land of achieved liberty, of republican citizenship. It seems that Shelley intended 'Sonnet: England in 1819' and the Ode to appear together with *The Mask of Anarchy* in a 'little volume of *popular* songs wholly political'.[10] The volume was never published, but his plans indicate his political radicalism and his desire to understand the implications of Phantom and enchanter: both are self-generating, self-directing forces. And although *The Mask of Anarchy* is written on the specific occasion of the Peterloo massacre, it, too, connects with a popular voice that defies all those other voices whose abstractive mode claimed the true authority of Englishness.

> Rise like lions after slumber
> In unvanquishable number –
> Shake your chains to earth like dew
> Which in sleep had fallen on you –
> Ye are many – they are few.

II

But while in *The Mask* Shelley responds strongly to particular events, his political thinking takes him far beyond Byron's scorn for 'cant political'. Of course Shelley has an unwavering hatred of all forms of oppression, which includes his detestation of orthodox religion and of those marriage vows which 'chain' men and women together for the longest journey. Moreover, in his loathing of England's brutality towards the Irish, Shelley writes and behaves as a political liberationist. This is no doubt why, as the facts of his life emerged, he became so shocking to those middle-class intellectuals who had earlier thought of him as an aerial, blithe spirit. Hence Arnold's famous account of Shelley as the beautiful, ineffectual angel. This is a form of containment masquerading as disinterested condescension. And although it has often been approvingly referred to, it is precisely how the author of *Culture and Anarchy* could be expected to speak of someone who says 'Ye are many – they are few.' Shelley must pose a threat to anyone who offers to speak from a position of liberal enlightenment and who regards the elite, the guardians, the remnant – call them what you will – as the true upholders of England, its culture and politics.

It will hardly do to argue that the full development of the division into the many and the few had to wait until later in the century, when such alignments were forced on intellectuals by events of which Shelley could have had no foreknowledge. His language of phantoms and enchanters allows him to foreshadow historical processes that anticipate (say) 1848. Shelley's radicalism is grounded in and sustained by a politics which is as grandly, as unashamedly utopian as Blake's, and which may be thought of as even more intellectually and imaginatively comprehensive, and therefore not merely utopian. As G. M. Matthews has shown in his suggestive essay, 'A Volcano's Voice in Shelley', Shelley's greatest mythopoeic work, *Prometheus Unbound*, provides both a utopian vision of man, 'Sceptreless, free, uncircumscribed', and an account of the transformation of present to future, rooted in imagery whose social and historical resonances are essential to the drama's meaning. *Prometheus Unbound* is not the vaguely 'sublime' work its casual detractors have presented it as being, nor is there any justification for seeing it as fundamentally escapist, a turning away from history.[11] In anticipating or rebutting these familiar charges, Matthews makes good use of the figure of Demogorgon. Demogorgon, he argues, 'is accurately described in terms of shapeless molten magma or lava; he erupts in order to overthrow Jupiter . . . Shelley thought his own contemporary society contained a force which was familiar and alien in the same way'. And Matthews adds that 'The basis of much of the volcanic imagery in Shelley's poetry . . . is the perception of revolutionary activity in the external world and in the human mind – or irrepressible collective energy contained by repressive power.'[12] The volcanic area around Naples is thus the perfect setting for the work, and the Italy of 1818 and 1819, when it was written, is equally apt.

Yet although *Prometheus Unbound* is universalist in its full implications, it is undoubtedly shaped by and responsive to contemporary events in England. This is made clear in the Preface.

> We owe the great writers of the golden age of our literature to that fervid awakening of the public mind which shook to dust the oldest and most oppressive form of the Christian religion. We owe Milton to the progress and development of the same spirit: the sacred Milton was, let it ever be remembered, a republican, and a bold enquirer into morals and religion. The great writers of our own age are, we have reason to suppose, the companions and forerunners of some unimagined change in our social condition or the opinions which cement it.[13]

Like Blake, Shelley looks to Milton for the authority of his own political imagination. But also like Blake he goes beyond Milton. For the 'fervid awakening of the public mind' is Demogorgon-like; it comes from *below*; and this characteristic way of thinking belongs to a development of radical thought that is inevitably post-Miltonic. It is able to read into contemporary events the rumblings of a volcanic voice which bursts, upward, into the world, illumining, transforming. Volcanic energy does, of course, transform a landscape, and lava eventually enriches the soil it invades. In a famous end-note to the poems of 1819, Mary Shelley wrote that:

> Shelley loved the People; and respected them as often more virtuous, as always more suffering, and therefore more deserving of sympathy, than the great. He believed that a clash between the two classes of society was inevitable, and he eagerly ranged himself on the side of the people.[14]

'Ye are many – they are few.' It has frequently been argued that Shelley's mind, his vast-ranging knowledge, his mythopoeic imagination, make it impossible to believe that he could ever hope to communicate with the many. (He says 'ye' rather than 'we', admits, that is, his own separation from 'the people'.) There is some truth in this, even if we discount the fact that we still do not have a proper edition of the works and even if we leave aside the debilitating effects of successive generations of Shelley's critics who have mostly disliked what they understood and misunderstood what they liked – so that, to take a representative example, Harold Bloom has twice managed to write about *Prometheus Unbound* without so much as suggesting it might have anything to do with radical politics.[15] But Shelley's poetry is not hermetic. Even the 'difficult' works like *The Revolt of Islam* and *The Triumph of Life* are more accessible than Blake's Prophetic Books. It is true that Shelley typically bursts the poetic forms he takes over, but that is an entirely proper aspect of his radical enterprise, as is his decision to make his book of the people not the Bible, as Milton and later Blake had done, but such works as Paine's *The Rights of Man* and Godwin's *Political Justice*, allusions to and echoes of which, as is well known, can be found scattered throughout his writings. Where Milton drew on the best available thinking about such matters as astronomy, geography, chemistry, Shelley does the same with the thinking of his day. This is the explanation for the wide range of speculative, scientific language that occurs throughout his work, and why his ambition may be called epic in its oppositional power. Erasmus Darwin could welcome the march of science as wholly beneficial to his class. Shelley, on the other hand, sees that if it is to be a glorious Phantom, it must be part of a genuinely progressive, transformative vision. It is this, I suggest, which critics have found it difficult to accept.

'So controversial were some of Shelley's ideas, that they were not printed until a century after his death.' These words appear on the dustjacket of David Lee Clark's edition of Shelley's prose, published in 1954. They bear compellingly on the great *Address to the People on the Death of the heiress apparent*, written late in 1817 and first published sometime in the 1840s.[16] The *Address* was prompted by the death of the heiress apparent, on whom, as is often the way with heirs to the throne, high hopes had been placed. She would wipe clean the monarchy's stained image, she was a true friend of the poor, she had a deep love of her country. So, at least, legend had it. But on 6 November 1817 she died. Earlier that year the march of the blanketeers had taken place and had been suppressed; Habeas Corpus had been suspended; and on the day following the Princess's death Jeremiah Brandreth, William Turner and Isaac Ludlam were brutally executed at Derby. They had been found guilty of high treason, or, more exactly, of organising an uprising in Derbyshire in June. Shelley's *Address* contrasts the death of the princess, which, however regrettable, was at least one of natural means, with the judicial execution of three labourers who also, as he points out, 'had domestic affections and were remarkable for the exercise of private virtues'.

> Their death by hanging and beheading, and the circumstances of which it is the characteristic and consequence, constitute a calamity such as the English nation ought to mourn with an unassuageable grief.

Shelley then goes on to note that 'kings and their ministries have in every age been distinguished from other men by a thirst for expenditure and bloodshed'. He writes at length about the conditions of the manufacturing districts and comments with bitter eloquence on the role of Oliver the spy and his masters in tricking the labourers into joining a possible insurrection, their purpose being 'to trample upon our rights and liberties forever, to present to us the alternatives of anarchy and oppression, and triumph when the astonished nation accepts the latter at their hands'. In conclusion he notes that the princess whose death should be universally mourned is not the Princess Charlotte but the Princess of Liberty:

> Let us follow the corpse of British Liberty slowly and reverentially to its tomb; and if some glorious Phantom should appear and make its throne of broken swords and sceptres and royal crowns trampled in the dust, let us say that the Spirit of Liberty has arisen from its grave and left all that was gross and mortal there, and kneel down and worship it as our Queen.[17]

This great address, which ought to be as well known as Byron's speech to the House of Lords, clearly provides a starting point for the 'Sonnet: England in 1819', and explains the androgyny of the glorious Phantom. But much of its intellectual energy is derived from Shelley's awareness of how working people are becoming the inevitable victims of a process over which they have no control. Rulers 'blind in blood' weren't simply fattened to excess by the events of Peterloo. We are led to reflect that the 'glorious Phantom' invoked in both the *Address* and the sonnet is an image of hoped-for potentiality, to be measured against the heavy odds which oppose it. Against the hermaphroditic Liberty must be set the official warrior, Britannia. Here again, there is nothing vague in Shelley's reading of contemporary history.

Yet it does raise a question that he cannot be blamed for overlooking, but which needs to be given some attention. In his 'New National Anthem', one of the popular songs of 1819, Shelley wrote:

> God prosper, speed, and save,
> God raise from England's grave
> Her murdered Queen!
> Pave with swift victory
> The steps of Liberty,
> Whom Britons own to be
> Immortal Queen.

An atheist appealing to God? It is possible to read this as the token of a secret despair, of a betraying belief that human energy is now incapable of raising the spirit of Liberty. But it is probably best not to do so. Instead, we may regard the blasphemy as a witty denial of God's special plans for kings, and thus equivalent to Byron's thrust at having George 'practising the hundredth psalm'. Nor need we be exercised over the slippage from 'England' to 'Britons'. Although Shelley is a true internationalist, he is especially preoccupied with England. The deaths of Brandreth, Turner and Ludlam make it plain that those who have the authority to speak for England do so in an entirely coercive manner. 'England' is then a contested term: who owns it, speaks for it, who is a true Englishman (or, but Shelley apart the question hardly ever surfaces, Englishwoman)?

E. P. Thompson has argued that the contest is fought out entirely within the developing history of England. This position has recently been challenged by such Scottish Marxists as Angus Calder, Cairns Craig and Tom Nairn, who have wondered whether the development of class-consciousness could be quite so fully determined by an internal national history as Thompson and others have asserted. In an important contribution to the debate, Angus Calder writes:

> Christopher Hill and E. P. Thompson see class struggle as fundamental to English history, but conceive that struggle to be 'shaped by the conflicts and the accommodations between classes which do not need to be understood except in their relations with each other'. Their work can be defended as seeking to capture tradition and continuity from the Right so that Left domination appears legitimate, and it might seem unfair to deny the English their own left-wing nationalism while the Irish, Scots and Welsh are permitted theirs. Yet as Cairns Craig suggests, no Scottish historian would dream of writing about the Scottish working class as if it had not experienced English influence. Despite their magnificent scholarship, there is something inherently implausible in Hill's and Thompson's view. . . . Their work takes it for granted that English history is in effect self-contained: the American experiences of Paine and Cobbett are left out of the story. The land, England within its 'natural' boundaries, is ultimately the key to everything.[18]

There is considerable strength in this argument, although a problem which confronts any historian of English working-class consciousness has been precisely those 'natural' boundaries, for they have made possible the growth and sustaining of a form of unreflective patriotism which is in essence xenophobic. (And it is in the interest of those who arrogate themselves the authority to speak for England to encourage such xenophobia.) One might also argue that the development of class-consciousness beyond the 'natural' boundaries was made especially difficult at the end of the eighteenth century. For example, when, in the 1790s, members of the London Corresponding Society met with radicals in Edinburgh, Robert M'Queen, Lord Braxfield, had the leaders transported for fourteen years, mostly on trumped-up charges. If this were not discouragement enough, one can add such various matters as the suspension of Habeas Corpus, the blatant acts of oppression by the judiciary, and the Combination Acts – whose institution in 1800 made it illegal for working men to form political clubs or societies and prohibited their attempts to argue for improved pay and conditions. Connections across boundaries could hardly be easy.[19]

But the question that must concern us has less to do with the difficulties of working-class consciousness developing across boundaries than whether and to what extent it can be thought of as national, as self-consciously English at all. Shelley, the internationalist, dreaming of a future utopian man 'Equal, unclassed, tribeless, and nationless', nevertheless called to an England who 'yet sleeps', while other lands summon her to take her place among the nations of the free. This is set out, very schematically it must be admitted, in the 'Ode to Liberty'.

> England yet sleeps: was she not called of old?
>   Spain calls her now, as with its thrilling thunder
> Vesuvius wakens Aetna, and the cold
>   Snow-crags by its reply are cloven in sunder:
> O'er the lit waves every Aeolian isle
>   From Pithecusa to Pelorus
>   Howls, and leaps, and glares in chorus:
> They cry, 'Be dim; ye lamps of Heaven suspended o'er us!'
>   Her chains are threads of gold, she need but smile
>   And they dissolve . . .

Chains don't of course dissolve at a smile, any more than do threads. This is nothing like the imaginative exactness of the glorious Phantom of 'Sonnet: England in 1819', and it indicates the difficulties Shelley sometimes had in attempting to realise his vision. More importantly, where the sonnet had been justifiably cautious in its reading of likely events (for to say that the Phantom *may* burst is to leave the way open for its not doing so), the rapturous prophecies of the 'Ode to Liberty' feel unfocused. Here then, we must suppose that the very vapourishness of Shelley's language conceals grave doubts about the ability of England to wake from its sleep. And if we seek an explanation for this it will not lie merely in Shelley's own psychology – those fits of dejection to which he was liable – but in the objective situation, especially as that might demonstrate less a united Englishness than a regionalism or series of competing local interests. In short Englishness may recommend itself more readily to Shelley's kind of political idealist than to those people on behalf of whom he urged it.

P. M. S. Dawson suggests that we should place some emphasis on the basic distinction between

> The *metropolitan* Reformers like Burdett, Francis Place, Leigh Hunt, and the more radical Whigs, and the *provincial*, working-class Reformers, who had their own local leaders, and followed the political line of the more extreme national figures like Cartwright, Cobbett, and Henry Hunt, who had recognised the potential of this large popular movement. There was

inevitable tension and even friction between the two groups. To a Manchester man like Samuel Bamford, for example, London was 'the great Babylon'.[20]

This usefully points up divisions which cannot be closed by the claim for an overall national class-consciousness. It is not merely a matter of agreed or contested aims or projects. Far more substantial as a basis for radical disagreement or failure of alignment is the fact of regionalism. And it *is* a fact. I have argued elsewhere that socialist historians – cultural as well as social and political – have consistently under-emphasised the importance of regionalism, and that as a result they have produced monolithic accounts of English working-class experience whose tendency is to impose uniformity and conformity where these did not necessarily exist.[21] Shelley's appeal to the men of England is as understandable as it is honourable, but it runs the danger of accepting that pattern of conformity which those whom it seeks to define neither feel nor desire to feel. For against the appeal to Englishness is a radical recognition of how any appeal to nationalism turns into an appeal to patriotism, which then seeks to legitimise the idea of the state as a hierarchically-ordered institution, imaged both macrocosmically in the relationship between king and commoners and microcosmically, let us say, in the relationship between admiral and ratings. There were, of course, expressions of struggle against this pattern of conformity as well as compliance with it. The various mutinies during the period of the Napoleonic wars can be read both as a protest against hierarchy *and* as a desire to produce a different, more truly democratic, society. But at the same time we have to recognise that indifference to the idea of nationhood implied a set of commitments that could offer themselves as attractive alternatives to that Englishness which all too plainly denied meaningful identity to those on whom it was conferred.

Shelley is perhaps the last considerable radical to identify England in ardently optimistic terms as, at least potentially, a land of liberty. From now on, it is the *loss* of liberty and liberties which will engage radical thinkers; and they will customarily be forced to dismantle the pretension that the events of 1688 had inaugurated a society in which 'liberty' and 'England' could be treated as virtually synonymous terms. Those who speak on behalf of such a pretension have no reason to feel that liberty has failed them. It hasn't. But it is clear that liberty does not belong equally to all English people; it is the possession of a certain number who use what 'liberty' has given them to deny it to others. As Goldsmith was the first to recognise – or to be disturbed in recognising – liberty is a function of class interest. England increasingly belongs to those whom 'liberty' favours, in the strict sense that they are enabled to take over more of the land and the culture. They appropriate Englishness. It should therefore come as no surprise that a possible alternative for those not appropriated might seem to be not so much 'un-Englishness' – for who, without going into exile, could wish to identify with such a term – as regionalism. (Though among many forced into such exile – as émigrés or, more extremely, transportees – few felt any commitment to the nation of their birth.)[22]

Regionalism could offer itself as an alternative to the concept of Englishness that required a person to identify with the monarchy, the Church, and all those structures of the state which upheld liberty for some. 'Nation heere! nation theere! I'm a man and yo're another, but nation's nowheere.' The words are spoken by Daniel Robson in Elizabeth Gaskell's *Sylvia's Lovers*. In the event, he turns out to be wrong. The state eventually orders his execution, as it had ordered the execution of the three Derbyshire labourers in 1817 and the transportation of the six men of Tolpuddle. *Sylvia's Lovers*, written in 1863, is set in the 1790s, and Mrs Gaskell does her best to make her novel as historically accurate as possible. Robson's denial of the reality of the nation is meant to belong to that decade and to sound a note of defiance to the England that was making war on revolutionary France. But inevitably issues relevant to mid-Victorian England are also signalled in *Sylvia's Lovers*. Mrs Gaskell is keenly alert to the undercurrent of regionalism, one which repeatedly comes to the surface of her work, disrupting the developing national self-consciousness that her more middle-class characters embody. It is no accident that it should be a working-class man who puts the case against such nationalism.

In his essay 'The Industrial Revolution and the Regional Geography of England', John Langton notes 'the considerable regional fragmentation of various social and political movements in the late eighteenth and early nineteenth centuries', and he shows how radical politics in the north and Midlands developed in quite separate ways from each other and from the radicalism of London. He also makes the valuable point that 'regional differences of preoccupation, generalised beyond particular issues, entered popular consciousness', a claim which any study of Mrs Gaskell's writing about Manchester will bear out.[23]

All this goes counter to the claim for a united 'people' that is evident in much of Shelley's writing. But it is not surprising that he should think in terms of such a totalising, near monolithic, image, nor that he should discount or be unaware of the kinds of regional pressures and distinctions to which Langton draws attention and which I suggest must condition our understanding of the political actualities of early-nineteenth-century English. Living when he did, it was more or less inevitable that Shelley should have adopted the terms he did. Living *where* he did – that is, in exile – made it even more likely. From far off it is always easier to see things steadily and see them whole. Shelley wanted 'the people' to be 'the men of England'. As Jack Common said of his friend Eric Blair's decision to take the name George Orwell: 'he did not borrow it but compiled it, seeking for something that sounded solidly English . . . The rootless, non-dialect speakers of the public-school elite are apt to overvalue nationality, just as exiles do.' But that was not how the people always, or primarily, saw themselves.

In addition, regional commitments and identification came more readily to those who had no good reason to think of themselves as primarily belonging to a nation. They did not speak 'proper' English. They were disadvantage to the extent of being 'placed' by their regional accents and/or dialect. They were also, by and large, without the vote. Again, many who might be thought to have shared the kinds of class interests that prompted members of the London Corresponding Society to travel to Edinburgh did not in fact share them, for the obvious reason that they were not 'mechanicals', 'manufacturers' or 'operatives'. As socialist historians have often pointed out, the difficulty of finding an inclusive term for what they wish to identify as intrinsic to working-class experience is one reason why the consciousness of and about that class is slow to develop. But this then ought to suggest that the absence of the term may well imply the absence of the consciousness it is meant to signify. And the problem becomes especially acute when such consciousness is supposed to include that of 'peasants'.

This does not mean that the impulse to think and speak in regional terms was objectively correct. Far from it. Robson may claim to be free of the nation, but in the end he is destroyed by agents acting on behalf of that nation whose unreality he had proclaimed. Nevertheless, it is not difficult to see why regionalism had its attractions, nor why they could be exploited. At its most graspable, that is as a sense of the local, it is both powerful and consoling. It is what is familiar. It seems to offer a way of belonging, of 'rootedness'. Hence nostalgia, which is so dominant a source of imaginative writing – and experiencing – in the nineteenth century. Yet as this testifies, what is rooted can be uprooted. Against the wish for stability have to be set the forces – often felt as intrusive – that make for instability, for exposure to the unfamiliar. They are those economic social processes which are intrinsic to the 'nation'.

Besides, 'organic' terms of belonging come more usually and more aptly to those who have a vested interest in promoting a sense of community as stable, even though they do not usually have the interest of the community at heart. 'Rooted', 'dwellers', 'native': these terms, this language, regularly mutate into the language and cultural formation of pastoral. It is a way of closing down a more complex awareness of the shaping of identities as they are formed by the economic social process. By what ought to be a recognisable tactic, the regional can be condescended to as the 'provincial'. In short, the language and thus the induced sense of experience of regionalism typically fosters a false consciousness in those at whom it is directed, and who can themselves sometimes be lured into identifying with it. This brings us to the subject of the next chapter.

CHAPTER 7

Peasants and Outlaws: John Clare

I

Johnson had defined 'peasant' as 'a hind; one whose business is rural labour'. A hind was 'a boor; a mean rustick'. Goldsmith tried to free the term 'peasantry' from the condescension and dismissal which characterised Johnson's definitions, but his success was limited. William Cobbett says that peasantry is 'a *new* name given to the *country labourers* by the insulting boroughmongering and loan-mongering tribes'. It was not new in 1830, when this comment was made, but Cobbett was right to be angered by the insulting, habitual use of a term which sought to deny the reality of labour, and thus serious identity, to the people to whom it was applied.

Yet 'peasants' were undoubtedly allowed an identity of sorts. From Stephen Duck onwards, peasant poets could be accommodated within shaping notions of literariness. For Duck this meant that he had to cease being a peasant. Fashions, however, change. Burns capitalised on the opportunities which 'polite' interest in the low or 'uneducated' poets provided for him. Uneducated poets might be city-based and even involved in trade: peasant poets were not. They seemed to possess a peculiar advantage in that their affixed identity offered a quick way out of Manchester. 'Peasant poetry' could be easily appropriated for a world which was always being lost: the land of lost content. The eighteenth century lacked a word for this world. It had to make do with the phrase 'rustic charm'. But crucially, in 1795, comes the first modern use of the word 'quaint'. Hitherto, it had meant 'clever', or 'ingenious', or even 'elegant'. These are still dominant meanings at the end of the century, but a new one is added: 'Unusual or uncommon in character or appearance, but agreeable or attractive, esp. having an old-fashioned prettiness or daintiness.'

Such a shift in meaning was inevitable. The new sense, one that would gain in currency throughout the nineteenth century, was needed. Quaintness now becomes culturally acceptable, marketable. If we require proof of this we have only to look at those many late-eighteenth-century painters – Morland, Opie, the Norwich School – who 'paint the cot', as Crabbe contemptuously remarked. Or consider the poets of whom Crabbe was equally contemptuous.

> Ye gentle souls, who dream of rural ease,
> Whom the smooth stream and smoother sonnet please;
> Go! if the peaceful cot your praises share,
> Go look within, and ask if peace be there . . .
>
> (*The Village*, Part I, ll. 172–5)

Looking within formed no part of the tactics of genre poets and painters. Or rather, on those rare occasions when they crossed the threshold it was to encounter that life of tranquil contentment recommended by Hannah More, in *The Shepherd of Salisbury Plain*. Here, the charitable gentleman, Mr Johnson, on being granted his first sight of the shepherd's cot, cannot believe that people manage to live well within it.

> 'What, that hovel with only one room above and below, with scarcely any chimney? how is it possible you can live there with such a family!'
> 'O! it is very possible and very certain too,' cried the Shepherd. 'How many better men have been worse lodged! How many good christians have perished in prisons and dungeons, in comparison with which my cottage is a palace.'[1]

Given that this was written in 1794, its politics of cheerful subservience need to be understood in the context of that potentially convulsive period. Such politics are implicit in the terms 'quaint' and 'peasant'; for these emphatically offer a view of rural England the nature of which implies that those who, so defined, occupy it, will comply with the 'proper' users of the language who introduce and employ the terms as a means towards social definition. And these 'proper' speakers of English use the language of pastoral convention to confuse or obliterate the complicated actuality of social relations. 'Peasants' know their place. A 'quaint' cottage is 'naturally' a bit tumbledown.

At this point we need to reintroduce the term 'bard', which by the end of the eighteenth century was frequently hooked onto the adjective 'un-lettered'. The phrase looks back to those associations on which Gray had drawn, and also allows for connections between 'barbaric' and 'rude', connections which can then be 'naturally' extended towards the regional, even the local. To take two examples more or less at random. First, Robert Anderson's *Cumberland Ballads*. This initially appeared in 1798 and subsequently went through a number of enlarged editions. Anderson is introduced to readers as 'The Cumberland Bard'.[2] His ballads are all set to 'airs', and this makes an interesting contrast with *Lyrical Ballads*, for that title poses the highly individual (lyrical) against the collective (ballad). Second, *Rhymes of Northern Bards*, published in 1812. The compiler of this 'curious collection of old and new songs and poems peculiar to the Counties of Newcastle Upon Tyne, Northumberland, and Durham' was John Bell. Like his father, Bell was a Newcastle stationer and bookseller, and his volume was based on his own collection of 'books, curiosities, songs and all manner of printed matter'. In its wide variety of dialect words and heterodox material, much that Bell includes is markedly different from Percy's *Reliques* (1765), Scott's *Minstrelsy of the Scottish Border* (1802) or, most relevant in this instance, the various ballad compilations of the Scottish lawyer Joseph Ritson, whose interest in 'local' work did not prevent him from 'polishing' it for the polite audience at which it was aimed. Ritson's editions of *Gammer Gurton's Garland* (1783), *Bishoprick Garland* (1784) and *Northumberland Garland* (1794) were all 'rather genteel chapbooks', and *Northumberland Garland* in particular – published in the same year as *The Shepherd of Salisbury Plain* – 'has a thematic insistence on the brand of local "patriotism" which was being used as an excuse to squash dissentient voices throughout the country'.[3]

Nevertheless, Bell sold his edition at six shillings, which put it well beyond the reach of less well-off readers. And against the comparative lack of 'beautification' we have to set the fact that

> those few songs which appear to reflect at all accurately working people's beliefs and culture in general tend to stand out from the fare included for the benefit of lovers of apostrophes to disembodied mistresses, patriotic hurrah-songs, anti-Tory satire and 'comic' 'descriptions' of working people as seen by members of other classes.[4]

Anderson's *Cumberland Ballads* and Bell's *Rhymes* may, then, be regarded as forms of cultural containment. The role of the bards is identified in a manner that prohibits them from being taken seriously, except when they offer to speak in patriotic terms for England, and at *this* moment dialect is dropped and a form of standard English substituted. 'Trafalgar's Battle' comes early on in Bell's anthology – presumably it is strategically positioned so as to reassure the six-shilling customers of the decency of his enterprise. It begins:

> In a battle, you know, we Britons are strong;
> A battle, my friends, is the theme of my song;
> Had it not been for this, and the sake of my king,
> No mortal, I am sure, had forc'd me to sing,
>   And Nelson, that great man,
>   Who bother'd the Frenchman,
>   At Trafalgar's great battle, and died.

There is no suggestion that this poem is an anonymous folk ballad. The author is, we learn, J. Stawpert, who in the previous poem had masqueraded as the patriotic local John Diggons ('John Diggons be I, from a Country Town').[5] The dangers of acceding to the comfortable, conformable, image of regionalism are plain.

It is nevertheless hardly surprising that poets should have been quick to latch onto the fashion for bards and ballads. James Hogg's volume of ballads, *The Mountain Bard*, published in 1807, is typical, as is his styling himself 'The Ettrick Shepherd'. Louis Simpson notes that the major weakness, of Hogg's uncertain handling of language

> points to his main weakness as a poet – he does not know for whom he is writing. Should he write in Scots, or in English, or in a mixture of Scots and English? Should he write for the English-speaking Union, and the approval of Tory Edinburgh, or for his own common people?[6]

To speak of Hogg as belonging to the 'common people' is hardly correct, although the error is pardonable. But Simpson is quite right to see that the problem of language is bound to be a problem of audience, and one that troubles much greater poets than Hogg. It is, moreover, pointed up by the fact that now is the moment when poetry becomes fashionable among large numbers of the literate. As Byron remarked in *Beppo*, 'I've half a mind to tumble down to prose,/But verse is more in fashion, so here goes'.

As evidence of the fashion for poetry we might note that large sums of money were at this time paid to poets for their work: £2,000 in 1812 to Scott for *Rokeby*; £3,000 in 1817 to Moore for *Lallah Rooke*; the same amount to Crabbe in 1819 for *Tales of the Hall*. And after the publication of *Childe Harold* Byron woke to find himself not only famous but rich. Poetry was fashionable, and fashion meant business. According to Lee Erickson, much of the explanation for this has to do with printing costs. During the Napoleonic wars the importation of rags, from which paper was then made, became inevitably curtailed; accordingly, the cost of paper rose steeply. 'The greater cost of books generally encouraged poetry at the expense of prose and made poetry a more important part of the publishing market.'[7] But this can hardly be the whole story. To Erickson's account we need to add the stocking of private libraries for gentlemen, which in its turn has to be linked to developments in domestic architecture, interior furnishings and design. Bookcases were becoming features of many a 'polite', middling residence, as Crabbe notes in 'Procrastination', one of his *Tales in Verse* (1812).

> Within a costly case of varnish'd wood
> In level rows her polish'd volumes stood;
> Shown as a favour to a chosen few
> To prove what beauty for a book could do.

Crabbe wittily unpicks the language of taste. 'Polished' and 'beauty'; these are the clichés of literary approbation. But such polish, such beauty, are also literally skin deep, a matter of leather binding. Binding is a form of packaging, a way of making books acceptable as the possessions of gentlemen and ladies and those who aspire to their ranks. Since poetry and literature were at the time virtually interchangeable terms – as the novel and literature assuredly were not – it is hardly surprising that Crabbe should identify the purpose of books which are used to furnish a room in a manner reminiscent of Wordsworth's attack on the world of taste in his Preface to *Lyrical Ballads*, whose members 'furnish food for fickle tastes and fickle appetites'. Wordsworth by implication rightly traces to its root meaning the newly-fashionable word 'aesthetic': ('received by the senses' – which definition the OED dates to 1798). And he sees the vendors of 'tasteful' literature as supplying 'gross and violent stimulants' to readers who then 'talk of Poetry as a matter of amusement and idle pleasure; who will converse with us as gravely about a *taste* for Poetry as they express it, as if it were a thing as indifferent as a taste for Rope-dancing or Frontiniac, or Sherry'.[8]

Wordsworth's scorn indicates clearly enough his understanding that although poetry may be fashionable, this doesn't mean that those who follow the fashion take a serious interest in poetry. Quite the reverse. The interest in local bards is nothing if not trivial. (Which is not to say that the 'bards' are themselves necessarily trivial). Trivial, too, is the overlapping and coincident interest in 'peasant' poets. Nor can it be assumed that the shifts in fashion are in any sense arbitrary. My present purpose is to suggest how political and social forces help to shape and partly determine fashions, tastes, modes.

Publishers are crucially significant as actors and acted upon, for they respond to and at the same time seek to direct their readers' tastes. When in 1820 the publishers Taylor and Hessey brought out Clare's first volume, *Poems Descriptive of Rural Life and Scenery*, Taylor provided for it an introduction which begins:

> The following Poems will probably attract some notice by their intrinsic merit; but they are also entitled to attention from the circumstances under which they were written. They are the genuine productions of a young Peasant, a day-labourer in husbandry, who has had no advantages of education beyond others of his class; and though Poets in this country have seldom been fortunate men, yet he is, perhaps, the least favoured by circumstances, and the most destitute of friends, of any that ever existed.[9]

There then follows an account of Clare's birth and early years.

Taylor means to be sympathetic. Yet that placing term 'Peasant' clearly reveals the publishers' shaping intentions, and these are underpinned by the design of the title page, which identifies Clare as 'A NORTHAMPTONSHIRE PEASANT'. Below that is affixed as epigraph:

> 'The Summer's Flower is to the Summer sweet,
> 'Though to itself it only live and die.'
>
> *Shakspeare*

Clare, the summer flower, the child of nature, is thus produced in a manner that inevitably calls to mind Gray's plangent description of the flowers, born to bloom and die, which waste their sweetness on the desert air.

The placing runs through the entire volume, and in so complete a manner that it is doubtful whether Taylor and Hessey have the right to speak of the book as housing Clare's 'genuine productions'. They alter his spelling and his punctuation, lay out the poems according to the dictates of acceptable literary conventions; and lines, stanzas and, on occasion, entire poems are dropped. In short, *Poems Descriptive* is editorialised to market Clare as a 'peasant poet'. The upshot is that he is denied his (own) voice, his (own) identity. (Though we shall see that Clare has a number of voices, and identities.) Moreover, Taylor and Hessey not only interfere with the poems to bring them more into line with what was expected of peasant poets, they also bow to the wishes of Clare's self-appointed patron, Lord Radstock, who had a very strong dislike of Clare's unsentimental writing about the society he knew intimately, and an even stronger dislike of Clare's politics. Yet again, regionalism has been captured and tamed.

Clare was therefore not likely to be mollified by the fact that *Poems Descriptive* was a publishing success. He would have bitterly assented to the truth of Blake's remark, one of the Marginalia to Reynold's *Discourses*, that 'The Enquiry in England is not whether a Man has Talents and Genius, But whether he is Passive and Polite and a Virtuous Ass and Obedient to Noblemen's Opinions in Arts and Science. If he is, he is a good Man. If not, he must be starved.' On the occasion of the third edition of *Poems Descriptive*, Clare wrote to Hessey:

> I am cursed mad about it the Judgement of T. is a button hole lower in my opinion – it is good – but too subject to be tainted by medlars *false delicasy* damn it I hate it beyond everything[10]

Clare is referring to Taylor's decision to drop 'My Mary' and 'Ways of the Wake', as altogether too strong for fashionable taste to swallow.[11] And there was worse to come. In the fourth edition Taylor cut lines from 'Helpstone' which detail the effects of enclosure. According to J. W. and Anne Tibble, Taylor 'was willing to omit the odd dozen lines out of gratitude for what Radstock had done for the Subscription list'.[12] It sounds innocent enough. But the Tibbles conveniently forget the letter in which Clare spits out his anger to Taylor over the loss of lines which Radstock had said were tainted with 'radical slang'. 'Damn that canting way of being forced to please I say – I cant abide it and one day or other I will show my Independence more strongly than ever.'[13] These are the lines that caused all the fuss:

> Oh who could see my dear green willows fall
> What feeling heart but dropt a tear for all
> Accursed wealth o'er bounding human laws
> Of every evil thou remainst the cause
> Victims of want those wretches such as me
> Too truly lay their wretchedness to thee

> Thou art the bar that keeps from being fed
> And thine our loss of labour and of bread
> Thou art the cause that levels every tree
> And woods bow down to clear a way for thee[14]

The first couplet seems initially to speak for that regret at the principle of change which we have seen to be at the heart of the picturesque aesthetic. This is often enough voiced through the 'fall' of trees, as in Cowper's 'Poplar Field': 'The poplars are fell'd; farewell to the shade,/And the whispering sound of the cool colonnade'. But, lovely though the aural effects of this poem are, they collaborate with Cowper's musings on 'the perishing pleasures of man', where the loss of such pleasures is taken to be inevitable. (The poplars 'are felled', and this passive construction implies that nobody and nothing need be identified as the agent of their felling.)

The drive of Clare's lines is very different. The cursed wealth 'o'er bounding human laws' is an echo of Milton's Satan who, on arriving at the heavily wooded entrance to paradise, 'Due entrance ... disdained, and in contempt,/At one slight bound high over leaped all bound' (*Paradise Lost*, Book IV, ll. 180–1). Human laws – natural rights – are helpless to oppose those thousands of Acts which in the latter half of the eighteenth century and early part of the nineteenth legalised enclosures and then dropped the bar on labourers, not necessarily in the sense that the labourers immediately lost employment (new improvements in arable farming led in some instances to an increased workforce), but because particular kinds of labour became obsolete and, more importantly, because the already poor relationships between landowners and labourers now deteriorated still further.

But after 1815 rural depopulation rapidly increased. The Corn Laws meant that farmers inevitably did deny labourers their bread. In addition, 'improving' landlords are from Clare's vantage point a malign power. There is a precise wit in his writing of those trees which, like a crowd of supplicants, 'bow down to clear a way for thee'. In his *Pastoral*: 'Summer' Pope had written:

> Where-e'er you walk, cool Gales shall fan the Glade,
> Trees, where you sit, shall crowd into a Shade,
> Where-e'er you tread, the blushing Flow'rs shall rise,
> And all things flourish where you turn your Eyes.

In this playful mythopoeia nature co-operates with human directives to bring about an Edenic fullness of being which amounts to a joyful plenitude. Clare's trees, on the other hand, are helplessly servile. They are like a crowd of men who co-operate in their own destruction.

Those who o'er bound human laws have state laws on their side. True, since 1722 it had been a capital offence to 'cut down or otherwise destroy any trees planted in any avenue, or growing in any garden, orchard or plantation, for ornament, shelter or profit'. But this law was directed towards the protection of private woodland. Where open woods began to come under law, the law worked against the common people. From 1766 wood gathering became a criminal offence. According to Robert Bushaway, 'where records survive, it would seem that wood theft was the most common form of crime in the countryside, possibly the most common way in which the laws and rights of landed property were infringed'.

During the Napoleonic wars timber for ships was in great demand. Nevertheless, in the shadow of the law

> forest communities . . . continued to affirm their customary rights, gleaning faggots and offal wood, cutting young trees for maypoles and green oak for Maytime processions and, on occasion, mutilating or destroying trees in plantations to signify their disaffection with the encroaching gentry.[15]

The woods which Clare is writing about are clearly those of customary rights (rights that Goody Blake affirmed against Harry Gill). Hence the cause of his bitterness that they should 'bow down', should lose their rights.

This brings us to a further point. Clare's woods provide a kind of sweet, equal republic, they are wild woods, whereas from the point of view of authority 'the most agreeable woodland was tidily planted or securely partitioned in great estates. Here trees confirmed power of property.'[16] By the same token, of course, authority sees in wild woods a condition of lawlessness. Such woods harbour outlaws.[17] That they now 'bow down' means therefore that they confess subservience to a greater, o'er bounding, power. It follows that Radstock was quite right to recognise Clare's 'radical slang', for the account of woods as ideally non-subservient implies a vision of society as essentially republican, egalitarian; and the sadness of Clare's lines comes from his recognition of the defeat of this vision. Such a defeat is made the more complete by Radstock's having the lines removed. They too bow down to clear a way for the safe 'peasant poet'.

Clare's comments to Taylor on Crabbe's *Tales of the Hall* are therefore instructive.

> Whats he know of the distresses of the poor musing over a snug coal fire in his parsonage box – if I had an enemy I coud wish to torture I woud not wish him hung nor yet at the devil my worst wish shoud be a weeks confinement in some vicarage to hear an old parson & his lecture on the wants & wickedness of the poor & consult a remedy or a company of marketing farmers thrumming over politics in an alehouse or a visionary methodist arguing on points of religion either is bad enough.[18]

Here, Clare speaks as one of 'the poor', although his use of such a phrase hints at his putting a certain distance between himself and those of whom he speaks. It was a distance that could be affected by his becoming 'independent' as a poet, or so he sometimes hoped, just as Stephen Duck must have hoped. But this was to prove impossible, and not because he could never become a part of literary orthodoxy. The problems lay elsewhere. For one thing, he was necessarily dependent on publishers, patrons and readers. For another, his fame, brief as it was, opened him up to inevitable and unresolvable contradictions. In the most obvious sense, he lacked an audience. Those who most fully shared his language and understood the sources from which his poetry was derived – it included that tradition of folk song and ballad which his father had passed onto him and which he himself added to,[19] as well as local knowledge, popular radical politics and ways of thinking – this audience was lost to a poet who was published in London, and whose work was, by the processes I have glanced at, offered for absorption into 'polite' literature and *its* audience as a species of harmless regionalism, as peasant poetry, the work of an unlettered bard.

Yet Clare was never, and could not be, absorbed. If we are tempted to see in this heroic resistance we would be wrong. We would also be guilty of ignoring what was conceivably the greatest problem confronting him.

> Chauncy Hare Townsend came to see me one evening in summer & askd me if John Clare lived there I told him I was he & he seemd supprised & askd agen to be satisfied for I was shabby & dirty he asked freely & was dissapointed I dare say at finding I had little or nothing to say for I always had a natural depression of spirits in the presence of strangers that took from me all power of freedom or familiarity & made me dull & silent for [when] I attempted to say anything I could not reccolect it & made so many hums & hahs in the story that I was obliged to leave it unfinished at last I often tryd to master this confusion by trying to talk over reasonings & arguments as I went about in my rambles which I thought I did pretty well but as soon as I got before anybody I was as much to seek as ever C H T was a little affeecting withh dandyism & mimicked a lisp in his speech which he owd to affectation rather than habit otherwise he was a feeling & sensible young man he talked about Poets & poetry & the fine scenery of the lakes & other matters for a good while & when he left me he put a folded paper in my hand which I found after he had gone was a sonnet & a pound bill he promised & sent me Beattie's *Minstrel* some letters passd between us & I sent him a present of my *Village Minstrel* when I never heard of him afterwards he has since published a volume of Poems.[20]

This extract from Clare's projected autobiography powerfully communicates a helpless feeling of social inferiority, where the power is all the greater for its occasional innocence ('a natural depression of spirits in the presence of strangers'). This is very like Pip's initial encounter with Estella in *Great Expectations*, still more like Joe's with Miss Havisham. Against Townsend's asking 'freely', we have Clare's 'hums & hahs'. It is recognisably the same man who notes that 'I had a timidity that made me very awkward and silent in the presence of my superiors.' Yet we cannot impute conscious snobbery to those 'superiors' in their dealings with Clare. On the contrary: they behaved to him better than he felt was true of the majority of those among whom he lived:

> I was courted to keep company with the 'betters' in the village but I never noticd the fancied kindness the old friends & neighbours in my youth are my friends & neighbours now & I have never spent an hour in any of the houses of the farmers since I met with my [success] or mixd in their company as equals[21]

Superiors in London really are superior. 'Betters' in the village aren't. The inverted snobbery implied by those quotation marks is deeply revealing of Clare's confused registering of gaps and separations in social relations that press in on him as he tries to negotiate a sense of himself as 'independent'. There is a variable stress on the terms 'peasant' and 'poet', which comes out again when he remarks that

> the lower orders of England from their almost total disregard of Poesy have been judged rather too harshly as destitute of the finer feelings of humanity & taste & it is a paradox yearly witnessed of the apparent apathy & unconcern with which they witness the tragedy of death displaying farces (sic) as seemingly happy as on a holiday excursion yet these very people will stand around an old ballad singer & with all the romantic enthusiasm of pity shed tears over the doggerel tales of imaginary distress[22]

Disregard of Poesy? But 'Poesy' itself is a 'polite' term, a way of putting what it stands for beyond the reach of the 'lower orders'. Poesy is for superiors. Yet Clare loved those ballads and 'doggerel tales' which he here seems to be condescending to, as though they aren't for him. (He collected them and found a means of notation to transcribe the tunes they were sung to.) And then we note that this implied denial of relationship is itself qualified by the repeated qualifiers: 'judged rather too harshly'; 'apparent apathy'; 'seemingly happy'. He is attempting to mediate for a 'polite' audience, and the strain shows.

It is particularly acute in *The Shepherd's Calendar*. Here, Clare on the one hand describes the work of various carefully identified kinds of labourers: ploughman, woodman, sower, for example; and on the other can find no collective noun for their activities other than 'Labour', which then leads him to use the placing term 'Clown'. At the conclusion to 'June' he writes of 'good old times' when farmers and hired hands came together in song and feast:

> When masters made them merry wi their men
> Whose coat was like his neighbors russet brown
> And whose rude speech was vulgar as his clown
> Who in the same horn drank the rest among
> And joind the chorus while a labourer sung

> All this is past – and soon may pass away
> The time torn remnant of the holiday
> As proud distinction makes a wider space
> Between the genteel and the vulgar race[23]

In the glossary of terms they add to their edition of *The Shepherd's Calendar*, Robinson and Summerfield identify 'clown' as 'yokel, rustic, labourer', without any apparent awareness of how their running the terms together is bound to collapse important distinctions between the purely literary and the socially exact.

But it is possible to recognise why Clare shifts between the two. 'Clown' is for his readers. 'Labourer' speaks from a knowledge that denies those readers their presumed authority, their knowledge that all peasants are clowns, rustics, yokels. Clare also identifies 'rude speech' as nowadays the clown's alone. But what and how does Clare himself speak? Merely to ask the question is to recognise the tensions within him and his work. He can't, surely, wish to be with the clowns, certainly not if that's how, in naming them, he thinks of them. And so in *The Parish*, written in the early 1820s but never published in his lifetime, he protests against Young Brag's 'illspelt trash' and 'bad English'. The whole enterprise of *The Parish* is fraught with contradiction. It is a satire on village 'pretension' and yet is written from the presumed standpoint of exactly that superiority or proud distinction which Clare distrusted and by which he was victimised. It is therefore significant that the lines from 'June' quoted above were cut by Taylor when the severely mauled *Shepherd's Calendar* appeared in 1827. Presumably he knew that Clare's ill-spelt and bad English made it impossible for him to stand with those of proud distinction.

Yet against this we need to recall Clare's remark that Chauncy Townsend 'has since published a volume of Poems'. Gentlemen, unlike jealously pretentious 'betters', do such things. Clowns don't. Peasant poets may, but the poems they write have to be appropriate ones. A late poem of Clare's, 'He Loved the Brook's Soft Sound', which was written in the Northampton asylum, ends:

> A silent man in lifes affairs
> A thinker from a Boy
> A Peasant in his daily cares –
> The Poet in his joy

This identification of the nature of 'the Poet' by means of the emotion of joy is familiar from Wordsworth and Coleridge. Clare claims this nature for himself and makes an absolute distinction between the accident of social identity – 'A Peasant in his daily cares' – and what he hopes to claim as a more 'essential' identity. But the fact that he writes of himself in the third person implies how little at ease he can be with the identity he lays claim to;

and whoever transcribed the poem for him added a title which, while it in one sense wickedly travesties Clare's meaning, in another goes far to explain his unease. The poem is called 'The Peasant Poet'.

I I

The writing and subsequent history of the poem we know as 'The Peasant Poet' between them make plain the tensions and contradictions in Clare's position. These are nowhere more eloquently brought out than in Chapter 10 of the autobiography, 'My Visit to London'.

> I started in the old Stamford Coach but I felt very awkward in my dress My mind was full of expectations all the way about the wonders of the town which I had often heard my parents tell storys about by the winter fire when I turned to the reccolections of the past by seeing people at my old occupations of ploughboy & ditching in the fields by the road-side while I was lolling in a coach the novelty created such strange feelings that I coud almost fancy that my identity as well as my occupations had changd that I was not the same John Clare but that some stranger soul had jumped into my skin.[24]

For all the self-consciousness about this there is no reason to question the painful care with which Clare sets down his sense of a divided, troubled identity. The manual labourer has become identified, as poet, with mental activity, and has thus acquired a special status. Clare is reformulating the issues we saw Wordsworth exploring in 'Resolution and Independence', though from a very different perspective. Here, it will help to refer to a remark of Raymond Williams:

> To be able to read and write is a major advance in the possibility of sharing in the general culture of a literate society, but there are still typically determinate conditions in which the exercise of these faculties is differently directed. Thus in late eighteenth-century England it was argued that the poor should be taught to read, but not to write. Reading would enable them to read the Bible, and learn its morality, or later to read instructions and notices. Having anything to write on their account was seen as a crazy or mischievous idea.[25]

There is a very real sense in which Clare's methods of articulating his poetry can be seen as a struggle to be free of the medium of writing, or at all events of print. His shaping of poems, of their rhymes, their syntax, even their use of dialect, is primarily for the ear. As Barbara Strang has importantly argued, 'reading Clare to oneself is unusually like reading aloud.'[26] Having your poems appear within the covers of a book makes for cultural and social respectability. Becoming a printed poet, and a London poet at that, emphasises a separation from that oral tradition in which Clare was deeply rooted. But the roots are partly bared by his publishers. He is a 'peasant poet'. Or, as variation, 'The Village Minstrel' (the title of his volume in

1821). That Clare sometimes co-operated with these stylings only rein-forces the impossibility of his ever realising his hope that he could be independent.

For *The Village Minstrel* was not Clare's choice of title. He wanted to call this second volume *Ways in a Village*. The title his publishers substituted makes plain their determination to market him in the manner we should expect. Minstrels are an even more limited species than bards. The next volume, *The Shepherd's Calendar* (1827), is so insistently editorialised that it can scarcely be called Clare's own work. As Robinson and Summerfield note, Taylor's acknowledgement to Clare that he had been compelled to 'cut out a vast many lines' tells only half the story.

> Every month of [the poem] was lopped with greater or lesser brutality . . . Most of Taylor's excisions are frankly unintelligible to us, unless on the supposition that he found many passages too 'unphilosophical', and too concerned with everyday events . . . On other occasions Taylor seems to have cut out lines because they did not agree with his sense of poetical fitness, as when Clare describes fairies crowding in cupboards 'As thick as mites in rotten cheese'. . . . In Taylor's version, too, the labourer, 'stript in his shirt', is not allowed to sit beside the maiden 'in her unpind gown'; no criticism of enclosing farmers or 'tyrant justice' appears; and labourers are not even allowed, in an age of industriousness, to be:
>
> > Glad that the harvests end is nigh
> > And weary labour nearly bye

It goes without saying that Taylor 'mended' grammar and punctuation throughout. He also removed dialect words. 'Similarly the names of country games are omitted because they are not familiar to the editor.'[27]

The unkindest cuts of all were aimed at the last volume published in Clare's lifetime. His proposed title for this volume, *The Midsummer Cushion*, was changed to *The Rural Muse*, and a number of crucial poems were omitted. They included 'To a Fallen Elm', a great poem whose starting point was a threat by Clare's parents' landlord to cut down the tree that stood behind their cottage. This becomes the occasion for Clare to voice his angry, bitter awareness of those who 'wrong another by the name of right'.[28] It is not to be wondered at that 'To a Fallen Elm' and others like it should be omitted. Yet again Clare was being fitted to a comfortable image, one which included silencing him as a politically radical poet, whose radicalism was an English radicalism if for no other reason than that it grew out of his experiences. And here we come to the heart of the matter.

'To a Fallen Elm' was probably written as early as 1821. It is one of a group of poems from the years between 1820 and 1824 which between them variously articulate Clare's sense of dispossession, his recognition of how his voice, his identity, is being shaped in a way that distorts to the point of lying. This is confirmed in the most savagely ironic manner when Taylor refuses to publish the very poems that explore and testify to the distortion. The double recognition feeds into the conclusion of Clare's sonnet, 'England in 1830'.

> And will these jailors rivet every chain
>   Anew, yet loudest in their mockery be,
> To damn her into madness with disdain,
>   Forging new bonds and bidding her be free?

'England in 1830', which naturally enough was never published in Clare's lifetime (Taylor trumping Clare's ace), identifies, and identifies with, an England of the dispossessed. 'To damn her into madness with disdain'. The line makes sense only if we understand that the damned are all those people subject to others who 'o'erbound Human laws', and who in doing so make endless laws which bind the rest ('Forging new bonds and bidding her be free'). This is the England in which, as Corrigan and Sayer remark, 'the most comprehensive battery of legislative, practical and other regulatory devices against the emerging working class is . . . established'.[29]

But it is also the England of Captain Swing; and the events of Tolpuddle are four years away. At the end of one of his greatest poems, 'The Flitting', Clare speaks of nature's love of 'little things', and keeps faith with those who resist bondage:

> And still the grass eternal springs
> Where castles stood and grandeur died.

Towards the end of the eighteenth century, it was not unusual for grass to be identified with the 'plebeians'. 'The more they are taxed and trod upon the more they multiply.'[30] Clare's springing grass is to be read as an invading army, breaking bonds, surging towards freedom by overwhelming castles and the grandees who die defending them.

It is tempting to relate this exuberant affirmation of continuous energy, this celebration of victory over disdain, to Shelley's glorious phantom. Not that Clare could have known Shelley's sonnet, because that was published for the first time in 1839. But their rhetorical devices may seem to develop out of a shared political radicalism. There are, however, important distinctions, which relate partly to the different moments at which Shelley and Clare write and the different positions they occupy. Shelley, the ardently optimistic radical, places himself 'on the side of the people', and foresees eventual struggle and triumph. Clare, endlessly exposed to the testing, bewildering and embittering experiences of separation and contradiction, of repeated defeats, of the legal appropriation of the people's – common – land, is not characteristically to be identified with the powerful affirmations with which he concludes 'The Flitting'. The very title of the poem tells how little he can make a stand. He is more often in a prolonged, conceivably unending retreat, partly occasioned by those experiences of separation that leave him deeply unsure about where to locate a sense of community other than somewhere 'back there', in the past.

Here, we may note Clare's praise of Cobbett as one of the most powerful writers of the day. The praise is, however, qualified.

> I am no politician but I think a reform is wanted – not the reform of the mob were the bettering of the many is only an apology for improving the few – nor the reform of partys where the benefit of one is the destruction of the other but a reform that woud do good & hurt none I am sorry to see that the wild notions of public spouters always keep this reform out of sight – & as extreams must be met by extreams – the good is always lost like a plentiful harvest in bad weather – mobs never were remembered for a good action but I am sorry to see it now & then verging into the middle classes of society whose knowledge ought to teach them commonsense & humanity for if they have it they never let it get into their speeches[31]

This was intended to form part of an essay on Industry, and Clare attempts an even-handed distribution of praise and blame, of non-party judiciousness, which is suspect if for no other reason than that he is aiming for an audience which was hardly likely to sympathise with those whose industry did not guarantee them the vote. In a sense, Clare doesn't know what he's talking about. In another, his rejection of both 'mobs' and 'middle classes' means he has nowhere to go except into retreat, or out of bounds. And this is the case with many of his finest poems, which are preoccupied with his sense of being an outlaw. They complement other poems where, as we have seen, he attacks the enclosers, those disdainful ones who make laws to suit themselves and fetter others.

For example, in 'The Mores', written some time between 1821 and 1824 and never published in his lifetime, Clare speaks of

> plains that stretched them far away
> In uncheckt shadows of green brown and grey
> Unbounded freedom ruled the wandering scene
> Nor fence of ownership crept in between
> To hide the prospect of the following eye
> Its only bondage was the circling sky . . .
> Now this sweet vision of my boyish hours
> Free as spring clouds and wild as summer flowers
> Is faded all – a hope that blossomed free
> And hath been once no more shall ever be
> Inclosure came and trampled on the grave
> Of labours rights and left the poor a slave . . .

'Uncheckt shadows' punningly echoes, in order to subvert, the 'chequered shades' produced by careful landscaping. Clare's shadows of 'green brown and grey' describe a natural scene, one that is the very opposite of emparkment, let alone 'improved' farmland. Such a scene may truly be called 'wandering'. Its freedom from rule, from the landscaper's art which 'directs' the eye, also testifies to the fact that those who inhabit the scene are free to roam or wander about it. They are not to be kept to paths or forced to view from a fixed prospect the land they share. This is not so much nature beyond bounds as unbounded nature. But bondage comes in the shape of those fences which creep in like spies or some sly intruder whose purpose is not known until too late. Now, wanderers become transgressors. Clare breaks the natural shape of the couplets at this point. The syntax runs on disruptively against the rhyme, although we only, suddenly, realise this as we come to the end of the line 'To hide the prospect of the following eye': the fracturing of the couplets' harmonies are until then hidden from us. (It is important to note this, because Clare so regularly works *with* line and rhyme that on those rare occasions when he works *against* them it is clear that he is doing so under exceptional pressure.)

Wandering guarantees human freedom. Bondage, on the other hand, leaves 'the poor a slave'. The agent of this bondage is 'Inclosure', whose values are characterised in terms of an orderly meanness, a deadly constriction of the human spirit.

> Fence now meets fence in owners little bounds
> Of field and meadow large as garden grounds
> In little parcels little minds to please . . .
> Each little tyrant with his little sign
> Shows where man claims earth glows no more divine
> On paths to freedom and to childhood dear
> A board sticks up to notice 'no road here'

('The poor should be taught to read . . . Reading would enable them . . . to read instructions and notices.') The 'no road here' notices which effectively proclaim 'earth glows no more divine' are, then, the signs of denial of God-given freedom: natural justice is forbidden to English men and women. God has absconded or been forced from his own creation, and Clare's trope voices a greater sense of loss than Wordsworth's failed visionary gleam, for where that had been about the failure of an individual imagination, this speaks of a deep, representative and most grievous loss of rights, freedoms, and even selfhood. Memory, after all, insists on recalling those now gone as forever lost, so that only in memory is Clare able to possess those spots of earth bound up in intimate knowledge and associations.

'The Mores' articulates a representative English experience, even though the voice through which the experience is uttered has that especial eloquence which belongs to a great poet. (No English poet apart from Dryden can match Clare for scorn or – even – disdainful handling of 'little minds'.) And if it is asked how representative claims can be made for an experience which speaks from outlawry, it ought to be enough to recall Lloyd George's question, put some forty years or so after Clare's death: 'Who made 10,000 people owners of the soil, and the rest of us trespassers in the land of our birth?'

This is not to suggest that we should place Clare and the class to which he problematically belonged in some romantic golden-world-turned-to-lead by the sudden intervention of law; they were not and had never been Merrymounters. As E. P. Thompson remarks:

> What was often at issue was not property, supported by law, against no-property; it was alternative definitions of property-rights; for the landowner enclosure – for the cottager, common rights . . . For as long as it remained possible, the ruled – if they could find a purse and a lawyer – would actually fight for their rights by means of law . . . When it ceased to be possible to continue the fight at law, men still felt a sense of legal wrong: the propertied had obtained their power by illegitimate means . . .
> law was often a definition of actual agrarian *practice*, as it had been pursued 'time out of mind' . . . The farmer or forester in his daily occupation was moving within visible or invisible structures of law: this merestone which marked the division between strips; that ancient oak – visited by processional on each Rogation Day – which marked the limits of parish grazing; those other invisible (but potent and sometimes legally enforceable) memories as to which parishes had the right to take turfs in this waste and which parishes had not . . .[32]

The loss of such rights through alteration of the law, and the alteration of the landscape which visibly insists on legal alterations – these are the tokens of that disorientation by means of which memory is at once made useless and at the same time presses in on the consciousness of the dispossessed with such urgency as to increase the disorientation. In which case the flight to the past, through memory, is a metaphoric attempt to stabilise a destabilised set of social arrangements and/or consciousness of those arrangements. This, I claim, is a form of outlawry, although the term will require justification.

Trespasser, fugitive, outlaw: these are the kinds of conditions, the forms of experience, which Clare addresses in his many poems about birds and animals. But the poems are not opportunistic metaphors of human circumstance. Where Shelley can unembarrassedly treat the skylark as a radiant image of the 'pure' poet, Clare's skylark is, always, a skylark. And yet his observations link the bird to the equally exactly observed hare, 'to terrors wide awake'. The lark lies in her nest, 'Where boys unheeding past . . . and so pass along/While its low nest moist with the dews of morn/Lye safely with the leveret in the corn'. Lying low offers, however, a temporary respite at best. When the corn is reaped the grown hare will be shot as it bolts from its last refuge. The poem doesn't say this, but then it doesn't have to. The vulnerability of little things, and the stratagems by means of which they try to keep beyond bounds, out of reach of destructive forces, is the subtext of nearly all of these poems. The reed bird which hides 'in thickest shade/Where danger never finds a path to throw/A fear on comforts nest securely made' leads to the reflection that 'man can seldom share/A spot as hidden from the haunts of care'. For the most apparently secure place – home itself – can be threatened by those who o'er bound human laws. Here, as so often, Clare speaks from an experience which is very plainly an English one. Yet such an experience runs counter to the Englishness that was developing and being endorsed by those voices which, like the later Wordsworth's, spoke for ownership, for belonging, and whose voting rights were secure. These are the voices of men who are able to think of themselves as 'free' Englishmen. Like Thomson and Dyer before them, but with even less excuse, they can plausibly assert England to be the land of liberty – *their* liberty – and claim for themselves an independence and a right to wander, to be 'free' to fix their habitations wherever they choose. For Clare, as for thousands like him, such freedom, such choice, remained a forlorn dream. This has a crucial bearing on much of his work.

'The Flitting', for example, was occasioned by Clare's removal from his cottage at Helpstone to one at Northborough, some three miles away. The move, engineered by well-meaning patrons, was intended to make him independent. Clare used the word in order to defend himself against charges that he had been 'given the cottage to live in'. But the poem is about insecurity, loss of relationship between self and place, and thus about a terrible disorientation: and it ends with the vision of future revenge to which I have already referred. In other words, it isn't about feeling grateful, nor does it give thanks for the good deeds of Mrs Emmerson *et al.*[33] The opening lines make this plain enough:

> Ive left my own old home of homes
> Green fields and every pleasant place
> The summer like a stranger comes
> I pause and hardly know her face . . .
> I sit me in my corner chair
> That seems to feel itself from home . . .

'I dwell on trifles like a child', he says later in the poem. 'Dwelling', as was noted in Chapter 5, is a key word. The loss of dwelling poses a decisive threat to a secure sense of self, and 'The Flitting' is about this, too. But then we may compare 'The Flitting' to 'The Mouse's Nest', for this poem, while it displays the 'insatiable habit of marvelling' which Arnold Rattenbury rightly attributes to Gilbert White and might even more rightly attribute to Clare, is also about a flitting. Clare disturbs a mouse which 'bolted in the wheat/with all her young ones hanging at her teats'. It is a grotesquely odd sight, one which at first brings disdainful laughter and aggressive curiosity:

> I ran and wondered what the thing could be
> And pushed the knapweed bunches where I stood
> When the mouse hurried from the crawling brood
> The young ones squeaked and when I went away
> She found her nest again among the hay

This dislocation in the mouse's secure activities is pointed by the verse itself. There are disruptions of the couplets' closures, and as with that moment in 'The Mores' to which I drew attention, so here: 'stood/brood' forces together lines which syntax divides. But order and harmony then return with the mouse's return to her home: 'and when I went away/She found her nest again among the hay'. Comfort is restored, but the pathos of the mouse's stratagems to avoid danger stems from our recognition of their inadequacy.

Yet stratagems, no matter how frail, are all that are available. The great poem 'To the Snipe' begins:

> Lover of swamps
> The quagmire overgrown
> With hassock tufts of sedge – where fear encamps
> Around thy home alone

> The trembling grass
> Quakes from the human foot
> Nor bears the weight of man to let him pass
> Where he alone and mute

> Sitteth at rest
> In safety near the clump
> Of hugh flag-forrest that thy haunts invest
> Or some old sallow stump . . .

It is not until we get to the third line of the second stanza that we can be sure that the snipe is in fact safe from the fear which encamps around its home like a besieging army ('trembling' and 'quakes' are literal and at the same time metaphorically charged terms and, to extend the line of argument about the available meanings of grass, I would argue that a fear of immediate invasion from 'human foot' springs from Clare's deep sense of rights trampled on). That the snipe should be safe here and here only gives deeper significance to what might at first seem the picturesque whimsy of the opening line: 'Lover of swamps'. In a later stanza Clare notes that 'in these marshy flats and stagnant floods/Security pervades'. Hence, other birds 'from mans dreaded sight will ever steal/To the most dreary spot'. At the end of the poem Clare tentatively claims to have derived comfort from his observations, and here, it might be said, he moves closer to Wordsworth and Shelley and to their observations about birds.

> Thy solitudes
> The unbounded heaven esteems
> And here my heart warms into higher moods
> And dignifying dreams
>
> I see the sky
> Smile on the meanest spot
> Giving to all that creep or walk or flye
> A calm and cordial lot
>
> Thine teaches me
> Right feelings to employ
> That in the dreariest places peace will be
> A dweller and a joy

Yet Clare refuses the opportunity for the kind of enthusiastic identification which characterises Wordsworth's address 'To the Cuckoo'. There, the bird's 'wandering voice' is made to tell of 'visionary hours'. That the cuckoo's *is* a wandering voice is undoubtedly important. It embodies or calls up that freedom which Wordsworth recalls enjoying as a boy and the memory of which is re-animated for the mature poet by the bird's song. (The poem is very similar in strategy and meaning to 'I wandered lonely as a Cloud'.)

> And I can listen to thee yet;
> Can lie upon the plain
> And listen, till I do beget
> That golden time again.
>
> O blessed Bird! the earth we pace
> Again appears to be
> An unsubstantial faery place;
> That is fit home for Thee!

Clare could never write like this, of course, because for him the earth isn't to be freely paced, let alone thought of as unsubstantial. The obstacles to such pacing, the fact of its substantiality, are indicated by notices which say 'no road here'. So that although 'the unbounded heaven' may esteem the snipe's solitudes and the sky smile on the meanest spot, the smile comes only after – and by means of – 'dignifying dreams'. Such dreams dignify, presumably because they affirm communality, a calm and cordial lot for all. But the unlikeliness of this ever becoming reality, or of 'right feeling' being widely shared, is evident throughout the poem. The only conceivably realisable hope is that 'in the dreariest places peace will be/A dweller and a joy'. This can be read as meaning *even* in the dreariest places or *only* in them.

Either way not much is affirmed, for 'will be' can do no more than utter a hope for that future which right feeling may help to bring about. And although those words 'dweller' and 'joy' carry a powerful and very recognisable charge, we have to reflect that for Clare, as for those creatures he is writing about, there can be no security of dwelling. (A note to the poem explains that 'Wittlesey Mere was the habitat of snipes and other water birds. In Clare's day a watery wilderness of some 2,000 acres, it was drained in 1850 and turned into arable land.') This is why the 'lawless laws' of enclosure are so threatening to him and why memory is more poignant in his work than it is in the work of any other Romantic poet. It must be so, because for Clare memory speaks of what is lost, not through the principle of change, but by means of those legally enforced processes which deny him any confident sense of self, insofar as self is to be defined in terms of relationship, of dwelling.

It is this particular significance of memory which explains the power of such poems as 'The Flitting', 'The Lament of Swordy Well', or 'Remembrances'.

> Here was commons for their hills where they seek for freedom still
> Though every commons gone and though traps are set to kill
> The little homeless miners . . .
> All leveled like a desert by the never weary plough
> All vanished like the sun where that cloud is passing now
> All settled here for ever on its brow

Clare presumably uses this long, loose line, which he handles with great rhythmic assurance, because its ballad-like measure implies that he is speaking out of a collective experience. The metre echoes 'Banks of Inverary', a ballad he collected and imitated in both 'When I Meet a Bonnie Lass', and 'I Met a Pleasant Maiden'.[34] This experience was not one with which he could always confidently identify; the separations saw to that. But when he here laments the killing of 'the little homeless miners' he is aware of that condition of the outlaw which he inevitably shared with many others. 'Speed the plough' was the farmer's and squire's exuberant, exhortatory cliché of the time. Change the angle of vision, the nature of experience, and the 'never weary plough' provides not wealth but devastation, 'a desert'. And it is, then, the ultimate irony that Clare's own poems themselves become out of bounds. For, with the exception of 'The Flitting', not one of the poems I have been discussing was published in his lifetime.

It is widely agreed that the second generation of Romantic poets died young. Yet Clare, born between Shelley and Keats, lived until 1864. How can it be that until very recently he has been so persistently overlooked, or belittled? To ask the question is to prompt the answer. His voice is not 'English'. As an outlaw he cannot speak for England, his experience is denied authority or authenticity even though he speaks for countless thousands of English people, so that neglect of Clare is neglect of them. And this remains true no matter how he might occasionally protest against that 'dull and obstinate class from whence I struggled into light'.

It is for this reason, no doubt, that Raymond Williams warns against seeing Clare's condition, his history, as exceptional. Williams describes Clare's voice as representing 'a very significant moment of change in English poetry: a particular arrival, through deep social alienation, at a lively natural participation . . . Clare put a specific new voice into English writing, and it was a voice of his class though not through his class.'[35] It is possible to sympathise with this while feeling that a phrase such as 'natural participation' requires amending. And anyway, did the change in English poetry actually happen? We have seen that Clare's voice was repeatedly silenced, distorted, 'shaped', so as to fit into an entirely artificial, literary and culturally orthodox notion of what was and was not possible for peasant poets, of what might be granted a regional experience. This being so, 'natural participation' becomes an impossibility. Besides, the representativeness of Clare's condition and predicaments should not blind us to the fact that he is a great poet. And this greatness holds, paradoxical as it may seem, even or perhaps particularly through the years of his 'madness', by which time he had intermittently at least lost all sense of who he was and where he belonged, and out of which loss he continued to make great poems.

In *A Real World and Doubting Mind*, Tim Chilcott remarks that during his asylum period Clare tried 'to preserve a selfhood not predicated upon the world's recognition'.[36] This is undoubtedly true, although we shall see that the poems which result from this are in a sense about the impossibility of preserving such selfhood. An alternative might be to construct a different selfhood. Clare had desired the world's recognition, but not the placing, limiting recognition that had been forced on him – that of the peasant poet. Not surprisingly, therefore, as his desperation increased he tried to establish himself in ways that would make him entirely acceptable. (The connection back to Stephen Duck is surely obvious.) At different times he seems to have thought of himself as Shakespeare, Lord Nelson (about whom he knew an astonishing amount), Burns, and the boxers Ben Caunt and Jack Randall. In the guise of the last he issued:

Jack Randalls Challenge To All The World

Jack Randall The Champion Of The Prize Ring Begs Leave To Inform The Sporting World That He Is Ready To Meet Any Customer In The Ring Or On The Stage To Fight For The Sum Of £500 Or £1000 Aside A Fair Stand Up Fight

He also, more predictably, imagined himself to be Byron, and in that name he announced:

A New Vol of Poems by Lord Byron Not Yet Collected in his Works.[37]

And he wrote versions of *Don Juan* and *Child Harold*.

Anyone inclined to doubt Clare's extraordinary technical prowess should read his *Don Juan*. It is a *tour de force*, a brilliant pastiche of Byron's poem. Nevertheless, the ache of not being Byron throbs through its stanzas.

> I wish I had a quire of foolscap paper
> Hot pressed – and crowpens – how I could endite
> A silver candlestick and green wax paper
> Lord bless me what fine poems I would write
> The very tailors they would read and caper
> And mantua makers would be all delight
> Though laurel wreaths my brow did ne'er environ
> I think myself as great a bard as Byron.

The final rhyme is certainly managed with Byron's *élan*, but the true feeling of the stanza is to be located in the blend of desire and wit, which both recognises that poetry as a fashionable art is for dandyish show (all those tailors and lacemakers), and disdains its showiness, its being the possession and accomplishment of gentlemen ('Lord bless me what fine poems I would write').

In *Child Harold* Clare adopts the persona of the misunderstood, suffering poet. But where Byron merely played the part, although occasionally almost persuading himself he meant it, it is for Clare of great personal significance. 'Fame blazed upon me like a comets glare/Fame waned and left me like a fallen star.' This is no more than the truth. And while Byron, true to his self-appointed image, chose like Harold to go into exile, Clare had outlawry, in the sense I have been using the term, thrust upon him. Inevitably, such a condition brings with it the gravest of doubts about selfhood, and it is out of such doubts – the paradox of non-referential identity, we may call it – that Clare writes a sonnet called 'I Am'.[38]

'I Am' is not among the greatest of Clare's poems, because it relies too heavily on that Romantic notion of the poet as someone set apart. He says of himself that 'I was a being created in the race/Of men disdaining bounds of place and time'. This is to affirm the identity of poetic genius, 'The Poet in his joy', and although for Clare such an identity is tied up with an idea of class superiority to which he here makes appeal (for we have seen how important 'disdain' is to him, and can then understand why he will want to think of the poet as disdainfully o'er bounding human laws), the poem provides a merely forlorn compensatory myth for a lost sense of self, in which the poet tries to assert the role of divinely-inspired bard: 'A soul unshackled – like eternity/Spurning earth's vain and soul-debasing thrall'. This myth is also affirmed in 'A Vision', which like 'I Am' has been widely anthologised and intemperately admired. Its ringing avowals are, however, delusive:

> In every language upon earth,
> On every shore, o'er every sea;
> I gave my name immortal birth,
> And kep't my spirit with the free.[39]

It is not difficult to sympathise with the reasons that made Clare write in this self-aggrandising manner. But the painful fact is that the affirmations sound hollow. The ambition of the poem is to make Shelleyan claims for the poet as free spirit, or to identify with Wordsworth's claim for the poet as the rock and defence of human nature. Or, more accurately, it is to lay claim to the idea of the poet as a 'clear and universal man', possessed of an 'essentially poetic' identity. As we shall see in the next chapter, Hallam would claim such an identity for Tennyson, and with as little plausibility. Clare comes at the end of that line of thought which develops from an entirely generous wish to free poetry from the grip of correctly-educated 'scholar poets', a line we have seen Gray, Collins and others inaugurating in order to widen the constituency of English poets, to allow others than the city poets to speak for England, *their* England. From this comes the images of 'inspired poet' and 'natural genius' which feed into the Romantic movement and are then hypostatised as 'the Poet'. It is only to be expected that Clare should eagerly grasp at this idea. But everything that happened to him pointed to its unreality.

This is why the tragic, hard-thinking and comfortless three-stanza poem called 'I Am' is infinitely superior to either of the better-known poems. It explores the issues which they shirk, issues involved in the attempt to preserve or identify a selfhood that seems everywhere to be slipping away or to be denied.

I

> I am – yet what I am, none cares or knows;
>   My friends forsake me like a memory lost: –
> I am the self-consumer of my woes; –
>   They rise and vanish in oblivion's host,
> Like shadows in love's frenzied stifled throes: –
> And yet I am, and live – like vapours tost.

2

> Into the nothingness of scorn and noise, –
>   Into the living sea of waking dreams,
> Where there is neither sense of life or joys,
>   But the vast shipwreck of my life's esteems;

158

Even the dearest, that I love the best
Are strange – nay, rather stranger than the rest.

3

I long for scenes, where man hath never trod
   A place where woman never smiled or wept
There to abide with my creator, God;
   And sleep as I in childhood, sweetly slept,
Untroubling, and untroubled where I lie,
The grass below – above the vaulted sky.[40]

The assertions, followed as they are by definitions and explanations which take away all certainty from what has been asserted, make the first two stanzas very remarkable. And although there may seem to be some self-pity about them, even an echo of Shelley's 'Stanzas Written in Dejection' ('I could lie down like a tired child/And weep away the life of care,/Which I have borne and yet must bear'), it is no more than a fact that friends such as Taylor and Mrs Emmerson and other patrons had as good as forsaken Clare precisely like 'a memory lost', that is, as a poet whose moment of fame had long gone. So that the last stanza not surprisingly yearns for the imagined peace of childhood, a time before life, like a prison or madhouse, closed about the man. In other words, the poem's ending imagines a pre-lapsarian, unenclosed, natural world, free from the threatening tread of men.

And, it must be noted, women. For by the time he wrote this poem Clare had become convinced that his childhood sweetheart, Mary Joyce, was being kept from him. In this he was certainly deluded, because Mary Joyce had died in 1838. There is, however, good reason to believe that her father had intervened to prevent meetings between his adolescent daughter and the young day labourer. Mary Joyce came of a family of prosperous farmers. 'They lived in a good, large stone house in Glinton and employed servants and labourers.'[41] The story of the separation of Clare and Mary Joyce and the motives prompting it are representative. (How representative we may judge if we think of the factual history of the relationship of Dickens and Maria Beadnell, or the fictional history of Grace Melbury and Giles Winterbourne, to take two very obvious examples.) In Clare's case it leads to the writing of a number of poems, the finest of which is the one beginning 'I hid my love when young'. Here, Clare makes a lyric poem whose language and syntax so blend woman and nature that you cannot tell which he is talking about. They are not to be separated. He feels for both a secret love which is at once right and wrong, is both joyous and a guilty secret. The guilt is most strongly experienced in a peopled place: 'I hid my love in field and town/Till e'en the breeze would knock me down'. The field he has in mind is presumably a cultivated one, and it and town imply a world of men which threatens his secret, fugitive love – for that is what it amounts to. The sense of paranoid dread is deeply distressing – 'even silence found a tongue/To haunt me all the summer long' – or would be were it not for the fact that the calm utterances hold in equipoise the paradox of an experience which is socially improper and yet essentially natural.

Of course there can be no such simplistic formulation. The dream of the essentially natural, like the desire for a secure identity and voice, something you can call your 'own', endlessly fractures on the obdurate reality of social relations and the separations, tensions and contradictions out of which they are made. Clare's poetry is about these matters, and as such is deeply representative of English experience, even if it is not usual to say so. For the habitual strategy is to try to accept divisions by imposing solutions – that is, identities – which can then be produced as evidence of agreed social arrangements in which separations are themselves somehow 'natural'. This, too, is deeply representative of English experience.

I may seem to have argued against myself by failing to make out a case for Clare as a poet who produces his own, imagined England. But beneath all I have been saying runs the tacit argument that, given his circumstances, he could not possibly do so. His experience – regional, partial, self-fractured and fracturing – forbids those totalising myths which in their different ways Shelley and Wordsworth, for example, develop. But precisely because Clare's voice challenges and disrupts these myths, as it *must* do, it has to be registered as specifically English. Not to attend to it is to deny Englishness in the very act of proclaiming it.

CHAPTER 8

Tennyson's Great Sirs

In 1832 Wordsworth added some lines to Book 7 of the unpublished *Prelude*. Here, addressing the shade of Edmund Burke, he begs forgiveness for his own early democratic republicanism, and envisages Burke as standing

> like an oak whose stag-horn branches start
> Out of its leafy brow, the more to awe
> The younger brethren of the grove. But some –
> While he forewarns, denounces, launches forth,
> Against all systems built on abstract rights,
> Keen ridicule: the majesty proclaims
> Of Institutes and Laws, hallowed by time;
> Declares the vital power of social ties
> Endeared by Custom; and with high disdain,
> Exploding upstart Theory, insists
> Upon the allegiance to which men are born –
> Some – say at once a froward multitude –
> Murmur (for truth is hated, where not loved)
> As the winds fret within the Aeolian cave,
> Galled by their monarch's chain. The times were big
> With ominous change . . .[1]

And so, by clear implication, are the times which prompted the writing of this cliché-stuffed passage. 'Upstart Theory', that underbred affair of uncertain parentage but violent intent, has now succeeded in widening the franchise and therefore severing the social ties of custom. Mere anarchy is about to be loosed upon the world. Aeolus has been unable to prevent the wild west wind of change from breaking free.

Given how little the 1832 Act changed anything, Wordsworth's fears seem extraordinary. They are at their most revealing in his move from the 'some' who murmur to the indictment of a 'froward multitude'. Blake's innocent multitude of lambs, raising to heaven their harmonious thunderings, has become a cowed, inchoate and merely perverse – but powerful – mob. And Burke is then the wise champion of a politics whose 'natural' authority is at one with its embodied images of leadership: of stags and monarchs. (I do not suppose Wordsworth knew that 'stag-horn' branches occur when a tree is already dying.)

It is hardly surprising that the poet who praised Burke for his insistence 'Upon the allegiance to which men are born' should in 1836 tell Henry Crabb Robinson that in Ebenezer Elliott's poetry 'there is a deal of stuff arising from his hatred of subsisting things. Like Byron, Shelley, etc, he looks on all things with an evil eye.' Crabb Robinson's explanation for this evil eye is that it 'arises naturally enough in the mind of a very poor man who thinks the world has not treated him well'. Presumably he and Wordsworth agreed that the Corn Law Rhymer was motivated by envy or self-pity. Yet, to his credit, Wordsworth was prepared to acknowledge Elliott's great gifts. 'None of us have done better than he has in his best,' he remarked, adding that Elliott's later poems were his most successful, and that in particular '*The Ranter* contains some fine passages.'[2] We do not know which passages Wordsworth had in mind, but given the poem's title and subject it may at first strike us as odd that he is prepared to find anything in it to praise. 'The Ranter' is the opening, key, poem to Elliott's volume *Corn Law Rhymes*, 1834, in which upstart Theory powerfully challenges social ties and allegiance, and raises a good deal more than a murmur on behalf of a multitude of English people for whom custom meant dear bread and slow starvation. How could Wordsworth admire such a poem? The answer may lie in the fact that when he came to read the volume he realised that his fears of 1832 had been exaggerated. Or it may be that the poem stirred some guilty memories of his own past radicalism.

The title 'The Ranter' proclaims its protagonist's identification with the values of the extreme radicals of the Commonwealth period. Here again, we have a link back to the tradition of dissent which was of importance to Blake, and which continued to surface late into the nineteenth century. Miles Gordon, Elliott's ranter, is a Sheffield labourer who is also a Sunday preacher: 'The Great Unpaid! the prophet, lo!' He preaches in the open air and his message is frankly political. 'Wo be unto you, scribes and pharisees,/Who eat the widow's and the orphan's bread,/And make long prayers to hide your villanies,' he begins.[3] Gordon is a Primitive Methodist, and to recognise what this entails helps to situate Elliott's poem and to point its radicalism.

The Society of Primitive Methodists had been founded in 1812, as a breakaway movement from the Methodist Conference and in protest against the Conference's determination to become respectable in politics as in other matters. Methodism's historian, Rupert Davies, notes that the Conference

> almost fell over backwards in the effort to make it clear that it had no truck with Radical or any other kind of agitators, and published annually a protestation of deep loyalty to the Crown and an instruction to Methodist people to abstain from political activity. Methodism had become middle-class conservative.[4]

In sharp contrast, the Primitive Methodists were mostly working class. Their early leaders, Hugh Bourne and William Clowes, began to hold open-air 'camp meetings' in the years between 1808 and 1812 (a fact which made it easier for Viscount Sidmouth, Home Secretary in Liverpool's government, to introduce in 1811 a Bill banning Methodist preachers on the grounds of their 'illiteracy'). Davies remarks:

> Primitive Methodists were active in trades unions almost from the moment in 1825 at which it became legal for working people to 'combine' for the purpose of redressing their grievances . . . It was natural that Primitive Methodists should act in this way. They themselves were mine-workers, mill-workers, agricultural workers. They knew all about the long hours and filthy conditions for men, women, and children.[5]

In view of this it is surprising that Davies does not appear to understand why Primitive Methodist preachers should have called themselves 'ranters'. But the meaning would not have been lost on Elliott. He came from impeccably radical stock. His father was known as 'Devil Elliott' and 'was in politics an extreme radical, and in religion an ultra-Calvinist'. Ebenezer Elliott was baptised by 'Tommy Wright, a tinker, of the same religious persuasion as the father'.[6] (Bunyan was a tinker: a 'tinker' was a wanderer often seen as a troublemaker.) Just how far Miles Gordon shares his creator's radicalism is made evident in his sermon. He refers to the fact that

> The slander'd Calvinists of Charles's time
> Fought, and they won it, Freedom's holy fight.
> Like prophet-bards, although they hated rhyme,
> All incorruptible as heaven's own light,
> Spoke each devoted preacher for the right.

Elliott plainly knows about the radical tradition of distrust for 'mere' poetry – that is, for the consolations of rhyme; and he also knows about the tradition of the unorthodox, 'unlettered' poets-as-bards. It is this which helps to explain Gordon's confident rejection of the heroes of orthodoxy, including the Duke of Wellington. This will certainly account for Wordsworth's linking Elliott with Byron and Shelley, 'looking on all things with an evil eye'. Nothing is sacred, not even the hero of Waterloo. Byron had anathematised Wellington for his 'luxurious meals' while the people suffer hunger. Elliott carries on the attack:

> The Cadi *amateur* – a devotee
> For drum-head justice famed, and parlour law,
> Hater evangelized of liberty! . . .
>   Who does not loathe
> His loathsome loathing of all liberal taint!
> Which of you hath not toil'd, to feed and clothe
> His lacqueys?

Here as elsewhere in his work Elliott traces the effects of the bread tax back
to the Napoleonic wars. *His* Wellington is then the 'Saint of Carnage' (cf.
Byron's use of Macbeth's 'y'are the best of cutthroats!'), whose remedies,
'*Alms for the rich! – a bread-tax for the poor!*' produce, now, an apocalyptic
vision of retributive justice:

> Sublime events are rushing to their birth;
> Lo, tyrants by their victims are withstood!
> And freedom's seed still grows, though steep'd in blood!

For Elliott, the times are big with hopeful change. He may have in mind the
activities of Captain Swing, he may be thinking of the sporadic insurrections
of 1831–2, the implications of which Wellington refused to take seriously –
'I defy those who would use such violence,' he famously told the House of
Lords;[7] or he may be thinking of that more widespread apprehension of
change which impelled Wordsworth to compose his prayer of gratitude to
Burke. No matter how we choose to read the lines we must acknowledge
their confident prophecy that vast changes are in the offing: the phrase
'sublime events' echoes the utopianism of Shelley and, though Elliott could
not have known this, Blake.

Elliott's voice of radical dissent could and should be connected to John
Clare. It is worth comparing 'The Ranter' to 'England in 1830'. But the
comparison will bring out distinctions. Elliott's education was a good deal
more complete than Clare's. He belonged to that tradition which Hugh
Bourne exemplified. By trade a carpenter, Bourne had taught himself –
among a great deal else – Greek, Hebrew, Latin and French, and in this he
was by no means untypical of the Primitive Methodists (a fact which throws
harsh light on George Eliot's condescension to Bartle Massey's school).
There is also the matter of regional differences, to which I have earlier
drawn attention and whose importance is accentuated by the fact that
Clare's experiences were largely determined by agricultural labour, Elliott's
by industrial.

But Elliott shares with Clare a sense of being excluded from dominant
formations of Englishness. At the end of 'The Ranter' he says of his hero,
'Nor shall the patriot bard refuse to pay/Melodious honours to the patriot
dead'. Here, the tradition which Gray had fitfully illumined is once again
touched on. True bards are true patriots, because they sing for the people. It
is clear, however, that although Elliott may want to see himself and Miles
Gordon in these terms (with Gordon as a last revisiting of the kind of subject
reproduced in 'The Bard' and 'The Minstrel'), he doubts that the
working-class poet has much chance of gaining a purchase on the national
consciousness. Patriots-as-bards have no specific *English* identity, because
a national culture is being produced in terms which exclude them. They are
not subjects, they are only objects.

I do not suppose that Elliott could formulate this issue – about which there will be more to say later – in any other than tentative and baffled ways. But it explains why the 'brief inscription' on Gordon's grave which 'few will seek . . . and fewer find' reads: 'Here lies the preacher of the plunder'd poor.' For all the defiance of the inscription, it is as though Elliott expects Gordon to become unheard and invisible, just as Sidmouth intended those Methodist preachers against whom he framed his bill to become silenced and thus invisible.

Yet this did not happen. In the Preface to the third edition of the *Corn Law Rhymes*, Elliott remarks:

> Two generous critics (one of them writing in the *New Monthly Magazine*, the other in the *Athenaeum*,) have praised so highly this little unpuffed, unadvertised book, that I am almost compelled to doubt whether I still live in England. What! in the land of castes and cant, take a poor self-educated man by the hand, and declare to the world that *his* book is worth reading?

This is where the distinction between Elliott and Clare becomes most acute. *Corn Law Rhymes* was not only praised, it allowed Elliott to become part of a group of radical writers and to be on equal intellectual terms with them, experiences which never came the way of the endlessly condescended-to Clare. The man at the centre of the group with which Elliott became associated was W. J. Fox, political radical and editor of the *Monthly Repository*, a journal which during the 1830s produced radical literature of great significance. (It ceased publication in 1838.) The forebears to whom it proclaimed allegiance included Milton, Shelley and Byron, it was self-consciously democratic, republican and feminist, it announced that modern poetry ought to take modern subjects and that poetry *by* the poor would be necessarily different from and of more value than poetry *for* the poor; and among its contributors, Elliott apart, were R. H. Horne and Robert Browning.

The *Monthly Repository* is a most important venture. It attempts to articulate a wide range of English experiences and thus to provide a decisive challenge to developing orthodoxies. Fox himself had started out as a weaver's boy, become a renowned Unitarian preacher, and had taken the decision to part from his wife, to whom he had been very unhappily married, and live openly with his ward, years younger than himself. The decision cost him some friends, but not presumably the friendship of those who knew that the girl in question, Eliza Flower, was an ardent admirer of Mary Wollstonecraft.[8]

This was the milieu into which Browning was introduced, and knowing as much helps us to understand the nature of his intense love for Shelley's poetry. It also helps to explain Browning's early commitment to drama. Quite simply, drama was a way of reaching a wider audience than poetry could command, and it could focus on issues which would challenge that audience. Fox's group as a whole took this view of drama's importance. (In passing it may be noted that until he realised the potentialities of the novel, Dickens also seems to have seen in drama a means of communicating with a wide – rather than a merely homogeneously large – audience.) Hence, Horne's *The Spirit of Peers and People*, a 'dramatic burlesque' published in 1834, which mounts a sustained attack on Church, monarchy and parliament, and which ends with a character called Robert Vision proclaiming: 'Gold is God and Labour is the Ass/But now 'tis ridden to the precipice.' Given that labour is the only source of wealth, power and vast inheritance, Vision continues, change must come soon, if it is to be accomplished 'Without the flow of fratricidal blood,/Ruin, or injury . . .'[9]

The Spirit of Peers and People, which Horne subtitles 'A National Tragi-Comedy, Allegory, and Satire', is obviously intended as an act of political intervention ('burlesques' could be staged in places not subject to the laws which governed the licensing of plays), and this accords with Fox's insistence that poetry is an integral part of cultural formations and that it both expresses and helps to create the process by means of which change occurs. This has its significance for Browning's play *Strafford*, which was acted for the first time on 1 May 1837, with Macready in the title role. It is not possible to know whether this date was deliberately chosen, but the significance of the year is plain enough. Everybody knew that William IV's death was imminent – he died on 20 June – and there was a widespread feeling among radicals and others that when he died the monarchy would die with him.[10] He had done nothing to restore the monarchy's reputation, to which 'Prinny' had virtually put paid. 'What eye has wept for him? What heart has heaved one throb of unmercenary sorrow?' *The Times* asked rhetorically when bringing its readers news of George IV's death in 1830. True, there was the usual sad flutter of anticipation that the next king might be a bit better. Even Elliott had written a poem welcoming William to the throne, anticipating that he would be the 'king for the poor'. This is on a par with those who had held out hopes for the Princess Charlotte. (And in our own days Prince Charles visits the inner cities.) But Elliott must have realised his mistake as soon as it became clear that William agreed with Wellington in opposing the Reform Bill.[11]

William then becomes another reason to anticipate the death of the British monarchy. There were many who expected Victoria to become 'plain Miss Guelph'. Why this did not happen is a complex story,[12] but *Strafford* is very much of the moment in advising its audience not to put its trust in kings. The real villain of Browning's play is not Wentworth, but Charles. Wentworth is the hapless victim of an entirely unscrupulous monarch, torn from his earlier friends and then sacrificed by royal expediency. Browning shows Wentworth as acting in order to save the king from the consequences of his own unprincipled actions. His reward is to be executed. Near the play's ending, Charles appears to awaken to some flicker of conscience, but even here he turns out to be altogether too pusillanimous to save the man who has repeatedly saved him. In despair, Wentworth mourns that 'the common songs will run/That I forsook the people', and he anticipates with dread his future reputation as 'the Apostate Strafford'. At which point his former friend, 'the patriot Pym', addresses him, calling him

> this Wentworth here, –
> That walked in youth with me – loved me it may be,
> And whom, for his forsaking England's cause,
> I hunted by all means (trusting that she
> Would sanctify all means) even to the grave
> That yearns for him. And saying this, I feel
> No bitterer pang than first I felt, the hour
> I swore Wentworth might leave us . . .[13]

The anti-monarchism of *Strafford* is ungainsayable. Wentworth himself, however, is presented more in sorrow than in anger, a fact which probably helped Macready to make up his mind to play the part. That Strafford is an apostate is clear; but he is genuinely mistaken in that he chooses the king's cause rather than the people's, hoping that they can be made one. The play shows this to be a forlorn hope. Not the people *and* the king will bring England together, but the people *against* the king.

Patrick Brantlinger has argued that *Strafford* is in no serious sense about history or politics.

> History in *Strafford* serves as mere 'decoration' for a tale of conflict between two old friends . . . Its theme is that of personal loyalty undermined by personal treachery . . . Instead of suggesting that one side is right and the other side is wrong, the play suggests that politics is dangerous – it destroys friendship and kills both body and soul.[14]

But a play which shows politics to be dangerous is very clearly about politics. And a king who is guilty of 'personal treachery' is guilty *as a king*. Besides, a play which appears in 1837 and which is about England and the monarchy can hardly be other than political. *Strafford* is written from a republican point of view. This is not to say that Browning reduces his characters to the level of caricature. On the contrary, Wentworth's dilemmas are made entirely credible. But the fact remains that in choosing king rather than people he becomes a lost leader.

This is of course why Browning attacks Wordsworth. He, too, had made the wrong choice, and with less excuse than Strafford, because he had had more opportunity to see how badly kings behaved and how they aligned themselves against the people.

Just for a handful of silver he left us
  Just for a riband to stick in his coat . . .
Shakespeare was of us, Milton was for us,
  Burns, Shelley, were with us, – they watch from their graves!
He alone breaks from the van and the freemen,
  – He alone sinks to the rear and the slaves![15]

'The Lost Leader' was first published in *Dramatic Romances and Lyrics*, in 1845, by which time Wordsworth had accepted a civil-list pension (in 1842) and the Laureateship (in 1843). Even if, as Tom Paulin has brilliantly suggested, it makes the best sense to regard the poem as a kind of Chartist marching song, it clearly enough has Browning's support. He doesn't think poets should abandon their responsibilities to a democratic vision of England. Browning, it is not irrelevant to note, had not submitted to the kind of education which Tennyson took for granted, and his friends were nothing like the high-minded Apostles: royalists, Anglicans, essentially anti-democratic.

The 'Cavalier Tunes' of *Dramatic Lyrics* (1842) are jokes at the expense of royalists. They are also jokes at the expense of those contemporaries who believed that the way out of England's presumed dark future lay through a retreat to the age of chivalry (a belief which produced among other things the Eglinton Tournament and some of Tennyson's early poems, about which there will be more to say later). Browning's note to the *Dramatic Lyrics* says that:

> Such poems as the majority in this volume might also come properly enough,
> I suppose, under the head of 'Dramatic Pieces'; being, though often lyric in
> expression, always Dramatic in principle, and so many utterances of so many
> imaginary persons, not mine.[16]

There then follow three roisterous, thumping poems, which have the collective effect of sounding at best cheerfully bullying as well as thoroughly philistine and, in the light of history, comically wrong. 'God for King Charles! Pym and such carles/To the Devil that prompts 'em their treasonous parles.' Well, no, God wasn't for King Charles.

And then, once past the tunes, we come immediately on 'My Last Duchess'. This is crucial. Browning was careful to put his poems in the order which would best bring out meanings that reinforce or upset one another. It is an essentially dramatic method which is also essentially democratic. It refuses, or at least impedes the recognition of, any one voice as taking precedence over any other, of being privileged with the authority which Wordsworth increasingly came to assume as his right. It also exposes the presumptions of authority. The cavaliers give themselves away, as much by their table-banging bluster as by their misplaced confidence in history; and the aristocratic spirit which breathes through the speaker of 'My Last

Duchess' inevitably opens up a variety of disquieting questions about just what chivalry, gentlemanliness and courtesy actually mean. Since he is a Duke of Ferrara we don't have to identify him as "for King Charles". But the fact that 'My Last Duchess' comes directly after the 'Cavalier Tunes' allows us to make the links for ourselves. In the tunes, Browning produces the champions of high culture as a set of hearties. *This* champion of high culture is a hater of women. And here we come to a matter of the utmost importance.

I have already noted that the radicals who grouped themselves round Fox were feminists. It is, however, more accurate to say that the men sympathised with the cause to which the women in the group openly committed themselves. Eliza Flower, for example, was unconventional enough to cause Harriet Martineau to declare that she was 'ignorant of the important proprieties of life'. The same holds for her sister, Sarah, who wanted to be an actress and who wrote plays and verses. Other women who belonged to the circle included the poet Harriet Taylor, Caroline Hill, 'daughter of Southwood Smith, an ardent feminist and educationist, and her two close friends, Scottish sisters Mary and Margaret Gillies, the one a writer, the other a successful portrait painter'.[17] In short, the people among whom Browning moved were as radical in their support of or identification with feminism as in other matters. It is therefore hardly surprising that 'My Last Duchess' should pose the connection between 'sophisticated' aristocracy and oppressive, even murderous, patriarchy, nor that Browning should want to tease out what may be implied in such connections.

> She thanked men – good! but thanked
> Somehow – I know not how – as if she ranked
> My gift of a nine-hundred-years-old name
> With anybody's gift. Who'd stoop to blame
> This sort of trifling? . . .
>
> I choose
> Never to stoop.

This is the voice of aristocratic hauteur, managing to appear hesitant, slightly vulnerable ('I know not how') while at the same time unsheathing the steel of authoritarian purpose. 'I choose/Never to stoop.' It is the voice in which a gift of name is conferred as a means of securing property. (Only a very few years away, if somewhat lower on the scale, is Mr Dombey's reflection that as the bearer of his name 'Mrs Dombey must have been happy'.) And its tones would surely have been heard at that muddy farce of revived chivalry, the Eglinton Tournament, where in the summer of 1839, 'a knight under an umbrella became the symbol of the tournament, and to many people seemed sufficiently ludicrous to burst the bubble of chivalry for ever'.[18]

The point of drawing attention to the tournament is not to suggest that knights under umbrellas might in different circumstances become wife-killers (though they might). It is rather to suggest that Browning's radicalism leads him to sardonically query a type of ideal Englishman which was being promoted during the 1830s and 40s and whose essential characteristics were linked to an imagined ethos of chivalry or of the cavalier, especially since those characteristics stretched beyond matters of pose to larger commitments: to England as monarchy and hierarchically structured state. And we have then to make a further point, which is that this atavistic imagining suited Tennyson, who seems indeed never to have lost his interest in the type of Englishman it proposes, even though it is possible that the death of Prince Albert in 1861 marked for the then Poet Laureate the final passing of the type. Hence, the dedication in 1862 to an edition of *Idylls of the King*, in which Tennyson speaks of the late Consort as

> Scarce other than my king's ideal knight
> 'Who reverenced his conscience as his king;
> Whose glory was, redressing human wrong;
> Who spake no slander, no, nor listened to it;
> Who loved one only and who clave to her –'[19]

As Hopkins remarked when he first read the *Idylls*, Tennyson 'should have called them *Charades from the Middle Ages*'.[20]

Admittedly these lines were written some thirty years after Arthur Hallam's claim that Tennyson's early poetry was of national importance and ideally suited for England's needs because 'he comes before the public, unconnected with any political party, or peculiar system of opinion'.[21] But Tennyson's championing of chivalry is indeed a system of opinion, one that might be called decidedly peculiar. And it is arguable that, if not connected with political party, Tennyson is at least as implicated as Browning's lost leader in supporting monarchy as though it is the 'natural' or only conceivable arrangement. It can also be argued that such support does not emerge only after he becomes Poet Laureate. The reason he became Poet Laureate was that he supported the arrangement.

Yet Tennyson is far less of a single-minded upholder of the monarchy than he is sometimes credited with being. If his championing of the ideas of chivalry appears forlorn, it at least provides him with the means to criticise dominant values of the middle years of the nineteenth century which were all too obviously coming to be 'English'. His position as Poet Laureate is, for a while at least, equivocal. Hallam of course had no chance to trace Tennyson's development into a more complicated figure than the one he projected in his famous essay of 1831. Hallam's intention is clear enough. He wants to promote a poet who can be seen as somehow above politics and therefore able to speak for the nation as a whole. In this ambition he reveals

himself to be very much an Apostle. The hope of that idealistic band of
Cambridge undergraduates was to revive a dream of a united England,
which would serve to offer a valuable alternative to the disunity they saw
around them. They anticipated the cry of those who identified England as
'the two nations', and like the Young Englanders they seem to have felt that
desirable change could come about, not through political action, but
through some sort of transformation of consciousness, a feeling which was
accentuated by their one brief flirtation with active politics. Two of their
members, Richard Trench and John Kemble, took part in an attempt to
restore the liberal pretender to the Spanish throne, an attempt in which
Tennyson and Hallam were also marginally involved. It ended with the
shooting of their friend Robert Boyd on the beach at Malaga in December
1831.

In his lucid account of the affair, R. B. Martin remarks that Boyd's death
marked the end of a romantic dream

> in which a number of well-intentioned young Englishmen learned that what
> had begun as little more than an undergraduate lark for them ended in death
> and in even greater repression for the Spanish people; revolution, once
> begun, had consequences more serious than any of them had foreseen. It is
> no wonder that Tennyson became increasingly chary of anything that
> undermined the stability of the world as he had inherited it.[22]

Martin gives away more than he intends. Tennyson might have inherited a
stable world, but for millions of English people there was no such stability –
except in the sense that they were expected to acquiesce in those forms of
oppression which, from a different, more privileged point of view, do indeed
look like stability. Not surprisingly, therefore, the Apostles who had
ventured on their Byronic lark in Spain – but without any of Byron's political
nous – seem to have been united in their opposition to the Reform Bill. That
was not the way to change England. Hallam's essay establishes the template
of their political thinking. The true poet, he writes, 'addresses himself, in all
his conceptions, to the common nature of us all. Art is a lofty tree, and may
shoot up far beyond our grasp, but its roots are in daily life and experience.'
And later, presumably drawing on the same metaphor, he remarks that true
artists 'keep no aristocratic state, apart from the sentiments of society at
large; they speak to the hearts of all, and by the magnetic force of their
conceptions elevate inferior intellects into a higher and purer atmosphere'.
At the top of the tree, there is no need for faction.

But Hallam is here talking of the past, when 'common nature' was
apparently uncontentiously recognised in and by all Englishmen: 'the
knowledge and power thus imbibed, became a part of national existence; it
was ours as Englishmen; and amid the flux of generations and customs we
retain unimpaired the privilege of intercourse with greatness'. The present

age has, however, fallen out of this paradisiacal land of common nature: 'we have undergone a period of degradation. "Every handicraftsman has won the mark of Poesy." It would be tedious to repeat the tale, so often related, of French contagion, and the heresies of the Popeian school.'[23]

Two matters need to be noted about all this. First, Hallam's contemptuous reference to handicraftsmen, although no doubt echoing the by then orthodox view that Pope and the Augustans typically lacked 'inspiration', also surely reveals a conviction that only certain people can be true poets, and that they will not include a Clare or an Elliott. Quite apart from Clare and Elliott being literally handicraftsmen (at best), they make no pretence to speak for the 'common nature' of all Englishmen. On the contrary. They take for granted that the stability the Apostles so prized is won only at the expense of coercing large numbers of English people, and that this as good as denies them their right to speak. The oppositional voices of Clare and Elliott are created out of and bear witness to social divisions which Hallam knew about but which he hopes the true poet can somehow suture by his appeal to 'sensations', since it is such 'sensations', so he argues, which bind 'us' together. At all events, nothing else will. He therefore warns against

> the decrease of *subjective* power, arising from a prevalence of social activity, and a continual absorption of the higher feelings into the palpable interests of ordinary life. The French Revolution may be a finer theme than the war of Troy; but it does not so evidently follow that Homer is to find his superior.[24]

This statement strikingly anticipates Arnold's insistence that the Romantic poets did not live at an apt historical moment because the French Revolution suffered from a 'mania' of converting ideas into action. But Hallam also wants to argue that 'higher feelings' are what can appeal to our 'common nature': this, one might say, is that true disinterestedness to which Arnold also appealed. Here, it is enough to remark that beneath Hallam's desire that poetry should once again operate as the annealing spirit for our common nature is the essentially anti-democratic belief that only certain people can be 'above' the blinding limitations of ordinary life, even if their roots are in it. The organic metaphor is intended to conceal the difficulties inherent in the idea on which it depends. 'Roots' disguises the fact that whole areas of 'ordinary life' must be mysterious to the 'true poet'. He therefore has very little in common with those whose nature he is supposed to share.

Hallam's is yet another attempt to invoke the disinterested authority of the poet, which we have seen to be a persistent feature of thinking about poets and poetry in the centuries under review. But authority does not now rest so much on the idea of the free citizen as on the entirely mysterious 'nature' of the poet. We have seen how and why the version of the nature of the poet as independent of schooling arose in the middle of the eighteenth century. There, it was generously intended to give a voice to those who were typically denied their language, as somehow not English. Now, it has become captured for an altogether narrower view: politically and socially reactionary and coercive.

This, then, brings us to a second point. The dream of unity and the claim that it has once been part of 'national existence: it was ours as Englishmen', connects to a myth of Englishness which becomes increasingly troubling as the century progresses because it is increasingly xenophobic and eventually racist. It would be impossible, given the scope of this book, to attempt to untangle the many strands of this particular version of Englishness, but we must note that even at its most innocent it includes an insistence on England's unique role in Europe. As J. W. Burrow has wittily remarked, this was a European preoccupation of the time: 'In the years after the Congress of Vienna there seems to have been virtually no country or ethnic group so obscure that it failed to find publicists ready to claim for it the role of the messiah of the nations.'[25] In the case of England this usually included warning against the false messiah – that is, France.

There was nothing new in such francophobia. We have seen that Landor in 1802 thought that France had ruined forever the cause of Liberty.[26] Throughout the nineteenth century francophobia could be and repeatedly was grasped as a stick with which to beat radicalism.[27] As a result, English radicalism frequently turned inwards, denying any taint of foreign, especially French, ideas, and thus constructed a native 'English' tradition which had always to refer to the Commonwealth as the great achievement of the past. Whatever the limitations of this, it might be thought that the episode of the Commonwealth would have caused Hallam some difficulty when he proclaimed our 'common nature'. Yet Burrow and others have shown that even the events of the 1640s and 50s could be accommodated into a developing history of Englishness. This is what poets and ordinary people have in common.

For Hallam, one suspects, the accommodation would have to be made by means of the useful concept of chivalry. *There* lay true Englishness, and it would eventually triumph over the puritans, those revolutionary Frenchmen before their time, sour republican democrats, a blip on the island story. Obviously this notion of 'our national existence' has no relationship with the universalism of Byron and Shelley, and indeed such confident universalism has a struggle to survive in Victorian England. It is exemplified if anywhere by the Spasmodics, whose vapid epics make a feeble attempt to envisage a world future, but whose visions are so unspecific as to imply a forlorn realisation on their authors' part that they lack any understanding of history or, at best, are floundering in a welter of possibilities that dare not speak their name. Poetry like this gives utopianism a bad name.[28] It is therefore not without significance that Tennyson should have shown some interest in their work, whereas Browning did not, even though his attempts to resist incorporation into a narrowing concept of Englishness might have made him vulnerable to the vagueness of Spasmodic utopianism. As one way of pointing this contrast, we may note that in 1846 the Brownings chose to leave England for Italy. The following year, Tennyson published *The Princess*.

As with many of Tennyson's early poems, *The Princess* can be read as both an attempt to bear the burden which Hallam had placed on him and an effort to throw it off. Given the lofty sense of the poet which Hallam inherited from certain strains in Romanticism – the poet as *vates*, as God-inspired truth-teller, as *national* bard – his claim that of all modern poets it was Tennyson who most fully embodied the true poet was tantamount to making him an official spokesman for Englishness, for taking on the conscience of the nation. This would have put any poet in a difficult situation. For Tennyson, the difficulties were bound to be extreme. And yet the two-volume *Poems* of 1842 may seem to show him prepared to cope with them. There are, for example, a number of poems which testify to a concern with and commitment to that concept of chivalric Englishness which the Apostles had formulated. But then as has more than once been pointed out, poems such as 'Sir Lancelot and Queen Guinevere' and 'Sir Galahad' are infected by an uncertainty of purpose which suggests that Tennyson was by no means at ease with the kind of image he is apparently upholding. If we seek an explanation for this, it is probably best to look at the poems which are meant to deal with contemporary English life, especially 'Audley Court' and 'Locksley Hall'.

'Audley Court' is an 'English Idyl'. It uses the framing device of a song contest to voice tensions which, if they have some origins in Tennyson's unhappy love affair with Rosa Baring, nevertheless point to more revealing uncertainties, particularly as they touch on modes of behaviour – ways of acting out Englishness – that are offered for approval.

> 'Oh! who would fight and march and countermarch,
> Be shot for sixpence in a battle-field,
> And shovelled up into some bloody trench
> Where no one knows? but let me live my life.
> 'Oh! who would cast and balance at a desk,
> Perched like a crow upon a three-legged stool,
> Till all his juice is dried, and all his joints
> Are full of chalk? but let me live my life.
> 'Who'd serve the state? for if I carved my name
> Upon the cliffs that guard my native land,
> I might as well have traced it in the sands;
> The sea wastes all: but let me live my life.

Christopher Ricks says that the poem allows Tennyson to 'give free play to, and good naturedly control, his deep need always to express a counterview'.[29] But good-natured control is a tactic for masking the seriousness of issues the poem takes up. The tone of forced jocularity can even be – and I should say, is – a device to cover Tennyson's awareness that he doesn't really know where he stands with regard to such issues. The need to express a counterview can then be understood as the promptings occasioned by a radical insecurity with the kind of Englishness which *Poems* keeps offering to substantiate. To make a very obvious point, the idyls are hardly idyllic.

For even if the counterview isn't always to be found in Tennyson's putting rival voices on offer – and he does have real difficulties in wanting to surrender his poet's 'authority' – it surfaces in the frequently odd inappositeness of style and subject. The result is that what Ricks calls good-natured can, from a different perspective, look a more desperate strategy, Tennyson's way of deflecting his readers' attention, or of leaving them uncertain how, or with what degree of seriousness, to take any one poem. But then this is to say that Tennyson himself is far from sure how to take or to treat his subject. Ricks quotes R. W. Dixon's remark that the versification of 'Locksley Hall' is 'most unfit for intense passion, of which indeed there is nothing in it, but only a man making an unpleasant and rather ungentlemanly row'.[30] Dixon intends the word 'ungentlemanly' as a mark of his disapproval of the poem's speaker. Yet 'Locksley Hall' permits a reading in which the very status of a gentleman can come to seem dubious, even if 'gentleman' and chivalric virtue are meant to be virtually synonymous. The man who speaks the poem wants to be done with the Hall itself, in spite of the fact that its status as country house ought to command his and, presumably, Tennyson's assent as the embodiment of cherishable English values. Should we perhaps see the house's actual money-grabbing ostentation as a steep falling off from a nevertheless valid ideal?

> Cursed be the sickly forms that err from honest Nature's rule!
> Cursed be the gold that gilds the straitened forehead of the fool.

Henry Kozicki has argued that here as elsewhere in the idyls we need to register Tennyson's adherence to the ideal of 'the English Great House of the period. Such houses were being built in great numbers (as money accumulated) either about the real ruins of earlier houses, "ivy-clad and mouldering," or, if lacking these, about fake ones.' According to his argument, Tennyson uncomplicatedly endorses such houses as 'burgeoning symbol of the form whose seed lay in medieval time'.[31] But this is to suppose more than the poem allows us to do.

On the other hand, it has to be admitted that Tennyson's position is extremely evasive. The question the poem's protagonist asks himself, 'Am I mad?', prompted a good many Victorian readers to answer, yes. And for good measure they added that he was extremely unpleasant. This is true. But it is also true that his deep self-division argues for an unsettling of the kind of virtues which the chivalric, conservative imagination of Tennyson is supposed to uphold. The speaker of 'Locksley Hall' in some ways anticipates the Pip of *Great Expectations*. He doesn't know where he belongs. What he does 'know' is that action is preferable to passive suffering, and this leads to his momentary identification with 'Men, my brothers, men the workers, ever reaping something new'. But we have then to reflect that by the time Tennyson was writing his poem men, the workers, were not typically reaping, either literally or metaphorically. They were in factories rather than on the land, and they certainly didn't reap the rewards of their work. To say this is to say that 'Locksley Hall' is an instructive muddle, its hero necessarily unable to make sense of the society which, at one Spasmodic moment, he attempts confidently to 'read'. 'For I dipt into the future, far as human eye could see,/Saw the vision of the world, and all the wonders that would be.' This is the most extreme example of what the poem repeatedly demonstrates: that its hero's affirmations are the near-hysterical strategies of a man trying to convince himself that he can make sense of himself and therefore of the world out there.

If we relate 'Locksley Hall' to other Tennyson poems of the period which focus on country houses (not necessarily the 'Great Houses' of Kozicki's misleading formulation), we notice that there are a number of occasions on which the houses are not offered as 'burgeoning' symbols. Quite the opposite. In 'The Lord of Burleigh', for example, Tennyson specifically rejects the idea which, no matter how problematically, had sustained Jane Austen's fiction: that new blood will invigorate the old house. The union of aristocrat and village girl ends in her death. 'Lady Clara Vere de Vere' is about a selfish noblewoman ('Are there no beggars at your gate,/Nor any poor about your lands'), although, typically, the poem's lyric simper takes away much of the force of what is ostensibly being said. Tennyson, we may feel, doesn't want to force the issue. Nor does he do so in 'Edwin Morris', an English idyl written in 1839, which opens with the narrator recalling pleasant rambles by the lake when 'I was a sketcher':

> See here, my doing: curves of mountain, bridge,
> Boat, island, ruins of a castle, built
> When men knew how to build, upon a rock
> With turrets lichen-gilded like a rock:
> And here, new-comers in an ancient hold,
> New-comers from the Mersey, millionaires,
> Here lived the Hills – a Tudor-chimnied bulk
> Of mellow brickwork on an isle of bowers.

The level tone refuses to turn Mersey millionaires into the objects of disgust which a Bradford millionaire became for Eliot in *The Waste Land*; nor are we required to nod approvingly at the Tudor-chimnied bulk which, for all its mellow brickwork, is suspended out of time, on its 'isle of bowers'. The gap between the new-comers and the old house is too great to be closed, either by facile reflection on the irony of improbable contiguity, or by a narrative stance that seeks to offer itself as able to 'read' the significance of the gap. There is a real blankness here, an acceptance of the necessary inadequacy of the point of view from which the events are narrated. Here, at least, Tennyson surrenders authority.

Commentators are quick to remark that 'Edwin Morris', like 'Locksley Hall', is partly motivated by Tennyson's unhappy love affair with Rosa Baring. But unlike 'Locksley Hall', 'Edwin Morris' proposes neither action nor, even, brotherhood as an alternative to or way out of suffering. Perhaps for this reason Tennyson chose not to publish it in his 1842 volumes (it appeared for the first time in 1851). He may have felt that the poem was insufficiently addressed to the time at which it was written, was too much an idyl. Even if he was not fully conscious of the unrest that led to the Chartist movement and the demonstrations of 1839 and 1842, it is unlikely that he would have been ignorant of the circumstances that prompted them. *Poems 1842* shows that Tennyson was uneasy with a complacently 'idyllic' view of England. But 'Edwin Morris' could be read as endorsing such a view. This, then, brings us to *The Princess*.

In his sympathetic and acute discussion of this ambitious poem, Kozicki remarks that 'Through the Idyl's ability to fuse past and present, history becomes palimpsest.' He then outlines the themes of *The Princess* in such a way as to highlight what he takes to be Tennyson's successful treatment.

> The prince in the middle shell of the poem's time frame is, in the outer shell, the speaker of the poem, the seven-headed narrator, Sir Walter Vivian, and the archetypal 'great Sirs' of all England. Beyond this, in the circumambient 'real' present, he is Edmund Lushington, about to marry Cecilia Tennyson, he is Tennyson himself estranged from Emily Sellwood, and he is also those friends since Cambridge days who often told such tandem stories. Receding into time, the prince is Sir Ralph and all the 'knights,/Half-legend, half-historic, counts and kings/Who laid about them at their wills,' won their ladies, and established their houses.

And later, by way of rounding out his claims for the poem, Kozicki says that

> The story told by the gathering in the Abbey ruin reflects the 'realized' ideal of the scene in the poem's frame. On these grounds, the historically productive embodiment of concatenated generations is the 'great broad-shouldered genial Englishman:' Sir Walter. He is the apotheosis of the interpenetration between the ancient feudal rights and those of the Reform Bill that Tennyson had so welcomed . . . In this ideal order – the foundation of the medieval ideal – all together are 'a nation yet, the rulers and the ruled,' in 'universal culture' under the aegis of the 'great Sirs' that keep England from the 'Revolts, republics, revolutions,' that rock France.[32]

I quote Kozicki at some length because his account very ably draws together what certainly seem to be some of the poem's leading concerns and because, unlike many commentators, he recognises that *The Princess* is about a vision of England. It cannot be treated merely as a diversionary medley which takes a fairly relaxed view of marriage and women's education.

Yet Kozicki fails to come to terms with the problems the poem raises, and which, as so often, focus on the question of tone, or of the gap between subject and treatment of subject. He would probably agree with Robert Pattison's suggestion that '*The Princess* is idyllic in its playfulness, for the comic mode of the poem is but an extension of the basic manipulative sportfulness of the earlier idyls.'[33] This is to endorse that good-natured control which Ricks says Tennyson typically demonstrates and which is, presumably, thought to be adequate as a mode of operating. I neither think it is nor believe that Tennyson thought it was. What of those genial broad-shouldered Englishmen, for example, and of the houses they occupy? Kozicki assumes that it is only the nouveaux-riches whom Tennyson had it in for, and that they are to be opposed to the owners of houses which breathe an atmosphere of 'concatenated generations'. I am not so sure.

For one thing, Tennyson has great difficulty in making convincing the very notion of the chain of generations, of suggesting how a family lineage survives healthily into the present. Nor was he alone in this. Those of his contemporaries who formed the Young England movement, in a bid to restore the medieval ideal which Kozicki sees *The Princess* as endorsing, have not only to invent a past to which they can make appeal, they are compelled to admit that such a past has hardly any connection with the present. Similarly, Carlyle and Disraeli utter threnodies for 'blood' and the pure English gentleman, but in doing so lament a lost tradition. This is a rhetorical tactic, but it is one which reveals the difficulty of converting the word into flesh. And to say this is to be reminded that the fleshly Sir Walter is in truth *only* word. He is also exceptional, as exceptional, say, as Egremont, the hero of Disraeli's *Sybil* (1845), who tells the heroine – believed to be working class but actually born of aristocratic parents – that 'the new generation of the aristocracy of England are not tyrants, not oppressors, Sybil . . . They are the natural leaders of the People.'

In the novel, however, the only such natural leader we see is Egremont himself; and Disraeli writes about him in so unfocused a way as to make Sir Walter appear by comparison to be a most subtle, restrained study of the gentlemanly Englishman, 'distinguished by the beauty of the noble English blood, of which in these days few types remain; the Norman tempered by the Saxon; the fire of conquest softened by integrity'. (This is Disraeli's comment on the portrait of a gentleman introduced into *Sybil* to make the point diagrammatically about such gentlemen, such blood.) Even so, it is far from certain that Tennyson unquestioningly endorses Sir Walter's values, or believes them to be as centrally important as Kozicki and other commentators assume. For if the 'seamless' treatment of history allows the past to elide into the present, it more significantly reduces the present to the past. 'England' then is a graspable entity only insofar as it is unlike the England of the 1840s.

Here it may help to draw attention to the irreconcilable ambiguities of the lyric 'Tears, Idle Tears', which Tennyson himself said he was moved to write while visiting Tintern Abbey, and which was to express 'the yearning that young people occasionally experience for that which seems to have passed away from them for ever'. Christopher Ricks quotes F. W. Bateson's powerful objection to this: '*Either* the days that are no more are the objective past of kings and monasteries, *or* they are the subjective past of the poet's and the reader's own earlier life. They cannot be both together.' Ricks follows Bateson's criticism by remarking that Tennyson fails to find 'a congruence between the public past and a private past', and he locates the cause of this failure in an unintegrated personality.[34] My own view is that the failure is more plausibly to be seen as the result of Tennyson's deep uncertainty about the worth of particular values – including a sense of the past – as they present themselves in the terms which Kozicki and others think he unhesitatingly accepts. There is more than one way in which tears can be idle.

With this in mind we can understand why, after reading *The Princess*, Elizabeth Barrett Browning wrote that poets should 'represent the age,/ Their age, not Charlemagne's . . . To flinch from modern varnish, coat of flounce,/Cry out for togas and the picturesque/Is fatal, – foolish too.'[35] Barrett Browning misunderstands Tennyson's intention, which Kozicki is right to see as the desire to make a case for 'concatenated generations'. Yet she is right to sense that Tennyson's method suggests a failure of nerve. It may be harsh to call this 'foolish'. In all probability it arose from his deep uncertainty about whether he was in any position to address issues he knew to be of contemporary importance, and which as Hallam's ideal poet he felt compelled to confront, but which the inherited politics of the Apostles left him ill-equipped to handle. We have also to consider the possibility that at quite another level he felt considerable doubts about the worthwhileness of the kind of Englishness the poem seems to invite us to register and accept. Even if the image of Sir Walter is supposed to be Tennyson's ideal Englishman, a truly 'great Sir', there is little doubt that the sonorous ending of *The Princess* brings down a darkness which feels more than literal: the melancholy of idle tears is not far away from the charmed circle who are

> rapt in nameless reverie,
> Perchance upon the future man: the walls
> Blackened about us, bats wheeled and owls whooped,
> And gradually the powers of the night,

That range above the region of the wind,
Deepening the courts of twilight broke them up
Through all the silent spaces of the worlds,
Beyond all thought into the Heaven of Heavens.

Last little Lilia, rising quietly,
Disrobed the glimmering statue of Sir Ralph
From those rich silks, and home well-pleased we went.

The final three lines attempt a return to the more playful tone which Tennyson has adopted elsewhere in the medley, but they hardly dispel those deeper doubts released by the previous passage. These include an awareness of multiple worlds and therefore a shattering of the insulating creed of Christianity and, then, of the claims of chivalry (which is an expression of Christian 'gentleness'). They also include that possibly fraught meditation on the 'future man', who may be very unlike the men of concatenated generations, may be unknowable, and who, *as* the future, exists in great numbers just beyond these protective walls. Such walls enclose a privileged space of no greater contemporary significance, it may be, than the 'Tudor-chimnied bulk . . . on an isle of bowers'. 'The creepered wall stands up to hide/The gathering multitudes outside'. Auden's lines can justly be applied to much of the poetry that Tennyson wrote during the 1840s, but with this proviso: that Tennyson himself sensed that the enclosed garden, while it may offer a consoling or even seductive set of images of Englishness, especially as they nourish versions of the 'great Sirs' and the values they embody, prohibits any understanding of the multitude, that different, essentially unknown and unknowable England, which exists beyond its privileged walls.

CHAPTER 9

'The World's Good Word'

I

By the time *The Princess* was published the Brownings had left England for Italy. Elizabeth Barrett Browning's *Casa Guidi Windows*, of 1851, about suppressed Italian nationality, is written very much from the standpoint of the liberal-radical perspective that one would expect of someone connected to Fox's circle. In England, in the same year, the Great Exhibition marked a public declaration of England's achieved nationhood. Tennyson, who was now Poet Laureate, might be seen as official spokesman for such nationhood. Martin says that Tennyson took his new duties seriously. 'He believed that his acceptance morally obliged him not to oppose the Queen, either publicly or privately.'[1] There is no reason to doubt the truth of this assertion, and yet the Great Exhibition very obviously celebrated that aggressive commercialism which was to madden the protagonist of *Maud* (1855). In other words, Tennyson's position exacerbated those doubts and uncertainties which, while they conditioned much of his poetry of the 1840s, now produce a series of irresolvable tensions. Such tensions could have been, and in a way were, predicted by the poet who at this time was urging all poets to stay out of politics as a way of guaranteeing an art of tranquil assurance.

> True poets, [Matthew Arnold wrote in the Preface to his *Poems*, 1853] wish neither to applaud nor to revile their age; they wish to know what it is, what it can give them, and whether this is what they want. What they want, they know very well; they want to educate and cultivate what is best and noblest in themselves . . . They do not talk of their mission, nor of interpreting their age, nor of the coming Poet; all this, they know, is the mere delirium of vanity . . . [the poet] will not, however, maintain a hostile attitude towards the false pretensions of his age; he will content himself with not being overwhelmed by them. He will esteem himself fortunate if he can succeed in banishing from his mind all feelings of contradiction, and irritation, and impatience . . .[2]

This is to spurn Hallam's claims for the poet as plainly as it is to reject strategies by means of which Tennyson managed to express and at the same time endeavoured to contain feelings of contradiction, which can also be feelings of irritation and impatience. In a different context I would want to argue that the writers whom Arnold's remarks most challenge are novelists, above all Dickens. His definition of the poet commits Arnold to that platonic aloofness which he assiduously cultivated, and as a result of which he could produce, as poet, very little of worth.

Yet as one would expect of so cunning a mind as Arnold's, the Preface carries a number of special, concealed, charges. In the first place, he is almost certainly directing his attack against his friend Arthur Clough, of whose poetry he had come thoroughly to disapprove. 'I have had so much reluctance to read these, which I now return, that I surely must be destined to receive some good from them', he told Clough when he sent back a body of poems his friend had asked him to read; and although he came to regret some of his more hurtful remarks, he refused to write a preface for the posthumous collection of Clough's poems. Clough's radical politics were more than Arnold could bear. *That* was not what poetry should be about. Clough's satiric bite, his analyses of English middle-class mores and ennui, of cultural pretensions that ignore the economic bases on which they rest and the injustice of a social system on which they depend, his attacks on the Church of England as the complacent upholder of class values which degrade the very morality it claims to embody – all this was plainly too disturbing for Arnold to cope with. It wasn't, it couldn't be, poetry.

The nature of Clough's radicalism has been most ably studied in John Goode's essay '1848 and the Strange Disease of Modern Love', which is particularly valuable for Goode's suggestion that 'Clough's whole poetic career seems tied to the curve of events on the continent . . . After the coup d'état [in France] at the end of 1851, Clough's poetry withers . . . Its clear development from affirmation to despair cannot be dissociated from the political fortunes of the democratic movement.'[3] This is certainly true, although Clough's early death forbids us from deciding that the despair was final. But it is clear that Clough was no more at ease in the England in which he grew up than were the Brownings. In many ways he is as self-consciously exiled from the values of his class and their presumed national significance (English values, the values of an Englishman), as is the hero of his *Bothie of Tober-na-Vuolich*, who with his Scottish, peasant-born wife, emigrates to New Zealand.

Nor was Clough at ease with current poetic practice. This shows in his ceaseless experimentation with form and metre, his wonderfully successful and disruptive hexameters, and his edgy, uncompromising wit, as a result of which he received from Arnold the rebuke that he did not care sufficiently for lyric grace, and that he, Arnold, had 'a growing sense of the deficiency of the beautiful in your poems'.

This cold, almost contemptuous rejection of 'citizen Clough' is consistent with Arnold's ambitions as a poet. True poetry was to be removed from 'the smoke of the market place'. It should exist in a pure world of ideas. This seems always to have been Arnold's credo. It can be detected in the early

Cromwell (1843), which concludes with The Protector's deathbed dream.
Here, Cromwell is made to see that all he had tried to accomplish is ruin and
destruction, including the wreck of his childhood friendship with King
Charles. (There was a legend that as boys the two had been friends.)

> He, too, was there – it was the princely boy,
> The child-companion of his childish joy!
> But oh! how chang'd . . .
> No – all was chang'd – the monarch wept alone,
> Between a ruin'd church and shatter'd throne.

This royalist poem dissolves the question of Charles's culpability into one of
the pathos of broken friendships, and offers an instructive contrast with
Browning's *Strafford*. For Arnold, Cromwell is somehow at fault, though
how we are not told; quietism is to be preferred to political intervention.

This is not to suggest that the relationship between the politically
iconoclastic Cromwell and Charles in any sense reflects Arnold's later
feelings for his relationship with Clough. But *Cromwell* can leave us in no
doubt that Arnold saw political activity as destructive of calm, and of those
habits of mind which true poets must cultivate. This is why he is so deeply
committed to producing a version of Wordsworth which he can then uphold
as the poetic ideal. 'The cloud of mortal destiny,/Others will front it
fearlessly –/But who, like him, will put it by.' These lines from 'Memorial
Verses, April 1850' make clear that for Arnold Wordsworth is no lost leader.
Arnold's Wordsworth had rejected the involvement in politics for which
Milton had praised Cromwell, in lines which Arnold must be remembering:
'Cromwell, our chief of men, that through a cloud/Not of war only, but
distractions rude,/Guided by faith and matchless fortitude,/To peace and
truth, thy glorious way has ploughed.'

As with Wordsworth, so with Milton. Arnold denies him his ideas, rejects
any suggestion that he had been involved in politics. Or rather, he sets them
aside as unimportant. Arnold's Milton is a champion of style. The power of
poetry, Arnold says in his 1888 address on Milton, 'resides chiefly in the
refining and elevation wrought in us by the high and rare excellence of
style . . . Now, no race needs the influence mentioned, the influence of
refining and elevating, more than ours; and in poetry and art our grand
source for them is Milton.' Arnold's deployment of the terms 'refining and
elevating' is sly, but pointed. Milton is here being explicitly denied the
image in which the Romantic poets had cast him: Arnold's Milton is no
precursor of democratic politics. In case we miss the point, he adds: 'To
what does [Milton] owe this supreme distinction? To nature first and
foremost, to that bent of nature for inequality which to the worshippers of
the average man is so unacceptable.'[4]

It is a commonplace that Arnold's desire for an art of eternal values cannot be separated from his desire to withdraw from what he on one occasion called these 'damned times'.[5] That he could not entirely withdraw is evident from his prose writings and from his work as a schools inspector. But as a poet Arnold succeeds only too well. His poetry has so little purchase on the times that it seems almost empty of a subject. As he wrote of his own scholar-gipsy, 'For most, I know, thou lov'st retired ground'. Such retirement feels like an abandonment of the world. It is not to be equated with that wandering which we have seen earlier generations of poets took to be integral to larger responsibilities.

Tennyson also loved retirement. But as Poet Laureate he was necessarily thrust onto public ground, and the consequences of this require some comment. One way of focusing on Tennyson's poetry of the 1850s is provided by Ernest Gellner. In *Nations and Nationalism* Gellner argues that as nations 'develop', that is move towards industrialisation, so it becomes increasingly necessary to produce a culture which, in its realisation through a formalised common language, seeks to homogenise all members of the nation.

> Culture . . . is no longer the adornment, confirmation and legitimation of a social order which was also sustained by harsher and coercive restraints; culture is now the necessary shared medium, the life-blood or perhaps rather the minimal shared atmosphere, within which the members of the society can breathe and survive and produce. For a given society, it must be one in which they can *all* breathe and speak and produce; so it must be the *same* (literate, training-sustained) culture.[6]

It is notable that the year of the Great Exhibition was the year in which the concept of received pronunciation became established. It is also notable that at this same period teacher-training colleges were set up, arts and craft schools established, education made more widely available. In short, many of the elements which constitute what is recognisably the culture of English nationhood came into existence at this time, or were progressively promoted, as were the structures by means of which the promotion of such culture could be made possible.

Two elements which require particular comment are xenophobia, specifically francophobia, and monarchism. This latter is an extraordinary matter. Whatever fears there had been that Victoria would live to be plain Miss Guelph were quite dissipated by 1851. David Cannadine's argument that it was only in the 1870s that Victoria's position becomes unassailable is vulnerable because he ignores all the evidence which shows how, from the moment of her coronation, and even more after her marriage, the monarchy had been self-consciously promoted.[7] Albert played the most significant part in this, and one of his shrewdest moves was to establish himself, and thus her, as a sympathetic champion of the arts, especially the manufacturing arts. As a result he 'naturally' aligned himself with middle-class tastes and interests. (His choice of pictures and sculptures to add to the royal collection was, as Winslow Ames has shown, almost aggressively safe.[8]) Even more important, his close involvement in the planning of the Great Exhibition identified the monarchy with commerce and manufacture, an identification virtually sealed by the prayer which the Archbishop of Canterbury uttered at the opening ceremony, in which he assured God that 'It is of Thee that there is peace within our walls and plenteousness within our palaces.' As Eric de Mare notes, 'The Deity was clearly on the side of expanding markets.'[9]

But this alignment of monarchy with commercialism was bound to present Tennyson with an acute dilemma. The new Poet Laureate was deeply distrustful of the society of the cash-nexus. His form of romantic conservatism was a reaction against precisely the kind of nationhood which the events of 1851 insistently celebrated. What price now Hallam's dream of a 'national existence' based on values which, no matter how loosely, could be identified with the chivalric code? To be sure, during the 1840s Victoria and Albert had often enough been imaged as the embodiments of that code. Henry Nicolas's frontispiece *The Order of Knighthood* (1848), depicting Victoria as Gloriana, is typical of many such images produced during the decade. But this had little to do with the spirit which the Great Exhibition symbolised.

Maud and Other Poems (1855) is Tennyson's attempt to resolve the dilemma. Its real interest lies in the tactic by means of which he tries to separate his crucial sense of what he regards as the destructive commercialism of the age from his desire to promote an alternative image of what the age might be or become. Not surprisingly, therefore, the volume was heavily criticised. Arnold told Clough that it was 'a lamentable production, and like so much of our literature thoroughly *provincial*, not European'. George Eliot reacted powerfully against the title poem and its 'faith in war as the unique social regenerater'.[10] They are both right. And yet it is possible to feel a good deal of sympathy with Tennyson, especially since 'Maud' in particular is a very considerable attempt to cope with the difficulties to which his position had exposed him.

Everyone who reads the poem recognises that its hero is in many respects similar to the hero of 'Locksley Hall'. Both are in love with a girl who is their social superior, both fear their love will not be returned or that even if it should be it will not be allowed to prosper, and both are driven to near madness by these fears. The intense mental anguish of each is finally assuaged by a decision to plunge into activity, and in the case of the hero of 'Maud', which is a poem written very much to the moment, this means soldierly activity. At the end he goes to do his duty in the Crimean War. Moreover, where in 'Locksley Hall' the hero's 'mad' loathing of 'the gold

that gilds the straitened forehead of a fool' had been directed specifically
against the inhabitants of the Hall, in the later poem the voiced hatred of
commercialism spreads wider:

> Why do they prate of the blessings of Peace? We have made them a curse,
> Pickpockets, each hand lusting for all that is not its own;
> And lust of gain, in the spirit of Cain, is it better or worse
> Than the heart of the citizen hissing in war on his own hearthstone?
>
> But these are the days of advance, the works of the men of mind
> When who but a fool would have faith in a tradesman's ware or his word?
> Is it peace or war? Civil war, as I think, and that of a kind
> The viler, as underhand, not openly bearing the sword.

(Part I, stanzas 6–7)

Four years after the poem's publication Gladstone wrote that 'we do not
recollect that 1855 was a season of serious danger from a mania for peace
and its pursuits'.[11] Which is clever, but misses the point. The man who
speaks the stanzas quoted above rages against that 'war' which for him
epitomises the commercial greed of mid-Victorian England, and in so doing
he has something in common with the Dickens who wrote *Bleak House* and
Little Dorrit.

But then this rage can be interpreted as paranoid frenzy. It is
self-reflexive rather than in any sense produced by and responsive to issues
of the moment. So at least it can be argued, and that it can allows Tennyson
to evade the possible charge of opposing monarchical interests. He would
need the escape route. For 'Maud' is a most un-Laureatelike poem, which
in no sense offers a unifying vision of the 'national existence'. The account
mediated by the poem's protagonist is one of schism, of negation and
hatred. Tennyson therefore requires explanations for this account that will
not lead back to him, but will instead focus on the protagonist himself as
mad for love or unhinged by his father's suicide, which we are told has been
brought about because 'a vast speculation had fail'd'. But then that, too, can
be read as disturbingly appropriate to a decade which produced the suicide
of, for example, John Sadleir MP, banker, company promoter, and forger.
(The fact that 'Maud' appeared before Sadleir killed himself strengthens
the poem's claim to be alert to particular pressures of the decade.)

Speaking of the horror of being exposed to detailed knowledge of
particular events, the historian J. A. Froude wrote that 'It is very lucky for us
that we are let to get off for the most part with generalities, and the
knowledge of details is left to those who suffer them. I think if it was not so
we should all go mad or shoot ourselves.'[12] The no-nonsense rejection of
Tennyson's poem by many of its reviewers can with some justice be
attributed to their refusal to confront more than generalities, whereas its

hero is deeply disturbed by and therefore hysterically responsive to 'knowledge of details', at least the guessed-at knowledge of what those details imply about the true nature of the 'great commercial nation', as Dickens sardonically put it. In short Tennyson uses his protagonist to explore his own deep disquiet about elements in the emergent nation for which as poet he rightly claims no objective or disinterested 'understanding'. But he needs to be devious about this. He has almost to trick his readers into understanding the impossibility of the Poet Laureate feeling at ease with the national identity as it was being brought to consciousness in those formations of the 1850s to which, precisely as Poet Laureate, he was supposed to pay allegiance.

It is therefore misleading of Christopher Ricks to argue that Tennyson's sense of 'the relationship between madness and monodrama enabled him to create a living representation of the way in which a morbid self-consciousness precludes the consciousness of others' selves'.[13] For the morbidity in question is at least partly formed by an indissoluble awareness of forces that underpin the society to which the poem's hero belongs but from which, by the same token, he feels necessarily alienated. The neurosis so evident in Tennyson's speaker is inseparable from considerations of class as they show themselves in his registering of such matters as the power of money, the institution of marriage, and social status. His sense of himself as inturned, separate, fearful, is then capable of becoming representative. Social relations are endlessly a source of threat, they *cannot* issue in a confident consciousness of 'others' selves'. The society of 'Maud' is atomistic, essentially unknowable.

But this is of course an impossible position for the Poet Laureate to adopt. Hence, the strategy to pin all these phantasmagoric visions onto the speaker's 'diseased' mind, as though that is spectacularly exceptional, even though the issues which cause his mental torment are deeply representative. Patrick Brantlinger remarks that choosing to go off to war offers the narrator a certainty of purpose which he cannot derive from sources associated with domestic tranquillity or commercial progress. 'And the same,' he continues, 'is true of Tennyson, who as Laureate must have felt grateful for a theme that allowed him to be unambiguously affirmative, since there was so much about which he felt equivocal or negative.'[14] This is to say that war brought out the Laureate in Tennyson, as indeed it did. And it brings us to an aspect of his work with which it is less easy to feel sympathy.

At the end of 'Maud' the protagonist announces that he has awoken from his mental torment to 'higher aims'. He will go to seek the 'blood-red blossom of war with a heart of fire', for now, 'I have felt with my native land, I am one with my kind'. This glib resolution, which denies the bulk of a poem where feeling one with the kind had been shown to be impossible, is one of noticeably abstract terms. It merely permits the flourish of a routine patriotism while evading all those problems to do with nationhood that 'Maud' implicitly raises. (It is worth remarking that the 'kind' were a good deal less ready to feel for the native land than these lines suggest; recruiting soldiers for the Crimean War was no easy task, although I do not suggest we are meant to read the passage ironically.[15]) Nor can it be said that the feeling of being 'one with my kind' is merely a further delusion of the protagonist. He didn't write 'Ode on the Death of the Duke of Wellington', nor 'The Charge of the Light Brigade', both of which poems appear in the volume.

Not much needs to be said about either poem. Kozicki claims that the hero of 'Maud', like his creator, hopes that 'somewhere out there a strong military ruler (like Arthur) is about to bring a tight order to the anarchy and civil war that presently characterise the nature of the state'.[16] By 'anarchy' Kozicki means commercial anarchy, and he thinks that Tennyson praises the Iron Duke not merely for his exploits as a soldier but for his statesmanship, and for somehow representing 'the people'.

> A people's voice! we are a people yet.
> Though all men else their nobler dreams forget,
> Confused by brainless mobs and lawless Powers;
> Thank Him who isled us here, and roughly set
> His Briton in blown seas and storming showers,
> We have a voice, with which to pay the debt
> Of boundless love and reverence and regret
> To those great men who fought, and kept it ours.
> And keep it ours, O God, from brute control;
> O Statesmen, guard us, guard the eye, the soul
> Of Europe, keep our noble England whole,
> And save the one true seed of freedom sown
> Betwixt a people and their ancient throne,
> That sober freedom out of which there springs
> Our loyal passion for our temperate kings;
> For, saving that, ye help to save mankind
> Till public wrong be crumbled into dust,
> And drill the raw world for the march of mind,
> Till crowds at length be sane and crowns be just.

The 'brute control' from which England is to be saved has presumably to be understood as mass democracy. Tennyson here undoubtedly identifies the admiration for the anti-democratic Wellington with that Carlylean worship of heroism on which the health of nations depends, or so we are to understand, just as England's depends on its 'loyal passion for our temperate kings'. Temperate? George IV? The sanctimoniousness of this is as hard to bear as the claim that Wellington has somehow brought the people together in spite of those 'brainless mobs' whom the Iron Duke opposed over the Reform Bill. We are a long way here from Ebenezer

Elliott's 'Hater evangelised of liberty', further still from Byron's address to the 'best of cut-throats'. But: 'we are a people yet'. The ode operates so as to dismiss oppositional voices by identifying 'the people' with monarchy, with Wellingtonian statesmanship and with God's will ('Thank Him who isled us here'). 'The people' is a variant on the 'kind'. In both cases the complexity and divisiveness of the experience of being English is simply denied. Tennyson calls Wellington a Briton and Wellington was born in Ireland. (Though Wellington indignantly rejected the suggestion that he was therefore Irish: 'You might as well call a man a horse because he was born in a stable.' But *England* is Tennyson's real concern.) And in the volume's concluding 'The Charge of the Light Brigade' we have an image of insouciant, chivalric heroism held up for us as unstated embodiment of the 'kind' with which the hero of 'Maud' eventually claims to be able to identify.

Yet the fine 'To the Rev. F. D. Maurice', which also appears in the volume, cannot rest content with this uninflected image.

> We might discuss the Northern sin
> Which made a selfish war begin;
> > Dispute the claims, arrange the chances;
> Emperor, Ottoman, which shall win:
>
> Or whether war's avenging rod
> Shall lash all Europe into blood . . .

Maurice, the Christian socialist, had been made to resign his professorship at King's College, London, because of his religious non-orthodoxy. (He had argued in *Theological Essays* that an eternity of punishment was incredible.) Tennyson's poem then pointedly and honourably aligns the Laureate with an outcast. It also allows us to recognise that the connections between Christian socialism and Tennyson's political position were many and strong. Both disliked the dominant features of emergent capitalism, both sought in 'chivalric manliness' an antidote to the selfish aggressions of the 1840s and 50s. Tennyson could therefore readily sympathise with Maurice, could see in his persecution an example of a selflessly high-minded man brought down by time-serving venality, or by a kind of petty-mindedness that stood at the opposite extreme from the dauntless grandeur of the men of the Light Brigade.

In an interesting account of 'The Charge of the Light Brigade', Jerome McGann argues that Tennyson is hoping to show that 'the English aristocracy has lost none of its leadership qualities', and that it can still supply 'spiritual models' to an admiring nation.[17] The difficulty with this argument has less to do with the adequacy of such a model than with the reflection that it was aristocratic qualities – Raglan's, for instance – that led to the pointless sacrifice of the brigade in the first place. I am more persuaded by McGann's suggestion that Tennyson sees in the charge an opportunity to win back for Englishness a glory that has been usurped by the French *chasseur*, but then this points to the unpalatable fact of Tennyson's hysterical francophobia in numerous poems of the 1850s, including 'Rifle Clubs!!!', 'Britons Guard Your Own', 'Riflemen Form!', 'Jack Tar' and several more. Agreed, one might try to argue that these poems are intended to do no more than warn against the possible aggressive intentions of Louis Napoleon; but when they are put beside other poems which come early and late, such as 'Hail Briton' and 'The Defence of Lucknow', we have to conclude that *this* Tennyson is a simple-minded xenophobe and imperialist, one who will come to endorse the concept of chivalry as it is presented in *Idylls of the King* which then founders, as it must, on the failings of individuals.

The *Idylls of the King* record a deep bafflement. On the one hand they unhesitatingly put their reliance on chivalric values. On the other, the fact that they are set in a legendary past cuts them off from present realities. And anyway, by the time they have come to an end Camelot has fallen. Tennyson, it is true, writes into this a divine purpose, as he had to do; but it seems proper to assume that by the close of the sequence he had written himself out of an effort to come to terms with the complex implications of nationhood over which he had laboured in *Maud and Other Poems*. The *Idylls* are history as non-history, their concern with moral exempla a way of sealing individuality off from those social pressures, of class, money, gender, which, in no matter how muffled or inconclusive a way, Tennyson had tried to work through in earlier poems. And the relatively simple paradigm of history as evolution which the *Idylls* sketch – those 'concatenated generations' again – cannot really be sustained, for the obvious reason that not only is the fellowship of Camelot itself dissolved but that Tennyson has no other way of accounting for transition except in terms of disaster. 'We are a people yet.' Tennyson might wish to proclaim that, but deep down he feared otherwise. Or rather, the only terms by which he could hold onto an idea of nationhood had little to do with the social actualities of mid-Victorian England, into which he necessarily read a chaos of unknowability. 'England' becomes a series of meaningless generalisations: a people, a kind, an existence, empty of realisable content.

II

Like Tennyson, Browning has his quest poems, and in the great 'Childe Roland to the Dark Tower Came' he combines the quest with an ideal of chivalric conduct, although being Browning he does this in a way which defeats expectations. The poem ends in confusion and the assertion of dauntlessness against impossible odds which, if in one sense it may connect with the kind of example set by the Light Brigade, in another calls the whole notion of chivalric individuality into question. Of what use is it in this overwhelmingly hostile environment? Or, of what use is an individuality which must regard the world out there as inevitably hostile? At the heart of the poem's unfathomable mystery is a sense that the seeker is perhaps being mocked: that this dauntless heroism is absurd. Romantic individualism is predicated on a distrust of others: heroes cannot be members of a community, and community threatens the status, the identity, of heroes. So, at least, 'Childe Roland' can be read, the more readily as we note how delighted Browning was to put down heroes, especially chauvinistic Englishmen. I think, for example, of the spokesman of 'Apparent Failure', visiting the Paris morgue, who

> plucked up heart and entered, – stalked,
> Keeping a tolerable face
> Compared with some whose cheeks were chalked:
> Let them! No Briton's to be balked!

This out-Podsnaps Podsnap. And, 'Briton'. As enlightened sports journalists often point out, when the English want to parade the virtues of English teams and/or their fans they insist on the 'English'. When things go wrong, it is the 'British' who are to blame. More importantly, however, the Brownings' decision to settle in Florence must be seen as a deliberate choice, not merely to identify with a nation which was struggling to gain its own national identity against outside oppressors, but also as a rejection of particular values associated with, and perhaps becoming oppressive in, England, and as an identification with a different set of values. These latter reach back to Byron and Shelley, as how could they not, although the choice of Florence rather than Venice puts a distance between the Brownings and 'the great sun-treader' and his friend.

Browning is not at all censorious about what Venice had come to mean by the time he and his wife left for Italy. In 'A Toccato of Galuppi's' the narrator, a musician, scientist, agnostic, ruefully accepts the cold futility of his own life, compared with which the fashionable world and the dear, dead women of the Venice he imagines glow with vital warmth and sexual ardency. But Florence is untainted by associations of that sexual irresponsibility which Byron, above all, had brought to it. (His responsible life belongs, in image at least, to Greece.) Florence was Dickens's favourite city: a city, he wrote at the end of *Pictures from Italy*, 'not of siege, and war, and might, and Iron Hand alone, but of the triumphant growth of peaceful Arts and Sciences'. Barbara Melchiori claims that 'Elizabeth Barrett was a much more ardent sympathiser with the cause of Italian freedom, but then she had a weakness for causes (varying from the fate of factory children to Louis Napoleon) which was notably lacking in her husband.'[18] This is to misunderstand, almost entirely, the radicalism that led the Brownings to Florence.

They were not unaware of its history, nor of the part that the Iron Hand had played in it. But as *English* people in *Florence* they were necessarily, self-consciously, enabled to redefine the possibilities of Englishness. This becomes clear as soon as we consider 'Love Among the Ruins'. Browning put this poem at the head of *Men and Women* which, like *Maud and Other Poems*, appeared in 1855. The poem's placing therefore has an obvious iconic importance. Isobel Armstrong helpfully comments that:

> Lawrence was quite right to make Birkin see 'Love Among the Ruins' as an apocalyptic poem set in a disintegrating society when he quotes it to Gerald in *Women in Love*. The girl waiting for the lover in the empty landscape of 'undistinguished grey', trying to pour all her energies into a single, solitary relationship, waits in the ruins made by a once vivid, aggressive and expansive society . . . Love *is* best, surely, but Browning's point, I think, is that one should not have to see the question as a choice at all. It should not be necessary to make a choice between love and society . . . How can a love relationship placed in an extra-historical, extra-social emptiness be made to bear the whole weight of meaning and value, the total significance of being? As if to enforce the point, 'A Lovers' Quarrel' followed . . .[19]

This is well said, although Armstrong misses an all-important point. We do not know exactly when the poem was written, nor where, nor about which city the narrator speaks. But he makes clear that where now are ruins

> Was the site once of a city great and gay,
> (So they say)
> Of our country's very capital, its prince
> Ages since
> Held his court in, gathered councils, wielding far
> Peace or war.

This is how the poem begins, and it ends:

> In one year they sent a million fighters forth
> South and North,
> And they built their gods a brazen pillar high
> As the sky,
> Yet reserved a thousand chariots in full force –
> Gold, of course.
> Oh heart! oh blood that freezes, blood that burns!
> Earth's returns
> For whole centuries of folly, noise and sin!
> Shut them in,
> With their triumphs and their glories and the rest!
> Love is best.

One can see why the poet who wrote this should have so admired the poet who wrote 'Ozymandias', and why, associated with Florence as he is, Browning emerges as insistently anti-masculinist in his rejection of the ideals associated with war and martial heroism. To repeat: 'Love Among the Ruins' appeared at the head of a volume which was published in 1855. It has therefore to be read as a rejection of those values associated with the frantic prosecution of the Crimean War. It is not, then, placed in an extra-historical, extra-social emptiness, as Armstrong suggests.

The contrast with Tennyson Laureate is instructive. The protagonist of 'Maud' awakens from his self-enclosed madness into a feeling of brotherly at-oneness with his 'kind', which will then be tested through war. Serving Queen and country is an ideal of exclusively male activity (Florence Nightingale – the symbolic appropriateness of that name seems almost uncanny – sweetens the ideal, but her moment comes later). And it is significant that the war is officially endorsed by the institution of the Victoria Cross. Browning will have none of it. His protagonist rejects the ideal of heroic comradeship in arms for 'a girl with eager eyes and yellow hair [who] waits me there/In the turret where the charioteers caught soul/For the goal,/When the King looked, where she looks now'. In the manuscript version the poem's last line reads '*This* is best!' and behind that emphatic utterance one hears an echo of Antony's 'The nobleness of life/Is to do thus,' a claim, it will be remembered, which comes moments after he has said 'Let Rome in Tiber melt, and the wide arch/Of the ranged Empire fall!' Browning presumably changed the line, not so much to obliterate the echo as because, once he had decided that 'Love Among the Ruins' was to be placed first in *Men and Women*, he needed a more aptly ironic movement to the following poem, 'A Lovers' Quarrel'. For Browning's understanding of the dynamics of sexual relationships will not allow him to settle for the confident stasis which is apparently signalled by the poem's closing assertion.

Nevertheless, the argument of 'Love Among the Ruins' may seem to bring it in some respects interestingly close to 'Dover Beach'. Browning could not of course have known Arnold's poem, which was first published in 1867, although written much earlier, any more than he could have known about 'Maud'. The point is rather that at this time all three poets came in different ways to see tensions between private and public life as producing stark choices or alternatives; and that these focused particularly on the aggressive forces of the emergent ethos which led not only to war within the state ('the heart of the citizen hissing in war on his own hearthstone'), but war between states, and therefore to choices about how to register Englishness. Tennyson, it is true, tries to ignore the impact of these divisive forces at the conclusion of 'Maud', but their presence at earlier moments is unmistakable – is, indeed, the real cause of what happens. As for Arnold, the famous ending of 'Dover Beach', with its carefully calculated echo of Thucydides' account of the Battle of Epipolae, makes the 'ignorant armies' not only metaphoric of conflicting faiths and contending ideologies, but of wider struggles. 'On the French coast the light/Gleams and is gone; the cliffs of England stand,/Glimmering and vast.' This hints at the possibility of confrontation between two nations which ought, as far as Arnold is concerned, to have interests in common beyond their rivalries. For Arnold is at his most sympathetic when he seeks to find grounds for validating a *European* vision against that Englishness which he found so 'provincial' in Tennyson. And unthinking endorsement of the cause of war, especially the Crimean War, *is* provincial. (Although, interestingly enough, Arnold came to be as chauvinistic about it as Tennyson.) Arnold thought of England as necessarily a province of Europe, as it had earlier been a province of the Roman Empire. For him to say as much is silkily to rebuke those who claim a special status for 'the island race'.

But in 'Dover Beach' the alternative to ignorant armies is not, after all, a wider vision, but a narrower one. With the plaintive appeal, 'Ah, love, let us be true/To one another!' the more generous vision fades and is replaced by a wished-for retreat into private relationship. This may seem close to the assertion which ends 'Love Among the Ruins'. But there are crucial differences. I have already noted that Browning's awareness of the dynamics of sexual relationships will not allow him to endorse so absolute a claim as being 'true to one another'. Then again, as Isobel Armstrong says, 'it should not be necessary to make a choice between love and society'; and in Browning's poetry it isn't: love is socialised. Its appearance and the tensions that accompany it are related, no matter how problematically, to forces at work within the social process of which men and women are inextricably a part. The effect of this is to deny a transcendent authority to the lovers' viewpoint – especially since that viewpoint is itself endlessly contested from within the relationship. In 'Dover Beach', on the other hand, Arnold's view is permitted an authority which is never challenged, so that although what it registers is a profound alienation from the world of ignorant armies, this is offered as definitive. The man not only speaks *to* the woman, he speaks *for* her, interprets the world for her; and what he sees is offered as a final truth.

J. Hillis Miller claims that 'Dover Beach' is about 'the modern sort of love', in which 'two people . . . need one another to fill up the void in their breasts. Such modern lovers plight their troth in the face of an awareness that there is no universal love to guarantee the particular acts of love. Aloneness is now man's real condition, and love is founded on its despair.'[20] But this is some way from Arnold's poem, in which we know only what one person thinks. Miller, that is, cedes Arnold the authority which Browning challenges. All that 'Dover Beach' can finally affirm is the speaker's belief in the validity of his reading of 'the world' as having 'really neither joy, nor love, nor light,/Nor certitude, nor peace, nor help for pain'. And such blank generalisations are bound to tell us more about the speaker's state of consciousness than the world, or that part of it called England.

In sharp contrast to Arnold, Browning constantly denies the authority of any one point of view. He unfixes certainty. And so, as has already been noted, the claim 'Love is best' is immediately followed by a poem called 'A Lovers' Quarrel'. This essentially democratic strategy is repeatedly used in *Men and Women*. One result is to deny the authority of 'the poet'. Instead, we have in the volume a variety of voices whose major significance is that between them they unsettle, discompose, offer contradiction and impatience as a denial of all those calm certainties which Arnold thought alone appropriate for poetry. This is why the ordering of poems is so important to Browning's great volume. Everything is to be contested.

'Childe Roland to the Dark Tower Came' is, for example, followed by 'Respectability'. The former, deeply mysterious as it is, seems to evoke a particular kind of consciousness through its hero: dogged, undeflectable, persevering. Childe Roland is a captain courageous, even, perhaps, an intrepid voyager into a heart of darkness, and as such recognisable to a readership which knew about Mungo Park and the earlier adventures of Livingstone.[21] He can be claimed for a particular kind of Englishness. (The fact that Park and Livingstone were Scottish notwithstanding. When Dr John Kirk of Forfar was on the trail of the Zambezi with Livingstone they had a rude reception from one village until the headman 'found that we were English'. He then 'began to change his manner'. Kirk goes on to say that although he wouldn't have minded shooting 'the low rascals', it was 'our respectability in England that kept us back'.[22]) Arnold evokes a similar mode of Englishness in 'Rugby Chapel', the poem he wrote in 1857 to his father's memory:

> We were weary, and we
> Fearful, and we in our march
> Fain to drop down and die.
> Still thou turnedst, and still
> Beckonedst the trembler, and still
> Gavest the weary thy hand

Dr Arnold, his son says, was a soul 'temper'd with fire,/Fervent, heroic, and good'.

When Browning was asked whether the meaning of 'Childe Roland' was that 'he that endureth to the end shall be saved', he apparently answered, 'Just about that.'[23] As a poem of its time 'Childe Roland' teases out and worries at qualities of conscience which form a habit of consciousness, affirming commitment to activity, to doing, which could be claimed for an especially cherishable kind of Englishness. This consciousness typically sounds out in a moment of unselfconscious bluster when Charles Kingsley writes of 'the true English stuff . . . the stuff which has held Gibraltar and conquered at Waterloo – which has created a Birmingham and a Manchester, and colonised every quarter of the globe – that grim, earnest, stubborn energy, which, since the days of the old Romans, the English possess alone of all the nations of the earth' (*Alton Locke*, 1850, Chapter 12).

Browning does something far better than satirise such crassness. Against the consciousness of the hero of 'Childe Roland' he sets 'Respectability'. Here, the male speaker murmurs to, or rather with, the woman with whom he has eloped. The tone implies loving familiarity. The man recalls how, had they obeyed the dictates of respectability, they would have wrecked their lives and have been in no position to find out the truth of what the world fears – that is, sexual love. The poem is wonderfully candid in its rejoicing in such love, but in no boastful sense: the speaker's voice is warm, tender, and also wittily confident in its assumption that his lover will share his benign contempt for the 'world and what it fears'.

> How much of priceless life were spent
>   With men that every virtue decks,
>   And women models of their sex,
> Society's true ornament, –
> Ere we dared wander, nights like this,
>   Through wind and rain, and watch the Seine,
>   And feel the Boulevart break again
> To warmth and light and bliss?
>
> I know! The world proscribes not love;
>   Allows my finger to caress
>   Your lips' contour and downiness,
> Provided it supply a glove.
> The world's good word! – the Institute!
>   Guizot receives Montalembert!
> Eh? Down the court three lampions flare:
> Put forward your best foot.

On 5 February 1852, at a ceremony at which Browning was apparently present, François Guizot had to welcome his enemy Charles Montalembert into the French Academy.[24] The end of the poem has the two lovers turn away from this show of worldly hypocrisy, secure in their relationship.

But in the next poem the world insistently presses in on a private relationship. The speaker of 'A Light Woman' is one of those that 'every virtue decks'. He appeals to the listener – who turns out to be Browning – to agree that he behaved honourably in saving his young friend from the wiles of a seductress. What he then testifies to is what the previous poem had shown to be the world's fear of sexuality and, as it turns out, male fear, even hatred, of women:

> And she, – she lies in my hand as tame
> As a pear late basking over a wall;
> Just a touch to try and off it came;
> 'Tis mine, – can I let it fall?
>
> With no mind to eat it, that's the worst!
> Were it thrown in the road, would the case assist?
> 'Twas quenching a dozen blue-flies' thirst
> When I gave its stalk a twist.

The masculinist arrogance of this is inseparable from its denaturing of the 'light woman'.

Men and Women is among many things remarkable for Browning's acute, troubled and troubling recognition of the construction of English masculinity as that is predicated on concepts of heroism, dauntless courage, which cannot easily be dissociated from the perversions and psychological malaise of the speaker of 'A Light Woman'. The strategy of the volume is such as to force these disconcerting matters into every reader's mind, and that includes Browning's. For as I have said, at the end of 'A Light Woman' the narrator's silent listener turns out to be Browning himself, and if one way to read this is simply ironic – as the author of this volume he is not to be identified with the hatreds and sexual fears of this speaker – another is to register the fact that the speaker confidently anticipates Browning's sympathetic understanding. Browning, that is, allows himself to be cast in the role of the English male who, from the point of view of other such males, can be expected to share this particular view of women. It may even be that he felt he had no choice in the matter: all men may be guilty of such a view, or of the temptations to surrender to it.

In *The English Novel from Dickens to Lawrence* Raymond Williams touches on an aspect of this issue when he speaks of what was excluded from 'the achieved social mode, social tone', of the 1840s and 50s, especially, he says, 'if we remember that in a more evidently powered society it was a masculine mode. I don't mean universally or generically masculine, but what manly was coming to mean . . . What was taught and learned was a new and rigid control, "self-control" – even weak men not crying and being very stiff and proud of it.'[25] Williams's own tone here is necessarily hesitant, exploratory. But what he senses about this 'masculine mode' is valuable when we come to look at what Browning was working at in his volumes of the 1840s and 50s, and above all in *Men and Women*.

This is why Browning's dramatic method is not some quirk of fancy, any more than his unusual prosody is proof of incompetence: of a poet of barbarism who does not know how to be civilised. The speaker of 'A Light

197

Woman' does not lack for civility, any more than the speaker of 'My Last Duchess'. But other, less 'civilised' voices, ones less attuned to or conditioned by the iambic, by the pentameter, are given utterance throughout Browning's key volumes, and in their very strangeness these voices compel our attention, require us to recognise that English speaking doesn't have to go all one way. 'We', here, encompasses a very wide constituency of possible readers. And insofar as we take on these voices in reading the poems we, too, are startled into strangeness, are made to renounce any one, authoritative mode of utterance. Propriety, appropriateness: these become testing issues. Who would wish to speak with the cultivated accents of the Duke of Ferrara? What man would not yearn to be free to speak as does the lover of 'Respectability'?

The questions are not entirely rhetorical. Not all Browning's male contemporaries were at ease with his work. Walter Bagehot spoke for many of them when he complained that Browning's popularity had come about because 'We live in the realm of the *half* educated.' He means that 'grotesque' art such as Browning's could only make an appeal to an audience which had no true 'cultivation'. Although Bagehot is prepared to acknowledge Browning's 'great ability' and 'his great *mind*', and despite the fact that he gives his apparent approval to the poet because Browning 'knows women, and therefore they wish to know him', it is clear that he intends to damn with faint praise. Behind the sneers lies the recognition that Browning's art is truly radical; and it is hardly to be wondered at that Bagehot should fear it, nor that he should use his polished cynicism – his 'civilised' tone – to try to assert his superiority to Browning, his right to sit in judgement on him.[26]

I do not know the extent to which Browning relied on his wife: on her opinions and on her own, liberating example. But it seems reasonable to assume that her influence was considerable. At all events, when he returned to England after her death he began that downward movement towards the bland, incurious kind of Englishness which so baffled and vexed Thomas Hardy. And it is significant that in republishing his earlier work Browning chose to alter the original order of the poems. He therefore prevented new readers from recognising just how discomforting the poems had at first been. As a result, the radical, democratic, anti-authoritarianism of the volumes was smoothed away, as were the problematic readings of Englishness to which they had given rise. It is as though return to England marks Browning's readiness to be absorbed into precisely those accommodating, containing versions of the English poet as upholder of orthodox 'truths' – monarchist, Anglican, even masculinist – which at his greatest, in Florence, he had opposed.

By revealing coincidence, 1861, the year in which both Elizabeth Barrett Browning and Prince Albert died, was the year in which Palgrave first published his *Golden Treasury of the Best Songs and Lyrical Poems in the English Language*, dedicated to 'Alfred Tennyson, Poet Laureate'. I have referred in an earlier chapter to Palgrave's insistence that the best poetry of the Romantic period owes nothing to politics. Here I should add that he praises Shelley for his style and for qualities that align him with Scott, Wordsworth, Thomas Campbell and Keats: they all apparently share a 'reverence for human Passion and Character in every sphere, and impassioned love of Nature'. The denial of political actualities in this act of accommodation is to be expected of Palgrave. In 1871 he published a book-length poem, *The Visions of England* (it presumably helped secure him the Professorship of Poetry at Oxford). Towards the end of this series of visions comes 'A Dorset Idyl'.

> Dear land, where new is one with old:
>   Land of green hillside and of plain,
>   Gray tower and grange and tree-fringed lane,
> Red crag and silver streamlet sweet . . .

There is no point in spending time on these sub-Tennysonian verses, Palgrave is too inept a poet. Nevertheless, the entire absence of people from his idyl is worthy of note, as is the fact that the England evoked is endlessly and entirely rural. There are no new cities or towns here, any more than there are tensions between 'green hillside and plain'. One would not know from Palgrave's poem that at this time Joseph Arch was moving to form the Agricultural Labourers' Union. Palgrave's mythic England is entirely remote from actuality, though not at all remote from what was to become a dominant strain of writing in the final decades of the nineteenth century, in which the obliteration of the new, city-based, industrial England would be no more remarkable than the production of a 'dear land' whose health did not apparently require people to live in it.

In the year Palgrave produced his *Visions* Gerard Manley Hopkins was writing his famous 'red letter' to Robert Bridges:

> it is a dreadful thing for the greatest and most necessary part of a very rich nation to live a hard life without dignity, knowledge, comforts, delight, or hopes in the midst of plenty – which plenty they make. They profess that they do not care what they wreck and burn, the old civilization and order must be destroyed. This is a dreadful look out but what has the old civilization done for them? As it at present stands in England it is itself in great measure founded on wrecking. But they got none of the spoils, they came in for nothing but harm from it then and thereafter. England has grown hugely wealthy but this wealth has not reached the working classes . . . The more I look the more black and deservedly black the future looks.[27]

The future Poet Laureate was so aghast at this letter that he broke off communication with Hopkins for over four years. Yet Hopkins's poetry could not have so disturbed him. (It disturbed him for very different reasons.) Hopkins never managed to work the perceptions of his letter into his poetry, and this is not merely to be explained by the fact that he modified his political views. Neither the 'flaming republican' Swinburne nor the marxist William Morris was able to write about the city, nor about those issues on which Hopkins's letter touches. None of them finds it possible to say much about England 'as it at present stands'. And if we turn to one of the finest poets of this period, Christina Rossetti, it is only to confirm that as a woman, operating within a specific frame of reference, she is as disadvantaged as were a number of regional poets, such as Edwin Waugh or Ben Brearley, or as was William Barnes, whose self-conscious adoption of Dorset dialect necessarily marginalised or contained him, as Waugh and Brearley's regionalism contained them.[28]

Given this, it was the more possible for Arnold and his heirs to promote that 'moral' tradition of English poetry which centred on Wordsworth. This tradition can and usually does distance the difficult, contentious questions with which this book has been concerned. The story is familiar. Milton is a master of style (or not, according to taste); Shelley can be written off as a beautiful, ineffectual angel; Byron praised for his satire on philistinism, his penetrating simplicity, but criticised for his lack of 'knowledge, self-discipline, virtue', which would have allowed him to find 'the way out of the false state of things which enraged him'. Arnold, it must be said, writes brilliantly about Byron, but then he could be more at ease with him than he could be with Shelley, of whom he found it necessary to say, 'the moment he reflects, he is a child'. Yet even Byron's politics are denied him. Arnold ends by comparing him with Wordsworth and making him Wordsworth's inferior. 'Wordsworth has an insight into permanent sources of joy and consolation for mankind which Byron has not; his poetry gives us more which we may rest upon than Byron's – more which we may rest upon now, and we may rest upon always.'[29]

This is to make large claims on behalf of mankind. It is even to make large claims on behalf of that small portion of it who are called English or, as their passports tell them, British.

AFTERWORD

Writing to his friend Robert Bridges in 1878, Hopkins complained of the difficulties of making poems in or about the city. 'My muse turned utterly sullen in the Sheffield smoke-ridden air', he told Bridges. This may be linked to Arnold's famous invitation to Clough to reflect 'how deeply *unpoetical* the age and one's surroundings are'.[1] Between them, these statements prompt the obvious reflection that the cities of the nineteenth century were difficult for poets to write about because as entirely new experiences they required an entirely new language. Such a language existed, of course: but it was the language of the streets, of industry, of machinery, and it was therefore of little use to poets, burdened as they were with that language of authority whose appeal lay precisely in its being distanced from the forces of anarchy – in a word, from the city. For the novelists it was a very different matter, but then they were free of the cultural assumptions which fastened onto Poetry, and, unless they were extremely rare spirits, poets.

This is not to say that there were no city poems. A number of poets tried to incorporate their responses to the life of the city into their work. But, Browning apart, no English poet of the nineteenth century found a satisfactory way of registering that most crucial element of city life, its heterogeneity. Or rather, when they did so it was to insist that the city effectively meant Bedlam, Babel – or hell. Thus 'The City of Dreadful Night', written by James Thomson ('B.V.') between 1870 and 1874, presents the city as a phantasmagoric, nightmare vision of a society devoid of all purpose and therefore meaning. Thomson's linguistic and imagistic resources are heavily dependent on the hells of Dante and Milton (or, more particularly, what was made of these in the nineteenth century). In this he is typical. Poets and artists drew so regularly on – and from – these models that it may be said that most contemporary verbal and visual representations of the city are less acts of discovery than foreknowledge.[2] The same point could be put rather differently: the stylistic means by which the city was to be confronted and accounted for were, in fact, a means of evading the experiences it actually offered.

This is scarcely surprising. We make the world out of the language we have available to us. But the language available to later-nineteenth-century poets trying to write about the city was so little suited to the purpose that they inevitably distorted or, more usually, gave up in despair. The city became 'indescribable', especially since beyond the word's literal meaning was the *frisson* which suggested that no description could encompass the city's wickedness, its in- or sub-human life. This leads to a further point.

The poet speaks from the position of authority. Yet that which is indescribable must also be unknowable. (For although it is true that to call something indescribable is, perhaps, to hint that you are party to knowledge which you dare not share with others, this only shows that what you dare not describe has power over you, rather than you over it.) The unknowable city therefore takes away the poet's authority. It silences him. And from a certain standpoint the city *was* unknowable. It harboured dark secrets, hidden places, areas where no 'respectable' person could go. It enforced the recognition that here at least a belief in social coherence was virtually meaningless. As Esther Summerson muses in the greatest of all novels about the city, 'what the poor are to the poor is little known' (*Bleak House*, Chapter 8). Little known to middle-class city dwellers, she means; and *Bleak House* is deeply concerned with how unknowable England is becoming, even or perhaps especially to those who think they have a 'natural' authority to speak for it. Church, monarchy, law, government: what they collectively 'know' of England is only what they know of 'England', a mythically simple, well-ordered land which has hardly anything to do with the teeming, multiple, separate lives of Dickens's novel. True, writers such as Mayhew, Booth and Mearns plunged into darkest, unknown London in order to bring back reports about its inhabitants, but their travellers' tales were bound to reinforce the feeling of the essential unknowability of those about whom they wrote. *Demos* spoke with the bestial roar of the jungle, and it is a much-remarked fact that late-nineteenth-century writing about the city employs a kind of social Darwinism in order to suggest that city life is dehumanised and dehumanising.

Writing about the city which seeks to re-impose authority does so only at the expense of writing the city off. Its abstract insistencies deny concrete, actual lives. It therefore betrays an anxiety which decisively undermines its user's claim to justifiable authority or knowledge. He cannot speak to and for *demos*: he can only speak about it. The city, the crowd, the people, are homogenised by tropes which are self-reflexive. They tell one about the writer rather than about his ostensible subject. An obvious case in point is Hopkins's 'Tom's Garland'. Given that the poem's subtitle is 'Upon the Unemployed', you might suppose that here at least Hopkins would be determined to confront that phenomenon of the nineteenth-century city, its industrialised workforce. Yet the bulk of the poem is taken up with the description of one employed man. Tom is an ideal labourer in the mould of those joyous workers of Ford Madox Brown's famous painting *Work* (1852–6), in the centre of which is, in Brown's own words, 'the young navvy in the pride of manly health and beauty; the strong, fully developed navvy who does his work and loves his beer'.[3] This is clearly the prototype for 'Tom-Heart-at-ease, Tom navvy'. (It is worth remarking that celebrating the individual navvy is one thing; trying to come to terms with gangs of navvies is quite another, especially when such navvies were full of the beer they loved. No workmen were more feared as hooligan elements.) Only in the last two lines of 'Tom's Garland' do the unemployed make an appearance:

> This, by Despair, bred Hangdog dull; by Rage
> Manwolf, worse; and their packs infest the age.

As John Robinson remarks, 'This is journalistic in its sensationalist generalisations. Is Hopkins' "their packs infest the age" an attack on the unemployed or upon their condition?'[4] The answer could well be – both. That is, Hopkins may intend to deplore the conditions, but in using the word 'packs' he betrays an inability to find a language equal to the actualities he wants to write about. His gesture towards knowledge only reveals his ignorance and his own ideological position (which feeds and is fed by his ignorance). The unemployed become animals, roaming out of control in the city jungle, where no decent poet would wish to go. A contemporary cliché substitutes for thought.

In a letter to Bridges, Hopkins remarked that 'this state of things, I say, is the origin of Loafers, Tramps, Cornerboys, Roughs, Socialists and other pests of society'. And earlier in the same letter he speaks of his attempt in the poem to do justice to the fact that 'as St Paul and Plato and Hobbes and everybody says, the commonwealth or well ordered human society is like one man; a body with many members and each its function; some higher, some lower, but all honourable, from the honour which belongs to the whole'.[5] Such abstractions have to be set against the 'pests' who presumably deny 'everybody's' version of the commonwealth. But given that the assertion requires and indeed cannot manage without a language at once journalistic and derivative (the echo of a famous Marvell conceit in the poem's final lines is as unmistakable as it is fatal), the implausibility of Hopkins's reading of the city unemployed decisively undercuts the implicit claim for authoritative utterance.

Like most poets of his time, Hopkins's attitudes are virtually deterministic because determined by matters of class and culture which leave him baffled at how little usable authority he has when it comes to writing about the city. Hence, the alternative of a 'truly' human life to be discovered in the country and endorsed as inherently valuable. The world which is shook with the grandeur of God has nothing in common with London or Liverpool or

Sheffield or Dublin. The 'health' of England is therefore 'rooted' in country living. At this point the story becomes familiar. It is that of the cultivated ruralism of late-nineteenth-century and Edwardian poetry. This is an ordered, orderly world. Just how widely shared was the commitment to this world hardly needs pointing up, and full explanation for its persistence would take another book.[6] Here, I will say only that the heterogeneity of Browning's voices, which do imply a city vision and a democratic one, too, are abandoned in the interest of producing a coherent, 'authoritative' account of a rural England, which is doubly mythic in that the ruralism is unreal (as Hardy's novels can show) and because by the end of the century very few people lived outside the cities and major towns.

It might be thought that two poets at least would stand out against this prevailing ethos. Morris and Swinburne were both socialists, and both were therefore ardent republicans in whom one might expect to find a swift contempt for that rural vision whose implicit politics of containment and hierarchical structures so infect English poetry at the century's end. Yet while Morris had no wish to bless the squire and his relations, his detestation of the city made it impossible for him to see it as other than the determining factor in the dehumanisation of its inhabitants. The visionary utopia of *News From Nowhere* is arrived at by a journey upriver from London and away from the symbol of its degraded work – Hammersmith Bridge. And Morris's poems promote a vision of England whose vitality is inseparable from its rurality.

As for Swinburne, in many ways the most radical of all late-nineteenth-century poets, especially in his determination to break with 'English' metres and subjects and in his eager championing of Baudelaire and Whitman, the one way in which he does *not* follow them is in responding to the city. Baudelaire's *flâneur* is by no means in love with the life of the city streets. As Walter Benjamin has shown, Auguste Barbier's cycle of London poems deeply influenced Baudelaire. He echoed the ending of Barbier's 'Londres' ('Enfin, dans un amas de choses, sombre, immense,/Un peuple noir, vivant et mourant en silence') in the final lines of his own 'Crépuscule du Soir': '. . . ils finissent/Leur destinée et vont vers le gouffre commun'. But Baudelaire absorbed city life in a manner that Swinburne could not.

> Tes yeux, illuminés que des boutiques
> Et des ifs flamboyants dans les fêtes publiques,
> Usent insolemment d'un pouvoir emprunté.

This both acknowledges the existence of others who do not acknowledge the existence of the poet (something on which T. S. Eliot draws in his city poems) and in its imagistic resourcefulness specifically relates this condition to the city. The *flâneur* as observer is keenly alert to his own reactions to the city crowds while recognising that they *are* his and do not amount to a final verdict on the crowds themselves.[7] There is nothing like that in Swinburne.

It is true that in the poetry of this period it is possible to find voices which speak out of the city: the voices of clerks, as in John Davidson's 'Thirty Bob a Week', the soldiers of Kipling's 'Barrack Room Ballads', the roustabouts in early Masefield and Wilfrid Gibson. But these are sport poems; they are versions of the quaintness which made its appearance earlier in the century as a form of containment, since what is quaint is essentially unserious. Hence the use of dialect and argot. Characters become 'characters'; they have significant connections with the containing forms of music-hall songs, which were mostly written 'by aspiring members of the middle class, with powerful upwardly mobile ambitions'.[8] They do not so much come to terms with city life as impose terms upon its variousness. They, too, are versions of pastoral and the England they imagine is as self-consciously mythic as the rural England of Alfred Austin, Alfred Noyes and the rest. Imagining England turns out to mean not imagining it at all. But then it can be argued that by the end of the century the poet's authority had dwindled to the point where it was to be identified with the consolations of withdrawal. Real authority had long since passed to the novelists.

Notes

Introduction

1 See esp. Anthony Giddens, *The Nation State and Violence*, Polity Press, 1985, and Ernest Gellner, *Nations and Nationalism*, Blackwell, 1983.

2 Quoted by John Barrell in *The Political Theory of Painting from Reynolds to Hazlitt*, Yale University Press, 1986, pp. 36–7.

3 This is a complex subject and one that still awaits its historian. But the line from Addison to Bishop Newton, say, is one that is marked by an effort to subdue the essentially combative features of Milton's poem, and explains why later poets like Blake and Shelley should – wrongly – think of Satan as the secret hero of *Paradise Lost*.

4 See D. G. James, *The Romantic Comedy*, Oxford University Press, 1948; Allan Rodway, *The Romantic Conflict*, Chatto & Windus, 1963; and Graham Hough, *The Romantic Poets*, Hutchinson, 1953.

5 I have tried to examine the making of the monarchy in an essay, 'Love of England: the Victorians and Patriotism', in *Browning Society Notes*, Vol 17, nos 1–3, 1987/88.

6 'Invisible *flâneur*' is an adaptation of the title of a seminal essay by Janet Wolff, 'The Invisible *Flâneuse*: Women and the Literature of Modernity', in *Theory, Culture and Society*, Vol 2, no 3, 1985. She takes it from Walter Benjamin's discussion of Baudelaire, for which see 'Afterword', below.

7 Browning as the poet of the grotesque, the half-educated (and by implication, the barbaric), was a formulation of Walter Bagehot's and was developed by George Santayana. Both writers had a vested interest in promoting particular ideas of the good society: orderly, hierarchically structured. It is no wonder that they saw Browning as a poet to be feared. That more recent critics have not understood the ideological bases of their attacks on Browning is, however, to be wondered at.

Chapter 1

1 William Myers, *Dryden*, Hutchinson, 1973, p. 120. For the 'correct' style, see J. Barber, *The Theme of Honour's Tongue: A Study of Social Attitudes in the English Drama from Shakespeare to Dryden*, Göteborg, 1985.

2 Raymond Williams, 'Marxism, Structuralism and Literary Analysis', in *New Left Review*, 129, October 1981, p. 53.

3 Hence, one of the explanations for 'Imitation', that staple, high, important form of translation of the period, which includes Pope's versions of Homer, *Imitations of Horace* and translations of Chaucer.

4 A. R. Humphreys, *The Augustan World*, Methuen, 1964, p. 225.

5 Marcia Pointon, *Milton and English Art*, Manchester University Press, 1970, p. 1. There is some evidence that the Expulsion scene should be attributed to Henry Aldrich. For this see S. Behrendt, *The Moment of Explosion: Blake and the Illustration of Milton*, New York, 1983, esp. pp. 91 and 196. Even were this to be proved it would not affect my argument, because whoever is responsible for the scene has explicitly denied Milton's 'hand in hand'.

6 Tonson became a prominent member of the Kit-Kat Club, which in its later years was known as the 'Whig dining society'. Yet Dryden held a place of honour in the club, which met the expenses of his funeral; and in his monograph on Tonson, G. F. Papali remarks that 'we know that the publisher's Whig sympathies became more articulate after Dryden's death'. They were certainly mute when he commissioned Medina to illustrate *Paradise Lost*. See G. F. Papali, *J. Tonson: A Publisher and his Circle*, Auckland Publishing Company, New Zealand, 1968, esp. pp. 88–93.

7 J. Dennis, *The Grounds of Criticism in Poetry*, 1704, Specimen (u.p) and p. 5 *et seq.*

8 On more than one occasion in his *A Tour Through the Whole Island of Great Britain*, Defoe gives it as his opinion that the Act of Union has left Scotland as no more than a province of England. See especially Vol 2, p. 187 (Everyman edition).

9 For this see Marina Warner, *Monuments and Maidens*, Pan Books, 1987, p. 45.

10 Christopher Hill, *The Century of Revolution*, Nelson, 1961, p. 199.

11 Douglas Brooks-Davies, *Pope's Dunciad and the Queen of the Night*, Manchester University Press, 1985, p. 3.

12 Pat Rogers, *The Augustan Vision*, Methuen, 1974, pp. 48–9.

13 *The Englishman, a Political Journal by Richard Steele*, ed. Rae Blanchard, Oxford University Press, 1955, pp. 23–4 and 344.

14 ibid., p. xi.

15 ibid., p. 32.

16 Quoted by Geoffrey Holmes in *British Politics in the Age of Anne*, The Hambledon Press, revised edition 1987, p. 67.

17 Martin Price, *To The Palace of Wisdom*, Southern Illinois University Press, 1970, p. 80.

18 Holmes, op. cit., p. 300.

19 Shaftesbury, *Characteristicks of Men, Manners, Opinions, Times* (first edition 1711), 1727, Vol 3, p. 156. For Bolingbroke see A. D. McKillop, 'Local Attachment and Cosmopolitanism', in *From Sensibility to Romanticism*, ed. Hilles and Bloom, Oxford University Press, 1965, p. 196.

20 For this see James Sambrook, *The Eighteenth Century: The Intellectual and Cultural Context of English Literature, 1700–1789*, Longman, 1986, p. 39.

21 Raymond Williams, *The Country and the City*, Paladin edition, 1975, pp. 76–7.

22 The Twickenham Edition of *The Poems of Alexander Pope*, 'Epistles to Several Persons', Vol III, ed. F. W. Bateson, Methuen, 1961, p. xxvi.

23 The Twickenham Edition, *Pastoral Poetry and An Essay on Criticism*, Vol I, ed. E. Audra and Aubrey Williams, Methuen, p. 192.

24 Reuben A. Brower, *Alexander Pope: The Poetry of Allusion*, Oxford University Press, 1968, p. 258.
25 Maynard Mack, *The Garden and the City*, Oxford University Press, 1969, p. 173.
26 Bateson, op. cit., p. 137.
27 Thomas Maresca, *Pope's Horatian Poems*, Ohio State University Press, 1966, pp. 159–60.
28 Brower, op. cit., p. 318.

Chapter 2

1 Thomas Docherty, *On Modern Authority*, Harvester Press, 1987, esp. pp. 244–52.
2 Quoted in *Victorian Studies*, Vol XXIX, no 3, p. 389.
3 The Twickenham Edition, Vol IV, ed. John Butt, Methuen, p. 96.
4 *The Correspondence of Alexander Pope*, ed. G. Sherburn, Oxford University Press, 1954, Vol III, pp. 132–3.
5 ibid., p. 143.
6 Raymond Williams, *The Country and the City*, op. cit., p. 89.
7 Philip Corrigan and Derek Sayer, *The Great Arch: English State Formation a Cultural Revolution*, Blackwell, 1985, p. 96.
8 Roy Porter, *English Society in the Eighteenth Century*, Penguin, 1982, p. 271.
9 Robert Crawford, in *London Review of Books*, Vol 10, no 2, p. 16.
10 Russell E. Richey, 'The Origins of British Radicalism: The Changing Rationale for Dissent', in *Eighteenth-Century Studies*, Vol 7, 1973–4, pp. 179–92.
11 G. R. Cragg, *The Church and the Age of Reason*, Penguin, 1960, p. 171.
12 Sambrook, op. cit., p. 35.
13 Porter, op. cit., pp. 195–7.
14 ibid., pp. 271–2.
15 Corrigan and Sayer, op. cit., p. 105.
16 *The Poems of Gray, Collins and Goldsmith*, ed. Roger Lonsdale, Longman, 1969, p. 453.
17 ibid., pp. 178–9.
18 ibid., p. 179.
19 ibid., pp. 487–8.
20 A. L. Owen, *The Famous Druids*, Oxford University Press, 1962, p. 174.
21 S. Piggott, *The Druids*, Penguin, 1974, p. 134.
22 See in particular Piggott's account of the illustrated title page for William Stukeley's *The History of the Temples and the Religion of the Celts*, drawn between 1723 and 1733.
23 I owe much of this information to Ms Carol Gardiner.
24 See for example Gray's letter to William Mason, in which he demonstrates his knowledge of such matters. Gray's *Selected Letters*, ed. J. Beresford, Oxford University Press, p. 170 and also p. 130.
25 For all this see Christopher Devlin, *Poor Kit Smart*, Hart-Davis, 1961, pp. 84–7.
26 See *English Critical Essays, XVI–XVIII Centuries*, ed. E. D. Jones, Oxford University Press, 1963, p. 289.

27 ibid., p. 291.

28 *Selected Letters*, op. cit., p. 210.

29 ibid., p. 250.

30 *The Poetical Works of Beattie, Blair, Falconer*, 1854, p. 1.

31 The cult of hermits, noble savages, and the like is one of those odd expressions of mid-eighteenth-century taste that it is difficult to dignify by the term 'soft primitivism'. However, for Omai, see Michael Alexander, *Omai: 'Noble Savage'*, Collins, 1977.

Chapter 3

1 Seamus Deane, *A Short History of Irish Literature*, Hutchinson, 1986, p. 126.

2 Donald Davie, 'Notes on Goldsmith's Politics', in *The Art of Oliver Goldsmith*, ed. A. Swarbrick, Vision, 1984, pp. 83–4.

3 Quoted by Lonsdale, op. cit., p. 653.

4 ibid., p. 653.

5 J. H. Plumb, *The First Four Georges*, Fontana edition, 1966, pp. 123–4.

6 Deane, op. cit., p. 126.

7 Plumb, op. cit., p. 103.

8 J. H. Plumb, *England in the Eighteenth Century*, Penguin, 1950, p. 182.

9 Plumb, *The First Four Georges*, op. cit., p. 104.

10 Mavis Batey, 'Oliver Goldsmith's "'An Indictment of Landscape Gardening'", in *Furor Hortensis*, ed. P. Willis, Elysium Press, Edinburgh, 1974.

11 William Whitehead, *Plays and Poems*, 2 vols, H. Dodsley, London, 1774, Vol 2, p. 234.

12 It seems that the following year he resigned over a quarrel with the prince's tutors who, he claimed, were too much in favour of Absolutism. This may be the origin of David Jacques's beliefs that Harcourt had republican leanings.

13 David Jacques, *Georgian Gardens: The Reign of Nature*, Batsford, 1983, p. 94.

14 More than one commentator has noted that in 'The Description of an Author's Bedchamber' Goldsmith speaks of his possessing a print of 'The Twelve good rules'. These rules were said to have been discovered in Charles I's room after his execution, and if you believe that the author's bedchamber is based on Goldsmith's own it follows that he is announcing himself as a monarchist. The lines are then transferred to the description of the ale-house in *The Deserted Village*. But one is entitled at the very least to feel that their being fervent monarchists hasn't done the villagers much good, especially since their plight had been caused by the king's friend. In which case the lines become inevitably ironic.

15 John Ginger, *The Notable Man: The Life and Times of Oliver Goldsmith*, Hamish Hamilton, 1977, p. 162.

16 Roy Porter provides a useful bibliography of contemporary foreign observers of England. See Porter, op. cit., p. 394.

17 For all this see George Rudé, *Wilkes and Liberty*, Oxford University Press, 1962, pp. 45–97 *passim*.

18 A. Lytton Sells, *Oliver Goldsmith: His Life and Works*, Allen & Unwin, 1974, pp. 132–3.

19 ibid., p. 135.
20 Corrigan and Sayer, op. cit., p. 96.
21 See, for example, the essay 'The Poor Man's Cow', in *An History of the Earth and Animated Nature*, 1774.
22 See especially *Whigs and Hunters*, Penguin, 1975, although this insight is one to which Thompson repeatedly returns in his work.
23 Corrigan and Sayer, op. cit., p. 102.
24 Walter Benjamin, *Illuminations*, Fontana edition, 1973, p. 258.
25 Raymond Williams, *The Country and the City*, op. cit., p. 78.
26 John Montague, 'The Sentimental Prophecy: A Study of *The Deserted Village*', in Swarbrick, op. cit., p. 96.
27 John Barrell, *The Dark Side of Landscape*, Cambridge University Press, 1980, p. 78.
28 The demystifying of the picturesque is an important part of much recent writing about the eighteenth century. Barrell's book is a most valuable contribution to the work, as is Raymond Williams's *The Country and the City*. And my own essay 'Wordsworth and the Anti-picturesque' (in J. Lucas, *From Romantic to Modern Literature*, Harvester Press, 1982), tries to tease out further strands.
29 The Preface to Johnson's edition of Shakespeare was written in 1765. My text is from *Johnson: Prose and Poetry*, ed. Mona Wilson, Hart-Davis, 1957, p. 497.
30 ibid., p. 318. The Preface to the *Dictionary* was first written in 1755.

Chapter 4

1 *The Poems of William Blake*, ed. W. H. Stevenson, text by David Erdman, Longman, 1971, pp. 13–14. Unless otherwise indicated, all future references are to this edition.
2 Leavis's championing of Blake as the poet of 'native English' is too well known to need documenting. But of especial relevance is his essay in *The Common Pursuit*, Chatto & Windus, 1952.
3 For this see Vic Gammon, '"Babylonian Performances": The Rise and Suppression of Popular Church Music, 1660–1870', in *Popular Culture and Class Conflict 1590–1914*, ed. Eileen and Stephen Yeo, Harvester Press, 1981.
4 Chauncy Tinker, *Nature's Simple Plan*, Oxford University Press, 1933, pp. 93–4.
5 Mona Wilson, *The Life of William Blake*, new edition, ed. G. Keynes, Oxford University Press, 1971, p. 63.
6 Edward Young, 'Conjectures on Original Composition', in *English Critical Essays, XVI–XVIII Centuries*, Oxford University Press, 1963, pp. 291 and 300.
7 Northrop Frye, *Fearful Symmetry: A Study of William Blake*, 1962, Beacon Press, Boston, USA, pp. 169–70. There are also helpful comments on this in Harold Bloom's *The Visionary Company*, Faber, 1961, esp. pp. 9–15.
8 For this see Martin Butlin, *William Blake*, Tate Gallery Publications, 1978, pp. 30–1.
9 Wilson, op. cit., p. 18.
10 David Erdman, *Blake: Prophet Against Empire*, Princeton University Press, third edition, 1977, see esp. pp. 30–55.

11 Much of this ground has been covered by James P. Boulton in his *The Language of Politics in the Age of Wilkes and Burke*, Routledge, 1962, and by Raymond Williams, in *Culture and Society*, Chatto & Windus, 1956.

12 Among the plethora of such publications one may mention Webster's *Dictionary* (1828), the work of Mary Wollstonecraft, esp. *Vindication of the Rights of Women* (1792), Horne Tooke's *Diversions of Purley* (1786–1805), and Cobbett's *English Grammar* (1818).

13 See Olivia Smith, *The Politics of Language, 1791–1815*, Oxford University Press, 1984.

14 See for this Thomas Paine, *The Rights of Man*, Part II, ed. Henry Collins, Penguin, 1969, pp. 242–3.

15 Heather Glen, 'The Poet in Society: Blake and Wordsworth in London', in *Literature and History*, no 3, 1976, p. 12.

16 Desmond King-Hele, *Erasmus Darwin and the Romantic Poets*, Macmillan, 1986, see esp. pp. 35–59.

17 Maureen McNeil, 'The Scientific Muse: The Poetry of Erasmus Darwin', in *Languages of Nature: Critical Essays on Science and Literature*, ed. L. Jordanova, Free Association Books, 1976, esp. pp. 168–73. Darwin's *The Temple of Nature* exists in facsimile reprint, together with *The Golden Age*, ed. Donald E. Reiman, Garland Publishing Co., New York, 1978.

18 For the beginnings of this, see, for example, Maureen Bell, 'Mary Westwood: Quaker Publisher', in *Publishing History*, no 23, 1988, pp. 5–66. Bell is no doubt right to argue that a great deal remains to be done in order to bring the history of radical printing/publishing to light. Interestingly, Darwin provides a long footnote to his enthusiastic encomium of 'The Immortal Press', in which he says that 'if the liberty of the press be preserved, mankind will not be liable in this part of the world to sink into such abject slavery as exists at this day in China' (*The Temple of Nature*, op. cit., p. 151). This suggests that Darwin, writing in 1800 or thereabouts, knew that at least some technological advances were not being used for the good of all. Censorship saw to that.

19 A. L. Morton, *The Everlasting Gospel*, Lawrence & Wishart, 1958, p. 35.

20 The references to and accounts of Los's building of Golgonooza are scattered about the late Prophetic Books. An able summary of their appearances is provided by S. Foster Damon in *A Blake Dictionary*, Thames & Hudson, 1973, pp. 162–5.

Chapter 5

1 Mary Moorman, *William Wordsworth: A Biography*, 2 vols, Oxford University Press, 1968, Vol I, p. 251.

2 V. G. Kiernan, 'Wordsworth', in *Marxists on Literature*, ed. David Craig, Penguin, 1975, p. 164.

3 Heather Glen, *Vision and Disenchantment: Blake's Songs and Wordsworth's Lyrical Ballads*, Cambridge University Press, 1983, p. 229.

4 Martin Price, 'The Picturesque Moment', in *From Sensibility to Romanticism*, ed. Hilles and Bloom, op. cit., pp. 260–4.

5 Quoted in Christopher Salvesen, *The Landscape of Memory*, Edward Arnold, 1965, p. 66.

6 Glen, op. cit., pp. 245 and 229–30.

7 Matthew Arnold, *Essays in Criticism*, Second Series, 1888, p. 125.

8 John Ruskin, *The Stones of Venice*, Cook & Wedderburn edition, Vol x, pp. 228–9.

9 David Trotter, *The Making of the Reader*, Macmillan, 1984, p. 16.

10 Mikhail Bakhtin, *The Dialogic Imagination*, ed. M. Holquist, University of Texas Press, 1981, p. 272.

11 Price, op. cit., p. 264.

12 Michael Friedman, *The Making of a Tory Humanist: William Wordsworth and the Idea of Community*, Columbia University Press, 1979, p. 191.

13 Glen, op. cit., pp. 328–9.

14 G. H. Hartman, *Wordsworth's Poetry: 1787–1814*, Yale University Press, 1964, p. 262.

15 *The Letters of William and Dorothy Wordsworth, 1787–1805*, second edition, ed. E. de Selincourt, Oxford University Press, 1967, p. 314.

16 Friedman, op. cit., p. 187.

17 G. E. Mingay, *Rural Life in Victorian England*, Heinemann, 1977, p. 125.

18 Glen, op. cit., p. 334.

19 *Letters*, ed. de Selincourt, op. cit., pp. 314–15.

20 F. M. Todd, *Politics and the Poet: A Study of Wordsworth*, Methuen, 1957, p. 109.

21 Hartman, op. cit., p. 262. H. A. Mason's essay may be found in *Delta*, Summer 1963, pp. 4–15.

22 Mingay, op. cit., p. 12.

23 Kiernan, op. cit., pp. 182–3.

24 Moorman, op. cit., Vol 2, p. 73.

25 *Wordsworth and Coleridge's Lyrical Ballads*, ed. Brett and Jones, Methuen, 1963, p. 235.

26 Quoted in Moorman, op. cit., Vol 1, p. 588.

27 For this see 'Beaumont and Coleorton', by Felicity Owen, in *Sir George Beaumont of Coleorton*, Leicester Museum and Art Gallery, n.d., pp. 22–4.

28 For the full account of this see 'The Poet in his Joy', in Lucas, *From Romantic to Modern Literature*, op. cit.

29 I use here the text of Helen Darbishire, *Poems Published in 1807*, Oxford University Press, 1914.

30 Glen, op. cit., p. 21.

31 Darbishire, op. cit., p. 382.

32 Raymond Williams, 'Culture', in *Marx: The First Hundred Years*, ed. D McLellan, Fontana, 1983, p. 33.

33 *Complete Works of John Keats*, 5 vols, ed. Buxton Forman, Glasgow, 1901, Vol 4, p. 109.

34 Raymond Williams, *Modern Tragedy*, Chatto & Windus, 1977, p. 121.

35 W. H. Auden, *The Enchaféd Flood*, Faber, 1951, p. 34.

36 Coleridge, *Biographia Literaria*, 2 vols, 1817, Vol 2, pp. 150–1.

37 Quoted by Paul Hamilton in *Coleridge's Poetics*, Blackwell, 1983, p. 161.

38 For this see Coleridge, *The Friend*, 'Section the First: On the Principles of Political Knowledge', Essay 5, 'On the Errors of Party Spirit: or, Extremes Meet'.

39 Hamilton, op. cit., p. 203.

40 There is an account in H. House *Coleridge*, Hart-Davis, 1953, which has been amplified by later commentators.

41 Hamilton, op. cit., p. 142.

42 Kiernan, op. cit., p. 198.

Chapter 6

1 Quoted in Moorman, op. cit., Vol 2, p. 338.

2 *Southey's Works*, one volume edition, 1859, pp. 766–85.

3 Hamilton, op. cit., p. 152.

4 I quote the phrase used by Andrew Rutherford in his *Byron: A Critical Study*, Oliver, 1961, p. 221.

5 *Shelley: Poetical Works*, ed. Hutchinson, revised G. Matthews, Oxford University Press, p. 189. The problem of Shelley's texts is immense, and until Kelvin Everest's edition appears the Oxford edition is probably the best we have.

6 *Lord Byron: Selected Prose*, ed. Peter Gunn, Penguin, 1972, p. 476.

7 ibid., p. 484.

8 Linda Colley, 'The Apotheosis of George III: Loyalty, Royalty and the British Nation, 1760–1820' in *Past and Present*, 102, 1984.

9 Jerome McGann, *The Beauty of Inflections: Literary Investigations in Historical Method and Theory*, Oxford University Press, 1985. McGann claims that the poem is 'dialectically called into being . . . as an active response to, and alteration of, the events which marked the late summer and early fall of a particular year in a particular place'. He goes on to argue that Keats cannot directly voice his concerns because, fearing hostile reviews, his publishers had warned him off politics. Hence the poet's wish to 'escape the period which provides the poem with its context' (pp. 54–62).

10 For this see P. M. S. Dawson, *The Unacknowledged Legislator: Shelley and Politics*, Oxford University Press, 1980, p. 196.

11 Edward Bostetter is typical of many who read Shelley in the terms Yeats made available, as the secret hater of life and the dreamer of escape from its constrictions. According to this, Shelley the Platonist was always eager to lift the painted veil. See E. Bostetter, *The Romantic Ventriloquists*, Washington University Press, 1963, esp. pp. 193–210.

12 G. M. Matthews, 'A Volcano's Voice in Shelley', in *ELH* XXIV, 1957, pp. 191–228.

13 *Poetical Works*, ed. Hutchinson, op. cit., p. 206.

14 ibid., p. 588.

15 See *Shelley's Mythmaking*, Cornell University Press, 1959 and 1968, and *The Visionary Company*, Anchor Books, 1961.

16 For this see Dawson, op. cit., p. 177.

17 In David Lee Clark, *Shelley's Prose*, University of New Mexico Press, 1954, pp. 162–9.

18 Angus Calder, 'Forever Walsall', in *London Review of Books*, 21 March 1985, p. 7.

19 For this see of course E. P. Thompson, *The Making of the English Working Class*,

Gollancz, 1963, esp. pp. 132–7; and G. D. H. Cole and Raymond Postgate, *The Common People, 1746–1946*, Methuen, 1946, pp. 155–8.

20 Dawson, op. cit., p. 170.

21 See my essays on Elizabeth Gaskell, Engels and Manchester, in *The Literature of Change*, Harvester Press, 1977; and 'The Idea of the Provincial', in *From Romantic to Modern Literature*, op. cit.

22 The Tolpuddle martyrs, for example, were, unsurprisingly, scarcely grateful for their pardon: after their return to England most of them moved on to Canada. And the case of Philip in Clough's *The Bothie of Tober-na-Vuolich* is instructive.

23 John Langton, in *Transactions*, Institute of British Geographers, n.s. 9, 1984, pp. 145–67, esp. pp. 150–6.

Chapter 7

1 Hannah More, *Stories for the Middle Ranks of Society, and Tales for the Common People*, 2 vols, 1808, Vol 2.

2 For a full account of Anderson's life as a local bard see the introduction by Sidney Gilpin to the edition of 1893, Bemrose and Sons.

3 John Bell, *Rhymes of Northern Bards*, facsimile edition, F. Graham, 1971, with introduction by David Harker, from whom I quote these words.

4 ibid., p. xliv.

5 ibid., pp. 16–19. Speaking on behalf of local patriots is thus institutionalised in a manner which will become almost definitive in Kipling's *Barrack Room Ballads*.

6 Louis Simpson, *James Hogg: A Critical Study*, Oliver, 1962, p. 57.

7 Lee Erickson, 'The Poets' Corner: The Impact of Technological Changes in Printing on English Poetry, 1800–1850', in *ELH* LII (4), winter 1985, p. 894.

8 *Wordsworth and Coleridge's Lyrical Ballads*, ed. Brett and Jones, op. cit., pp. 241 and 250.

9 *Poems Descriptive of Rural Life and Scenery*, London, 1820. The introduction is unsigned.

10 *The Letters of John Clare*, ed. J. W. and Anne Tibble, Dent, 1951, p. 58.

11 'My Mary' is an earthy parody of Cowper's poem of the same title. 'Ways of the Wake' ('Dolly's Mistake') is a variation on a well-known folk song about a girl who is made pregnant by a young man, a casual encounter at a fair.

12 *The Letters of John Clare*, op. cit., p. 334.

13 ibid., p. 49.

14 I use the text of the Oxford Authors *John Clare*, ed. Eric Robinson and David Powell, 1984, p. 4. The state of Clare's texts is of course a tangled matter which, thanks to the work of these editors, is now at last becoming unravelled.

15 For all this see 'The Political Iconography of Woodland', in *The Iconography of Landscape*, ed. D. Cosgrove and S. Daniels, Cambridge University Press, 1988, esp. pp. 44–50.

16 ibid., p. 44.

17 Perhaps the last such blatantly ideological handling of the wild woods and their harbouring 'outlaws' comes in *The Wind in the Willows*, where the wild wooders – weasels and stoats – who try to capture Toad Hall are obvious stand-ins for an unruly working class threatening the proper ordering of English society.

18 *The Letters of John Clare*, op. cit., p. 75.

19 For an invaluable account of Clare's knowledge and acquisition of folk songs (including the music, which he set down), see George Deacon, *John Clare and the Folk Tradition*, Sinclair Browne, 1983. Deacon shows how Clare took over and adapted the song on which 'Dolly's Mistake' was based.

20 *The Prose of John Clare*, ed. J. W. and Anne Tibble, Dent, 1951, pp. 71–2.

21 ibid., p. 66.

22 ibid., p. 221.

23 *The Shepherd's Calendar*, ed. E. Robinson and G. Summerfield, Oxford University Press, 1973, pp. 68–9.

24 *The Prose of John Clare*, op. cit., p. 79.

25 In *Marx: The First Hundred Years*, op. cit., pp. 37–8.

26 John Clare, *The Rural Muse*, Carcanet, 1982, p. 161. Barbara Strang's invaluable essay, 'John Clare's Language', appears at the end of the volume.

27 *The Shepherd's Calendar*, op. cit., pp. ix–xii. The allusion to 'unphilosophical' passages glances at a letter of Taylor's to Clare, in which the publisher urges the poet to take a more philosophical view of nature.

28 For a fuller account of this poem see my essay 'Places and Dwellings', in *The Iconography of Landscape*, op. cit., pp. 95–6.

29 Corrigan and Sayer, op. cit., p. 111.

30 See 'Places and Dwellings'. The information about grasses . . . plebeians comes from Keith Thomas, *Man and the Natural World*, Allen Lane, 1983, p. 66.

31 *The Prose of John Clare*, op. cit., pp. 221–2. For Clare's probable awareness of protest songs etc, see, 'The Time's Alteration: Popular Ballads, Rural Radicalism and William Cobbett', by Alun Howkins and C. Ian Dyck, *History Workshop*, no 23, Spring, 1987.

32 E. P. Thompson, *Whigs and Hunters*, Penguin, 1977, p. 261. Fears of wandering and of wanderers are endlessly an expression of authority's determination to prevent mobility. Christopher Hill shows how this worked in the 17th century. See *John Bunyan and His Church*, OUP, 1988 esp pp. 112–13.

33 For all this see Edward Storey, *A Right to Song: The Life of John Clare*, Methuen, 1982, pp. 228–41.

34 For this see Deacon, op. cit., pp. 130–2.

35 *John Clare: Selected Poetry and Prose*, ed. Merryn and Raymond Williams, Methuen, 1986, p. 17.

36 Tim Chilcott, *A Real World and Doubting Mind*, University of Hull Press, 1985, p. 195.

37 Storey, op. cit., pp. 267–8.

38 Inevitably with the asylum poems we have to make do with transcripts, and the titles and punctuation are of course not Clare's.

39 The punctuation of this poem is especially unreliable. Geoffrey Grigson praises the poem both in his Muses' Library edition of Clare's poems and in his edition of *Poems of John Clare's Madness*, Routledge & Kegan Paul, 1949, p. 30, where he calls it 'the most visionary, complete poem that Clare wrote'.

40 The punctuation of this poem is deplorable and cannot possibly be by Clare.

41 Storey, op. cit., p. 81.

Chapter 8

1 *The Prelude 1799, 1805, 1850*, ed. Jonathan Wordsworth, M. H. Abrams and Stephen Gill, Norton Critical Edition, 1979, p. 255.

2 See *Henry Crabb Robinson on Books and Their Writers*, ed. Edith Morley, Dent, 1938, Vol II, p. 485.

3 I use the text of the Garland Series facsimiles: *Romantic Context; Ebenezer Elliott: The Village Patriarch: Corn Law Rhymes*, 1978. All future references will be to this edition.

4 Rupert E. Davies, *Methodism*, Penguin, 1963, p. 135.

5 ibid., pp. 137 and 153.

6 I take this information from the *DNB*, which relies heavily on Elliott's own *Autobiography*.

7 For this, and Wellington's obstructive tactics, see Michael Bentley, *Politics Without Democracy*, Fontana, 1984, pp. 75–82.

8 For this see Anne Blainey, *The Farthing Poet: A Biography of Richard Hengist Horne 1802–1884*, Longman, 1968, pp. 58–9. For a full account of the journal and of the period of Fox's editorship, see F. E. Mineka, *The Dissidence of Dissent: The Monthly Repository, 1806–1838*, Chapel Hill, 1944.

9 For a fuller account of Horne's radical poetry see my essay 'Politics and the Poet's Rule', in *Literature and Politics in the Nineteenth Century*, ed. J. Lucas, Methuen, 1971 and 1974.

10 See, for example, John Wardroper, *Kings, Lords and Wicked Levellers*, John Murray, 1973, pp. 239–40.

11 Elliott's song, one of the *Corn Law Rhymes*, ends:

> Free men! Free Bread! great William said,
> And like a second Alfred stood,
> King of the happy and the good;
>   While the free, from sea to sea,
>   Sang, Great William Rules the Free!

12 The fullest account is to be found in Tom Nairn's *The Enchanted Class: Britain and its Monarchy*, Radius Books, 1988. There is also an important essay by David Cannadine, 'The Context, Performance and Meaning of Ritual: The British Monarchy and the "Invention of Tradition" 1820–1977', in *The Invention of Tradition*, ed. E. Hobsbawm and T. Ranger, Cambridge University Press, 1983, although, as will become apparent, I disagree with some of Cannadine's arguments and conclusions.

13 *Strafford*, v, ii. I use the Dent edition of *Poems and Plays*, Vol I, p. 204.

14 Patrick Brantlinger, *The Spirit of Reform: British Literature and Politics, 1832–1867*, Harvard University Press, 1977, p. 165.

15 For this and all future quotations from Browning's poems I use *Robert Browning: The Poems*, ed. John Pettigrew, supplemented and completed by Thomas J. Collins, 2 vols, Penguin, 1981, Vol I, p. 410.

16 ibid., p. 347.

17 See Blainey, op. cit., pp. 59–60.

18 Mark Girouard, *The Return to Camelot: Chivalry and the English Gentleman*, Yale University Press, 1981, p. 103.

19 *The Poems of Tennyson*, ed. C. Ricks, Longman, 1969, p. 1467.

20 *The Correspondence of G. M. Hopkins and R. W. Dixon*, ed. C. C. Abbott, Oxford University Press, 1938, p. 24.

21 Hallam's essay 'On Some of the Characteristics of Modern Poetry and on the Lyrical Poems of Alfred Tennyson' first appeared in *The Gentleman's Magazine*, August 1831. I quote from the reprint in *The Emergence of Victorian Consciousness*, ed. George Levine, New York, 1967, p. 122.

22 R. B. Martin, *Tennyson: The Unquiet Heart*, Faber, 1980, p. 122.

23 In Levine, op. cit., pp. 405–7.

24 ibid., p. 408.

25 J. W. Burrow, *A Liberal Descent: Victorian Historians and the English Past*, Cambridge University Press, 1983, p. 32.

26 See R. H. Super, *Walter Savage Landor*, Calder, 1957, p. 65. More revealing, perhaps, is Landor's remark that 'Doubtless the government of Buonaparte is the best that can be contrived for Frenchmen. Monkeys must be chained.'

27 A good account of francophobia can be found in Gerald Newman's essay, 'Anti-French Propaganda and British Liberal Nationalism in the Early Nineteenth Century', in *Victorian Studies*, Vol XVIII, 1975, pp. 385–418. Newman errs, however, in labelling this phobia 'British'. It is *English*.

28 For more on the Spasmodics see my essay 'Politics and the Poet's Role', in *Literature and Politics in the Nineteenth Century*, op. cit.

29 Christopher Ricks, *Tennyson*, Macmillan, 1972, p. 167.

30 ibid., p. 165.

31 Henry Kozicki, *Tennyson and Clio: History in the Major Poems*, Johns Hopkins University Press, 1979, p. 57.

32 ibid, pp. 60–5.

33 Robert Pattison, *Tennyson and Tradition*, Harvard University Press, 1979, p. 94.

34 Ricks, *Tennyson*, op. cit, pp. 199–200.

35 Quoted by Cora Kaplan in her introduction to *Aurora Leigh and Other Poems*, The Women's Press, 1978, p. 28.

Chapter 9

1 Martin, op. cit., p. 352.

2 Quoted in *The Poetical Works of Matthew Arnold*, ed. Tinker and Lowry, Oxford University Press, 1957, pp. xxviii–xxx.

3 In *Literature and Politics in the Nineteenth Century*, op. cit., pp. 45–76. The quotation is on p. 52. I greatly regret not having the space to offer a more extended account of Clough's poetry.

4 The address is to be found in Arnold's *Essays in Criticism: Second Series*. It is worth remarking that the address is also calculatedly and woundingly anti-American, even though its occasion was the donation of a window to St Margaret's Church, Westminster, by a G. W. Childs of Philadelphia. The nation whose white forebears were puritans is upbraided for political beliefs of which Milton might be supposed to have approved.

5 In a letter to Clough of 1849. The entire, deeply instructive correspondence (at least from Arnold's side, Clough's letters are lost) is to be found in *The Letters of Matthew Arnold to Arthur Hugh Clough*, ed. H. F. Lowry, Oxford University Press, 1932.

6 Ernest Gellner, *Nations and Nationalism*, op. cit. p. 138.

7 See Cannadine's essay 'The Context, Performance and Meaning of Ritual', op. cit.

8 Winslow Ames, *Prince Albert and Victorian Taste*, Methuen, 1967.

9 Eric de Mare, *London 1851*, The Folio Society, 1972, unpaginated.

10 Quoted by Martin, op. cit., pp. 389–90.

11 ibid., p. 390.

12 Quoted by Burrow, op. cit., p. 238.

13 Ricks, *Tennyson*, op. cit., p. 250.

14 Brantlinger, op. cit., p. 191.

15 In *Culture and Anarchy* Arnold refers to a conversation he once had with the manager of the Clay Cross Works in Derbyshire, who told him that 'when our want of soldiers was much felt and some were talking of a conscription, that sooner than submit to a conscription the population of that district would flee to the mines and lead a sort of Robin Hood life under ground'.

16 Kozicki, op. cit., pp. 98–110 *passim*.

17 McGann, op. cit., pp. 191–201 *passim*.

18 In *Writers and Their Background : Robert Browning*, ed. Isobel Armstrong, G. Bell, 1974, p. 170.

19 ibid., p. 284.

20 J. Hillis Miller, *The Disappearance of God*, Harvard University Press, 1965, p. 251.

21 Livingstone's full apotheosis was to come, but by the early 1850s he was widely regarded as a great, intrepid explorer.

22 I owe my knowledge of this to Angus Calder, who drew my attention to Kirk's *Zambezi Journal*.

23 *Robert Browning: The Poems*, ed. Pettigrew and Collins, op. cit., Vol I, p. 1117.

24 ibid., Vol I, p. 1119.

25 Raymond Williams, *The English Novel from Dickens to Lawrence*, Chatto & Windus, 1970, pp. 51–2.

26 See Walter Bagehot, *Literary Essays*, 2 vols, Dent, 1916, Vol 2, 'Wordsworth, Tennyson and Browning: or, Pure, Ornate, and Grotesque Art in English Poetry', 1864, pp. 305–51.

27 Gerard Manley Hopkins, *Selected Prose*, ed. G. Roberts, Oxford University Press, 1980, p. 55.

28 For this, see John Langton's essay 'The Industrial Revolution and the Regional Geography of England', op. cit., esp. pp. 159–61.

29 In *Essays in Criticism: Second Series*.

Afterword

1 I have taken these references from William B. Thesiger's essay 'Gerard Manley Hopkins's Responses to the City: the 'Composition of the Crowd', in *Victorian Studies*, Vol 30, no 3, spring 1987, p. 387.

2 I have in mind such painters as 'mad' John Martin and Gustave Doré, whose Dante-esque engravings for *London*, the work on which he and Douglas Jerrold combined in 1872, are often, and incautiously, used as though they provide documentary accounts of later-nineteenth-century low life. In 'The Partial View: The Visual Representation of the Early Nineteenth-Century Industrial City', Caroline Ascott, Griselda Pollock and Janet Wolff demonstrate how the pictorial language of city painting was inevitably indebted to traditions which required the artists to produce images of the city in a manner that was accommodating and partial (where not downright false). See *The Culture of Capital: Art, Power and the Nineteenth-Century Middle Class*, ed. Janet Wolff and John Seed, Manchester University Press, 1988.

3 Quoted in Timothy Hilton, *The Pre-Raphaelites*, Thames & Hudson, 1970, p. 158.

4 John Robinson, *In Extremity: A Study of Gerard Manley Hopkins*, Cambridge University Press, 1978, p. 100.

5 *The Poems of Gerard Manley Hopkins*, ed. W. H. Gardner and N. H. Mackenzie, fourth edition, Oxford University Press, 1967, p. 291.

6 I have made some attempt to deal with this in *Modern English Poetry: From Hardy to Hughes*, especially Chapter 3, but I now feel the subject requires more careful analysis than I was there able to give it. See also M. E. Weiner, *England and the Decline of the Industrial Spirit*, Cambridge University Press, 1982.

7 Walter Benjamin, 'On Some Motifs in Baudelaire', in *Illuminations*, Fontana, 1973.

8 For this see Laurence Senelick, 'Politics as Entertainment: Victorian Music-hall Songs', in *Victorian Studies*, XIX, 1975, and Penelope Summerfield, 'The Effingham Arms and the Empire', in *Popular Culture and Class Conflict, 1590–1914*, ed. Eileen and Stephen Yeo, Harvester Press, 1981.

INDEX